THE POLITICAL THOUGHT
OF KARL POPPER

THE POLITICAL THOUGHT OF KARL POPPER

Jeremy Shearmur

London and New York

First published 1996
by Routledge
11 New Fetter Lane, London EC4P 4EE

Simultaneously published in the USA and Canada
by Routledge
29 West 35th Street, New York, NY 10001

Typeset in Baskerville by Keystroke, Jacaranda Lodge, Wolverhampton
Printed in Great Britain by Mackays of Chatham PLC, Chatham, Kent

British Library Cataloguing in Publication Data
A catalogue record for this book is available from the British Library

Library of Congress Cataloguing in Publication Data
Shearmur, Jeremy, 1948–
The political thought of Karl Popper / Jeremy Shearmur.
p.   cm.
Includes bibliographical references and index.
ISBN 0–415–09726–6 (alk. paper)
1. Popper, Karl Raimund, Sir, 1902—Contributions in political science.
I. Title.
JC257.P662S47   1996
320′.092—dc20   96–7016   CIP

To Colin, Mary and Pam

CONTENTS

ACKNOWLEDGEMENTS

The contents of this volume draw upon reading and discussion with those interested in Popper's work, over many years – in which connection I would particularly like to thank my teachers at the LSE Philosophy Department, and Karl Popper himself. It would be futile to try to refer to all those from whom I have gained, through discussion on these issues, but I would particularly like to thank the following: Bill Bartley, Larry Briskman and Ian Jarvie (especially for his comments on a late version of the manuscript); Malachi Hacohen and Geoff Stokes for recent work on Popper's political thought which I have found particularly stimulating; the Austrian Wittgenstein Society, the Departments of Philosophy at the University of Montreal and York University, Toronto, and the Department of Economics, University of Vienna, for the opportunity to present some of this material; and Liberty Fund for invitations to conferences which, in retrospect, have been important in shaping my ideas on issues discussed in this volume.

I would also like to thank the Earhart Foundation for financial support which allowed me to undertake research in the Popper Archives at the Hoover Institution, upon which I have drawn in writing this volume, and I am grateful to the staff at the Hoover Institution Archives for their unfailing help, assistance and consideration.

In addition, I would like to thank Mr and Mrs Mew for their permission to quote some unpublished material from the Popper Archives at the Hoover Institution, and to mention that portions of the material in the present volume were first published as:

'Philosophical Method, Modified Essentialism and *The Open Society*', in I.C. Jarvie and N. Laor (eds) *Critical Rationalism, the Social Sciences and the Humanities*, Essays for Joseph Agassi, volume

ACKNOWLEDGEMENTS

II, Boston Studies in the Philosophy of Science, Dordrecht: Kluwer, 1995; 'Epistemological Limits of the State', *Political Studies*, 1990; 'Il liberalismo a la societa aperta', in *Popper: il metodo e la politica, Biblioteca della Liberta 84–5*, 1982; 'Abstract Institutions in an Open Society', in *Wittgenstein, The Vienna Circle and Critical Rationalism*, HPT, Vienna, 1979.

Finally, some of the ideas which have influenced my approach to Popper are explored further in my *Hayek and After*, London and New York: Routledge, 1996.

Jeremy Shearmur,
Bungendore, NSW
March 1995

BIBLIOGRAPHICAL INFORMATION

The Logic of Scientific Discovery (1934), London: Hutchinson, 1959.

The Poverty of Historicism (1944–5), London: Routledge & Kegan Paul, 1957.

The Open Society and Its Enemies (1945), London: Routledge & Kegan Paul, fifth edition, 1966.

Conjectures and Refutations, London: Routledge & Kegan Paul, 1963.

Objective Knowledge, Oxford: Clarendon Press, 1972.

Unended Quest, London: Fontana, 1976.

The Self and Its Brain (with Sir John Eccles), Berlin, etc.: Springer International, 1977.

Postscript to The Logic of Scientific Discovery: Realism and the Aim of Science, London: Hutchinson, 1983; *The Open Universe*, London: Hutchinson, 1982; *Quantum Theory and the Schism in Physics*, London: Hutchinson, 1982.

In Search of a Better World, London: Routledge, 1992.

The Myth of the Framework, London: Routledge, 1994.

Die beiden Grundprobleme der Erkenntnistheorie (1930–3), Tuebingen: J.C.B. Mohr (Paul Siebeck), 1979.

P.A. Schilpp (ed.) *The Philosophy of Karl Popper*, La Salle, IL: Open Court, 1974.

David Miller (ed.) *A Pocket Popper*, London: Fontana, 1983, contains useful selections from Popper's work.

INTRODUCTION

I was lucky enough to be taught by Karl Popper, and also to work with him as his assistant for some eight years, between 1971 and 1979. While I gained immensely from this experience, I do not claim, by virtue of this, a privileged position for my interpretation of his views. In addition, any reader of Popper will be familiar with his argument that philosophers have sometimes been betrayed by those who were close to them. This was his view of the relationship between Socrates and Plato, and also between Kant and Fichte.[1] I am, accordingly, acutely aware of the fact that were Popper still with us, he might well see my work in the same light; not least because, as the reader will discover, I wish to argue that Popper's work has consequences in the political realm which are suggestive of views which are different from those which Popper himself espoused, especially as a young man.

My approach to Popper's early work – notably *The Open Society and Its Enemies* and *The Poverty of Historicism* – has been influenced by the older Popper, who in some important respects held views which were different from those of his younger self. I do not mean just his explicitly political views, although there are some differences here. More significant are differences in his views within philosophy. Popper was never a positivist. But the older Popper's approach was less positivistic than that of the author of *The Open Society*. The older Popper was more overtly a scientific realist (although realism in some form was clearly one of Popper's long-standing concerns[2]); he also took the view that metaphysical theories could be made the objects of rational appraisal.[3] In addition, there is a sense in which the author of *The Open Society* exhibits some affinities with post-modernism; something with which I have no sympathy whatever.

1

The younger Popper and post-modernism share a rejection of historical teleology. With this I am in full agreement. What seems to me less acceptable is the younger Popper's coming close to the rejection – in some of his criticisms of 'essentialism', and in his pursuit of a resolutely pragmatic orientation towards the social – of a realist approach to social science. I will also take issue with his emphasis on individual moral decisions, some of his views concerning which, despite his frequent disclaimers of relativism, come unacceptably close to a form of ethical subjectivism. I will argue in some detail that there is a – to me more acceptable – fallibilist moral realism to be discerned in his work. I also criticize his account of the value of (subjective) historical interpretation. By way of contrast, I make use of aspects of Popper's work which are in tension with these ideas. I have in mind here not only his realism, which I will suggest can be extended to the social sciences, and which seems to me to constitute a significant improvement upon the ideas on the status of social science which inform *The Open Society*. Perhaps even more important are his Kantian-derived ideas about interpreting objectivity in terms of inter-subjective acceptability. These play an important role in Popper's work. But their application there is unsystematic, and is intermingled with themes which seem to me more subjectivist in their character. I argue that this Kantian theme should be adopted more systematically. Doing this would allow one to interpret Popper's work in a way which avoids those elements that are subjectivist and, to the contemporary palate, post-modernist in their flavour. It would also bring out the respects in which his ideas are close to some themes in the later work of Juergen Habermas.

This volume is preliminary in its character – and not only in the sense in which this would be said by any fallibilist. I am acutely aware that my own views on the issues which I am here discussing are themselves in flux, not only as I discover more about Popper's work, but also as I consider it in relation to other material. But as the search for an interpretation of Popper's work in which I can have any real confidence seems to me not only an unended quest, but also possibly an unending one, I feel that I should write now, rather than wait for a conclusion to my research, at which I may never arrive. At the very least, this will mean that others can join in the criticism of the views to which I have at present been led.

In this volume, for the most part I consider only Popper's own views, rather than discussing his interpretation of the work of other people. However, in the re-reading of Popper's work that I undertook prior to writing the final version of this volume, I was struck, as I had been when working with him, by the immense range of his knowledge. It is one thing to agree or to disagree with the views that he takes upon various issues; and there have been some serious and interesting treatments of his interpretation of the work of some of the figures whom he discusses. But I found it striking that, for example, *The Open Society* has been so frequently the subject of disparaging comments from people whom it is difficult to imagine having actually grappled with the work with the effort that it demands. Popper believed that simplicity in writing was an important virtue, not least because of its relation to the possibility of fruitful and rational interchange between people from different backgrounds and intellectual environments. He has commented, when writing about *The Open Society*, that he had tried to make it readable, and in ways that might mask the scholarship that went into it.[4] It is sad that he was all too successful, in the sense that some of his readers do not seem to have had the patience to consider how seriously his argument should be taken.

Popper has also suffered from what Russell Jacoby has described as the decline of the public intellectual.[5] During Popper's lifetime, intellectuals have typically been in retreat from the public realm into the specializations of their varied academic disciplines. It is increasingly expected that academics will address only their peers, and that if anyone is to express a view upon any topic, they must have served their academic apprenticeship in the discipline of which it is a part. The result of all this, however, is a disaster. The non-specialist writers who address some issue with which academics have been concerned are all too often received in an ungenerous manner. They are treated as if they have written a poor-quality, specialized article, and criticized for not having taken into consideration every point raised by specialists; sometimes, one feels, whether it is relevant or not to the broader argument that they are advancing. As a result, specialized academic discussion becomes closed to the stimulation that can be brought to it by educated outsiders, while it also becomes difficult for specialists to contribute to public discourse. For the customary style and expectations of the academics become tailored to their academic audience, and they forget how to address the non-professional.

This, in turn, leads to the danger that the public forum (such as it now is) becomes dominated by the proponents of a succession of fads, or by figures for whom drums are beaten by a variety of special interests. Further, because reasoned exchanges between public intellectuals who are in significant disagreement with one another are not now so common, it also becomes more difficult for those taking decisions, and more generally for the public, to evaluate what they are offered by specialists. At the same time, decision-taking in significant parts of modern 'Western' societies often seems to be in the hands of people who do not have to answer to those who disagree with them, or even to explain to them, in ways that they can understand, why they believe that decisions should be taken as they think they should.[6]

All this, I should stress, is not a matter of special pleading because I am dealing in this volume with the work of a writer much of whose output is not specialized in its character. There is something more important at stake. For if it is important that ideas that make a difference to the world be open to criticism, and that decisions be informed by critical discussion as to the pros and cons of different options, it is necessary that there be places (actual, or virtual) within which such discussion can take place: places to which those with a concern for issues can get access, and into which such more specialized work as is pertinent is injected, in an appropriate form. Jacoby, it seems to me, is correct not only about the disappearance of the public intellectual, but also about the way in which much vital work, undertaken within universities, becomes almost irrelevant to public decision-taking. Accordingly, if ideas about accountability within a public sphere are important, we may need to think very carefully about the impact of various social changes (from specialization within universities, to changes in the media) upon how this may take place, and to consider what would be needed to reconstruct a public sphere, within which such discussion can take place.

These were issues with which Popper himself was in some ways concerned. In *The Open Society*, Popper responded in a hostile way to Arnold Toynbee's claims about the division of labour in the field of science. Popper argued, against Toynbee, that:[7] 'What Toynbee calls "division of labour" could better be described as cooperation and mutual criticism.' At the time at which Popper was writing, there would seem every reason to suppose that he was correct. At the very least, it was possible for a talented non-professional, such as Popper, to keep abreast of many scientific debates, and even to make serious contributions to some of them. The issue is significant, just because the hope that we could extend what he believed to be the rational approach of science to the sphere of politics represents an important strand within Popper's work. It is in relation to this issue that one might usefully interpret Popper's comments on the significance of Kuhn's criticism of his work (comments which surprised some of Popper's closest associates[8]), and in particular his reaction to Kuhn's discussion of 'normal science'.

In Popper's 'Science: Problems, Aims, Responsibilities', which originated in a talk that Popper gave in the year after Kuhn's work was published but does not yet show any sign of its impact, Popper writes critically about scientific specialization. He depicts such specialization as serving to remove those who are involved in it from 'participation in the self-liberation through knowledge which is the cultural task of science'.[9] He further argues that, in order to help others learn, the use of scientific jargon should be limited. Popper argues that we should:[10] 'speak as simply and clearly and unpretentiously as possible, and . . . avoid like the plague the suggestion that we are in the possession of knowledge which is too deep to be clearly and simply expressed'. He sums up what he believes to be the wider significance of this point, in the following terms:[11]

> This, I believe, is one of the greatest and most urgent responsibilities of scientists. It may be the greatest. For this task is closely linked with the survival of an open society and of democracy. An open society (that is, a society based on the ideas of not merely tolerating dissenting opinions but respecting them) and a democracy (that is, a form of government devoted to the protection of an open society) cannot flourish if science becomes the exclusive possession of a closed set of specialists.

The significance of Kuhn's work, it seems to me, lies less in its challenge to Popper's ideas about the rational assessment of scientific change than in his account of the *social* organization of modern science. This – and Kuhn's picture of the 'normal scientist' – Popper accepted as at least in part correct;[12] while at the same time he found it horrifying. Popper offered a response to it, not only in his explicit responses to Kuhn,[13] but also in his

'Moral Responsibility of the Scientist'.[14] However, the character of Popper's response – including his calls for changes to scientific education, and for public discussion among students and their teachers, centred on something like a modified version of the Hippocratic Oath – seems to me ultimately insufficient, and to highlight a problem that arises not only in his philosophy of science, but also in his political philosophy.

This problem concerns Popper's view of the relationship between norms and social organization. Popper's writings in the philosophy of science and on social philosophy offer two contrasting approaches to these matters, neither of which seems to me fully acceptable. Popper's philosophy of science is written (for example, in his discussion of 'methodological rules') in terms which invite interpretation as if he was dealing with norms that directly govern – or could govern – scientists' behaviour. Similarly, problems facing science are seen in terms either of the effects of inappropriate norms, or of the use of political power to suppress criticism.[15] In the field of politics, Popper offers us an account of what he thinks to be desirable aims for politics (and which he hopes also would be the result of an attempt at social consensus, directed towards identifying remediable evils). These are to serve as the goals for political initiatives, which are to be controlled by critical feedback from all citizens. In *The Open Society*, he also frequently suggests that we should construct institutions in order to achieve some specific goal. But Popper does not discuss *how* such institutions are to function in order to achieve the goals in question.

I would like briefly to postpone the analysis and discussion of these points until I have considered another theme in Popper's work. For there is a sense in which some of his writings after *The Open Society* – notably his 'Towards a Rational Theory of Tradition' – pose a significant problem for his ideas about institutional design. In that paper, Popper describes traditions as standing between people and institutions, and stresses the way in which the proper functioning of an institution may depend upon tradition. But while, in that paper, Popper has some interesting things to say about the tradition of rationalism, and about the importance of the critical scrutiny of tradition more generally, what he does not tell us is how one is to design institutions if their workings depend upon tradition. How, as it were, does one *create* a tradition which has desirable social consequences of a particular kind?

Popper does at one point mention that, around the time at which he left New Zealand, the chancellor of his university undertook an investigation and, continues Popper,[16] 'as a result of it made an excellent critical speech in which he denounced the university for its neglect of research'. Popper continues, however, to say:[17]

> But few will think that this speech means that a scientific research tradition will . . . be established [Popper clearly in this context may be understood as meaning: simply as a consequence of this speech having been made], for this is a very hard thing to bring about. One can convince people of the need for such a tradition, but that does not mean that the tradition will take root and flourish.

But Popper seems to me to have raised, here, what is also a significant problem for his own views. For how, given what seems to me this important point, are we now to interpret his own demands for the creation of various social institutions? How, as it were, is his 'social engineer' to create traditions? Popper has hit what could be called a Burkean constraint upon the research programme of *The Open Society*. For not only is there a problem as to how new traditions are to be created, but we also face the problem that we are, ourselves, the products of various other traditions; ones which impose limitations upon the options that are now open to us. To this, one might add that Popper later also argued that the individual is a social and cultural product; ideas which he has discussed in connection with what he calls 'world 3'. How, again, is the 'social engineer' to create institutions which will realize specific goals out of such material?

In this volume, I will take this argument one step further. For I will suggest that we need to see existing social institutions as manned by people who behave in ways that make sense to them in their various institutional settings. They are also typically subject to a variety of forms of accountability, and also to the influence of various social institutions that perform a selective role concerning the possibilities open to them. What is significant about all this, is that what Popper is writing about in his work both on epistemology and methodology, and on politics, must be understood as the products of such activity. That is to say, both knowledge as Popper understands it and the broadly negative utilitarian agenda that he commends to us as a goal of political activity are, in both cases, things which are the products of the actions of individual members of society, acting in their various social and institutional settings. But such goals are typically not – and as social institutions become more complex, they can hardly become – the *direct* object of the activities of those people: things which each individual, in his or her day-to-day life, is deliberately aiming to bring about. While each of these people must play a part if the goals that Popper is commending to us are to be achieved, what he is discussing are the by-products of interactions between many different people. But those people would not typically see themselves as playing a part in the realization of such goals; rather, they would just see themselves as going about their day-to-day tasks.

This, however, opens up a problem. A collective decision that we wish to bring about the goals that Popper favours may not in itself be of much moment. For this decision may not have any effect upon the conduct that either directly or in interaction with the conduct of others gives rise to the effects in question. It may have roughly the same character – and effects – as someone's new year's resolution to lose weight, where this is not accompanied by a detailed analysis of what specific changes would need to be made to bring about this consequence, and of whether, in fact, they were feasible. Criticism on the basis of our failure to meet such goals may tell us something important. But – not in respect of methodology, politics or weight loss – does it, in itself, tell us whether, to say nothing of how, those goals can actually be reached. In addition, once we have seen what their achievement would actually require, we may well wish to revise our initial decision that they were things that we would wish to achieve, at all.

Popper was himself fully aware that there are barriers to the realization of our normative goals. But his typical image is of us as being engaged in a process of social engineering, in which we, armed with knowledge from the social sciences, try to impress our ethical concerns onto an almost amorphous social stuff. As our knowledge is fallible, and as our actions will generate unintended consequences, he sees us as involved in a process of learning by trial and error. I will argue, in this volume, that such an approach is defective. For it does not take sufficiently seriously the character of the material upon which such 'social engineering' is working – the way in which there is something real behind it. This consists in part of structural arrangements which, while they are in place, impose constrains upon what else we can accomplish, and in part of the very meaning and significance that their own behaviour has for people, in the various historical and social situations within which they are acting, and into which they have been socialized. These points are of significance, in terms of the fact that they impose limitations concerning what, as a matter of fact, can be accomplished by means of 'social engineering' – especially a social engineering that, as Popper would wish, takes the freedom of the individual seriously; limitations which can be understood, through our understanding of these relationships by means of a realist approach to social science. But the latter of these points, in my view, points to ethical limitations upon the project of social engineering, too. For if a particular goal is put before us as desirable, it is not enough that it seems to us ethically attractive in itself. We must also consider what its achievement would mean, in terms of the actions that would have to be performed by the various people upon whose actions its realization would depend. And there is, to say the least, no reason to suppose that everything that looks attractive at the macro level will turn out to be constructable from actions which themselves are morally reasonable for the people concerned to take. If this is the case, it seems to render the claim that we should achieve these goals morally problematic.

What is needed, I would suggest, is a detailed concern not only for the design of institutions, but also for what practices, forms of accountability, and conduct would be needed in order to achieve what we tentatively take to be desirable goals. For such goals to be achievable, both practically and morally, we stand in need of an account of conduct that can make sense to individuals in the situations within which they are acting (or within those settings which are the products of feasible modifications of the institutions and settings within which they are at present operating), such that the goals in which we are interested arise as an emergent product from those actions, and from their interactions with other people. In this connection, it is vital to bear in mind that not every goal that might be set, or every suggested way of proceeding, will, in fact, make sense to the people who will be taking the actions in question. It may not make sense simply because what they would have to do in order to achieve it cannot, in fact, be undertaken in the ways suggested, or, say, in ways compatible with the rules or kinds of accountability in which they are involved,[18] or because it would involve them working in ways which they would find ethically unacceptable.

Let me offer a concrete illustration, which may give some substance to what is, otherwise, in danger of being an an over-abstract discussion. In his work on what he called 'street-level bureaucracy', Melvin Lipsky discussed the role of those people within bureaucracies who interact with members of the public. Examples might include police on the beat, those who actually deal with people making claims for social security, and so on. Lipsky, in writing about his work, says:[19]

> I argue that the decisions of street-level bureaucrats, the routines they establish, and the devices they invent to cope with uncertainties and work pressures, effectively *become* the public policies they carry out.

This, it seems to me, is to be interpreted as saying that the actual outcomes of public policy are the products of actions and procedures of the sorts to which Lipsky has referred (although clearly one needs here to take account also of the forms of accountability to which the street-level bureaucrats will be subject; although street-level bureaucrats will, again, develop routines which will enable them to cope with these). In this context, it will not make one iota of difference what goals had, formally, been decided upon by politicians or those running the agencies in question . . . unless it is shown how these goals can be achieved on the basis of actions that the street-level bureaucrats are currently taking or could, feasibly, take. It is simply pointless, in such circumstances, to tell people to act on the basis of a rule book which does not allow for the combination of discretion and rules of thumb that are needed actually to accomplish the tasks which the people in question are being required to undertake. But much the same, it seems to me, is true of all of us, in our various different social situations.

Alternatively, some task which is allocated to us may not make sense, given who we are. One must here take Burke seriously, and see ourselves as formed by our past and our traditions. This does not mean that we cannot do new things. But what we can do is limited by who we are, and by the fact that we are the products of our history, to date.

Indeed, it is in this respect that one theme of *The Open Society* – Popper's criticism of an approach to social institutions that is concerned with their history[20] – seems to me in need of modification. For if we take seriously Popper's ideas in 'Towards a

Rational Theory of Tradition', we must be concerned not just with the appraisal of institutions in the light of our current aims, but also with the (historically generated) limits on how we – and thus our institutions – can be modified. One might even draw much the same consequence from one strand of argument in *The Open Society* itself. For Popper there emphasizes the priority of sociology over psychology, arguing, for example, that even a *prima facie* psychological idea like his notion of the 'strains of civilization' is to be interpreted as a sociological as well as a psychological concept.[21] But if human psychology is seen by Popper as, in significant respects, a social product, it would seem as if we need to understand it in historical terms, in the sense that we need to understand how it has been constituted by specific historical and social situations, and the limitations that this, in turn, may impose upon the changes that we may undertake. . . .

From all this, let us return to Popper's notion of 'social engineering'. This terminology might sound strange – and even sinister – to our ears. But there is a sense in which that with which he is concerned *must* be one of our concerns. For what we care about ranges not only over our actions, as individuals, but also over the products of our – and other people's – actions. And while, as Hayek has stressed, it is important to bear in mind that valuable social outcomes may be the products of human action but not of human design, the results of the actions of ourselves, and of other people, often seem very different from what all of us would have wanted. Accordingly, how – and whether – we may improve the collective results of our actions, and the working of our institutions, is a legitimate matter of concern.

At the same time, the pursuit of such concerns (Popper's 'social engineering') must, if it is to respect individual freedom, be consensual in its character, in the sense of being of a kind with which we would be happy, if it were applied to ourselves. It would need to take us all not only ethically, as ends in ourselves, but as people who have their own concerns, desires, opinions and perspectives on things, which it makes no sense for those undertaking the 'engineering' to disregard.[22]

How might such 'social engineering' be undertaken? To my knowledge, some of the most interesting discussions of this occur within the literature of management theory and, in particular, in discussions of so-called 'market-based management'.[23] This literature (which is to be distinguished from approaches which seek to create quasi-market relationships within companies) has been concerned with a problem that one can usefully see as emerging from Hayek's work. As is well known,[24] Hayek stressed the significance of the way in which markets – and, more specifically, the price system – may enable us to utilize knowledge which is socially distributed, and which in some cases could not in principle be centralized. The problem addressed by these management theorists is posed by the issue of how such knowledge can be utilized in non-market settings; for example, within an individual firm. Related to this is the problem to which I have alluded more directly above: of how conduct that grew up – and is intelligible – within one setting, can be changed so that it better relates to some other goal. People may give this goal their rational consent. But it may well not be possible for them to pursue it directly, and in some cases the prerequisites to its achievement may not even be fully understandable to them. (For example, even in the case of a firm, consider how various possible practices in, say, a department that does not deal directly with what is marketed are to be related to a particular technical conception of the firm's profitability. It is by no means obvious how decisions about, say, production – where these relate to the expert or tacit knowledge of an engineer and a production manager, taken in the situations that confront them – are to be related to the firm's other goals.) The solution that was adopted in this management literature was, typically, that of articulating a goal, and then breaking down how the overall goal of the organization relates to people's day-to-day conduct in different settings – such that there could be changes to their routines in the light of the goal as it was disaggregated, so as to relate to their situation. This might be considered, even more usefully, as a *two*-way process, in which people's input based on their situational and often tacit knowledge might influence the organization's goals.[25]

This material seems to me both illuminating and important; not least because it highlights ways in which older, authoritarian management styles – within which people in positions of authority often gave instructions to those beneath them about how they should do things which may have made no sense whatever in those people's actual situations – are defective. It is also clearly in the spirit of Popper's work. At the same time, the application of such an approach is no easy matter, and may pose particular problems

12

in a non-commercial setting in which output cannot be judged in terms of a financial 'bottom line'. It is even more problematic if we think of it as operating not within an organization which people can choose to join – and which they can freely leave – but within a society in which nominally collective decisions are imposed upon its members. Such an approach would suggest the advantages of non-authoritarian forms of organization. But at the same time it suggests the need for a degree of openness of people's conduct to critical scrutiny, and of its control by others, of a sort that might seem worrying if we are concerned about individual liberty. In a manner that is perhaps suggestive of Foucault's discussion in *Discipline and Punish*, one might worry that while we may happily shed older authoritarian patterns of organization and the exercise of power, we may, in turn, be replacing them by something that, while softer, is more insidious, in that it relates more directly to our selves and to the patterns of conduct in terms of which we constitute our personalities. The people who are ordered around by a tyrannical boss may, as a result of this very process, develop a clear sense of their own individuality, and of their identity as something *other* than followers of what seem to them to be crazy orders, given to them by someone they do not respect.[26] The people who, by way of contrast, open up the details of their day-to-day conduct, and even aspects of their personal style, to interpersonal scrutiny and to improvement, to the better achievement of some nominally agreed goal, may in some ways be in a much better situation; but there is also a sense in which one might see their very personalities as being colonized. . . .

In *The Open Society*, Popper himself suggested that the 'greatest danger' of the form of interventionism that he favoured was that it 'might lead to an increase in state power and in bureaucracy'.[27] This misgiving seems to me of added significance, in the light of the ideas I have just discussed. In later editions of *The Open Society*, Popper argued that the interventions he favoured should take an institutional rather than a personal form. He developed these ideas by drawing a parallel with Hayek's discussion of the rule of law. Popper clearly thought that operating in this way might mitigate the risks that his preferred approach might otherwise seem to pose for individual liberty.[28] However, it is not so clear that the problems we have been discussing can be solved in such 'institutional' terms.

Popper's own discussion of the contrast between a personal and

an institutional approach is interesting. He argues for its importance in terms of our ability to learn more effectively by trial and
error (i.e. that an institution can, in a sense, be an object on which
we can work, in a way in which we cannot upon individual acts
of discretionary decision-taking). He also argued – along lines of
which Hayek had made much in his discussion of the rule of law
– that it creates a framework which 'can be known and understood
by the individual citizen', and the functioning of which is thus
'understandable' and 'predictable'.[29]

There is much to be said for Popper's and Hayek's approach.
But at the same time, it would not seem to me adequate to the
kind of task that I have discussed. First, there is a problem posed
by the very features that Popper and Hayek consider desirable:
that people may be able to understand and predict the workings
of the institutions in question. The problem is that these very
features also enable people to adjust their conduct to the forms
of institutional control to which they are subjected, so that they
treat these things not as something that gives them guidance in
the achievement of an agreed aim, but, rather, as constituting
obstacles around which they must negotiate, in the course of their
achievement of their own goals. Compare, in this context, the way
in which a wealthy person might, on the advice of an accountant,
respond to a change in the taxation code in the country in which
he or she is living.

Second, it is not clear how one could address the reshaping
of people's conduct, and even of their personalities, by means of
institutional changes of the kind that Hayek and Popper favour. To
be sure, there is a sense in which the changes in question would
respond to a concern of Hayek's: as compared with a dictatorial
regime, approaches which take individuals' knowledge and characters as the object of their concern really do take seriously each
individual's motivation and perspective. But while such approaches
allow for the individual's input, the institutional designer also
treats these things as objects to be subjected to critical re-direction
by others. But this would seem a *totally* inappropriate task for
government; or, indeed, for *any* authority, private or public.

All this might seem to leave us at an impasse. For once we take
seriously the importance of habit, custom, the social and cultural
formation of people's identities, and how people act and make
sense of their lives in specific institutional settings, our ability to
engage in social engineering seems limited. If we take individual

freedom seriously, it looks as if we might not be able to achieve much of what we want. While, if we do not, our approach starts to look like something out of *Brave New World.*

However, I would suggest that the changing of our habits, traditions, and even characters and personalities *may* be acceptable, if the acceptance of the discipline in question is both initially and on a continuing basis genuinely a matter of each individual's choice. Let me offer as an illustration here, a homely example.

Suppose that someone wishes to lose weight. One is here dealing, on an individual level, with something that is closely analogous to our problem. For the overweight person's concern relates to an object that, in Hayekian terms, is the product of their action, but not of their design. It is clearly a product of their habits and of the institutions within which they are involved, and also of their patterns of social interaction with others. Further, it is hardly itself something that *can* be the minute-to-minute object of their attention. As in the case of the institutional reforms that I have discussed, what is needed is a change in their behaviour and routines, so as to generate the desired result. This they may be able to do, by finding alternative courses of action which in themselves are desirable, and which have the effect of generating weight-loss as a by-product. (Indeed, while they may not be able to pursue the loss of weight directly, they may be able to exercise choice between otherwise attractive options, in the light of which of these also lead to the kind of large-scale outcome that they desire.) This, however, may not be enough, and they might well need much more by way of monitoring and control of their conduct. For example, they may need detailed suggestions as to what they should do; the criticism and support of others, and so on; and, indeed, they may need to follow a draconian regime.

If this were to be *imposed* upon them, however paternalistically, it would be an outrageous interference with their liberty. However, provided that the ways of proceeding within the group in question are not themselves subversive of their liberty,[30] and they could genuinely choose to leave, there would seem to me no reason whatever against their deciding voluntarily to join a group – such as Weightwatchers – within which such discipline would be imposed upon them. (Although, as distinct from the actual Weightwatchers model,[31] it would seem to me best thought of as an organization which those joining would have to understand as involving active membership, for life, and to relate not so much to their conscious pursuit of particular goals, as to how they are affected by the institutions and patterns of behaviour of which they are a part.)

Insofar as our problems require the kind of solution that I have suggested, it would seem to me inappropriate, because of its ability to use coercion, that the state itself be directly involved in the shaping of people's conduct to the achievement to some specific goal (other than, say, in the socialization of public servants, whose involvement with it would be a matter of free decision, and whose relations with it would need to be made subject to legal contracts, the mechanisms for enforcing which were themselves autonomous of the state). However, it, or some surrogate, would seem to me to have a legitimate role in ensuring the equity of the contracts, should people join institutions which play such a role; the right to leave and – though this gets more tricky – the role of sustaining and ensuring our exposure to the kind of background culture which would ensure, in the best manner possible, that decisions concerning the membership of some more specific community could be taken freely. Accordingly, a useful model would be that of people forming voluntary organizations, or of taking up commercial services, which offer solutions to these problems for them, but where their membership of the organization in question is voluntary. I am not sure of the cogency of these ideas, and I would wish to insist that the legitimacy of the problems that I raise for Popper's views does not stand or fall by their success. But one distinctive argument which I will develop in this volume will be that Popper's ideas, and the problems that are raised within them, may sometimes call for remedies that involve a degree of (freely chosen) collective control over the individual of a kind that Popper might not have welcomed. At the same time, I will argue that the proper role of the state[32] is the protection of the liberty of citizens where this is to be understood in a manner more restrictive than that which Popper himself would favour (my arguments are for something that is more clearly classical than welfare liberal). To this, however, I will add the idea that an important task for the state is the maintenance of, and the ensuring of our exposure to, a public forum. All this contrasts with Popper's own moderate, rational, and liberty-respecting but more substantively interventionist, statism.

In a manner which parallels this, I would urge the supplementation of methodology by a critical sociology of knowledge. This would address the task of how we might improve our knowledge, not just by formulating methodological rules but by examining, in detail, how knowledge is currently produced, and the various incentives and forms of accountability with which we are currently involved in the production of knowledge. It would then – subject to the considerations discussed earlier in this Introduction – address specific ways in which our knowledge-related institutions might be changed, so as better to produce the kinds of outcome that we desire. This would hold good not only for the production of knowledge within different particular specialisms, but also in respect of the reconstruction of a public sphere.

It was because of the differences from Popper's own views as to what are desirable social arrangements to which all this leads me and, in particular, because my own view is closer to classical liberalism in respect of what we owe to others, that I earlier suggested that the reader who finds what I have to say in the rest of this volume plausible – if there should be such – should be warned. Where I depart from the discussion of views with which Popper would himself identify, and from raising problems which face his work, and canvass views of my own, Popper's own reaction might well have been that I should be added to the list of those who have betrayed their teachers, along with Plato and Fichte. At the same time, as a fallibilist, Popper would have had to admit that, in principle, it is possible that one or other of these 'betrayers' might be right, although I am hardly the person to judge whether this is the case here.

1

THE DEVELOPMENT OF POPPER'S POLITICAL PHILOSOPHY

INTRODUCTION

Karl Popper was born in Vienna in 1902, into an upper-middle-class family of Jewish extraction. Popper has described his background in some detail in his autobiography, *Unended Quest*, and I will not repeat here more than I have to of this by now well-known story. In addition, I do not wish here to enter the realm of intellectual biography, not least because such work would require a knowledge of the wide range of Popper's interests and of their Austrian background, to which I cannot aspire. My concern, rather, will be to give a rough and speculative impression of the development of Popper's political views, which will serve also as an introduction to them. In this connection I will draw upon some of the material that has become available through the Popper Archive at the Hoover Institution, as well as on the work of Bartley[1] and of Hacohen;[2] but in the light of the huge quantity of material in the Popper Archive, this account should be understood as, very much, a first cut.

Popper was a highly precocious youngster, with wide-ranging intellectual interests which his early circumstances gave him every opportunity to pursue. His circumstances were to change, however, after the end of the First World War, which left Austria an impoverished rump, and subsequently with inflation which ruined his family financially. Popper describes himself as having moved away from his home into a converted military hospital,[3] in order to reduce the pressure on the family finances.

These changes in the circumstances of Vienna clearly had their effect upon many young people who experienced them. Friedrich Hayek has described the way in which they moved him to a concern with economics, because of wish to relieve suffering.[4] Popper was also profoundly affected, politically. He joined a

18

students' socialist society,[5] and subsequently moved further to the left. In *Unended Quest*, he described himself as having been a Marxist.[6] In fact, things went further than that for, as Bartley has described, he went to work, as a teenage volunteer, in the office of the tiny Austrian communist party.[7] It was from this setting that he experienced the trauma, which clearly played an important part in his intellectual development, of witnessing the loss of life that followed a demonstration in June 1919, with the organization of which that group had been involved.[8] As Popper has told us, this led to a personal crisis, in which he was led to re-evaluate whether he had been correct in the confidence that he had placed in these ideas, and decided that he had not. Bartley has claimed that this led Popper to question his faith in reason itself, and eventually to the adoption of Kantian ethics by decision, under the influence of Kierkegaard.[9] Whatever the basis of his views, it is striking that a rejection of heteronomy – whether from authority or history – is thereafter a key feature of Popper's ethics.

One practical product of this period, however, would seem to have been a first draft of the criticism of Marx that he eventually offered in *The Open Society*.[10] He has also indicated that some ideas which eventually went into *The Poverty of Historicism* stem from this period.

As Popper has described, he was able to study at the University of Vienna, as an auditor,[11] where he attended a wide range of courses. In addition to the study of physics and mathematics, he developed a particular interest in psychology. This was important, as he was in this context exposed to ideas influenced by Kantianism; to Buehler; and to the Wuertzberg School in theoretical and experimental psychology.[12] In philosophy, he was also strongly influenced by the work of Leonard Nelson's Fries'schule (on which see his 'Julius Kraft 1898–1960'),[13] and, as he has recounted, he benefited from interactions with Gomperz.[14] All this, together with his own realism, gave his thought a character somewhat different to that of the empiricism of the Vienna Circle. At the same time, Popper's concerns were strongly scientific. He was interested in contemporary developments in physical science and in mathematical logic, and he clearly shared with the Vienna Circle not only these concerns, but also the view that science was an examplar of rationality, from which we should learn in other fields.

In *Unended Quest*, and in other of his writings, Popper has described the way in which, as a result of his encounter with Marxism and also because of his sceptical reaction to the use of confirmatory evidence that he experienced at a time that he spent in a clinic for children run by Alfred Adler, he was led to concerns with the problem of demarcation, and more generally to issues in the philosophy of science. These were pursued in connection with his work in psychology, from which, however, he describes himself as having made a shift to more specifically philosophical interests, when he discovered the extent to which ideas which he had been developing had been anticipated.[15] I will not pursue these matters here, other than to note that the result was his *Die beiden Grundprobleme der Erkenntnistheorie*, in which he set out the views to which he had been led, in a systematic manner, comparing his ideas about induction and demarcation with those of other writers, including Wittgenstein. This, and his interests in science and logic, led to contacts with members of the Vienna Circle, and he seems to have been a significant influence on, for example, the development of Carnap's ideas about protocol statements.[16] At the same time, Popper was far from in agreement with Otto Neurath, who played an important role in the organization of the Circle. Neurath was at odds with Popper's philosophical views, and he championed political ideas with which Popper was also in disagreement.[17]

As Popper has described in *Unended Quest*, his work in this area eventually became *The Logic of Scientific Discovery*. All of this is import-ant, in signalling just what his concerns were – and were not. For when that work was published in 1934, his central preoccupations seem to have been ideas in the philosophy of science and develop-ments in logic – not least Tarski's theory of truth – the theory of probability, and issues relating to the interpretation of quantum theory. Thus, when Popper visited England – he spent a good part of 1935–6 away from Austria – it was with those associated with this kind of work with whom he spent time. These included Ayer (whom Popper had met in Paris in 1935, and who took him to Oxford, to the Aristotelian Society, and to Cambridge, and who introduced him to such people as Ryle, Price, Braithwaite and Ewing, and who, as Popper later said, 'looked after him as a hen looks after a chick');[18] Susan Stebbing (at whose invitation he delivered some lectures at Bedford College); and Woodger (who was later to produce a translation of *Logik der Forschung*). Indeed, as Popper was to write many years later, he was 'neither by inclination nor by training a student of society or politics'.[19]

This is not to say that Popper did not have concerns other than with epistemological, logical and scientific issues. His work at the university had qualified him as a school teacher, and he had also been involved in the intellectual activity associated with the Viennese School Reform movement. This movement had political and intellectual aspects, so that a politician who was a leading light within it, Gloeckel, had a role in Buehler's invitation to a Chair in Vienna. As Bartley has stressed, the school reform movement caught the interest of people as otherwise diverse as Popper and Wittgenstein.[20] Popper himself contributed to its journal, and Hacohen has argued that one of Popper's contributions has some political interest.

That being said, however, Popper's interests, when he was in England, were very much in the field which later would have been described as the philosophy of science. It was for this reason striking that he gave a paper to F.A. Hayek's economics seminar, at the LSE. It was on 'The Poverty of Historicism', and seems to have been strongly critical of Mannheim.

The Poverty of Historicism appears to have existed in some form or other in 1935,[21] a text having been the basis both for a talk in Brussels in 1936 and for Popper's talk to Hayek's seminar at the LSE. Further, in a letter to Edward Goodman of 27 April 1967,[22] Popper wrote something about its prehistory: 'The ideas of *The Poverty of Historicism* were *in part* conceived as early as 1919 or 1920. My views on piecemeal engineering have constantly developed since about 1922 when I first realized the problem of bureaucracy and the fact that none of my socialist friends (I was a socialist then) was interested in this awful problem, but were on the contrary for further bureaucratization of our life.'

Popper and Hayek did not know one another prior to this, and they seem to have met only occasionally when Popper was in England,[23] Hayek having referred him to the Academic Assistance Council, a body which was concerned with trying to place refugee academics in teaching positions in the UK. (This was eventually to lead to his being offered a refugee position at Cambridge, which, however, he turned down when he was offered a position in New Zealand.) There were, already at this point, certain resemblances between the views of Popper and of Hayek. Hayek had had his attention drawn by Haberler to *Logik der Forschung*, when it was first published, and he seems to have been broadly sympathetic to its approach. Indeed, as he was to write to Popper later, Hayek had himself expressed views which cohered with Popper's ideas on the theory of knowledge, prior to its publication.[24] In addition, he was clearly sympathetic to Popper's criticism of historicism. At the same time, it should be stressed that they did not know one another well, and that while they corresponded briefly after Popper's talk, it was mostly not on issues to do with social philosophy. (They do, though, relate to prediction and determinism, and it is possible that these topics had figured in Popper's talk, or in their conversations and Popper mentions having read, and agreeing fully with, Hayek's pamphlet 'Freedom and the Economic System'.) Accordingly, while Popper read some of Hayek's writings when he was in New Zealand and made acknowledgement to them in his work, and while he was later to be influenced by some of Hayek's ideas that he came across after writing *The Open Society*, there does not then seem to have been any close intellectual link between them. This made it something of a shock to Popper when, after he had completed *The Open Society and Its Enemies*, he found that Hayek – from what I will suggest were very different premises – had come to conclusions in some ways similar to his own, in *The Road to Serfdom*.[25]

NEW ZEALAND

As I have indicated, Popper was offered a teaching position in New Zealand, at Canterbury College. The transition must have been something of a shock: a move from a centre of intellectual activity to what must then have been the back of beyond. The UK representative of New Zealand universities had already warned Popper to take books with him, as there were not many there ('libraries etc. are poorly equipped');[26] and indeed, as Simkin has reported, the total library at Canterbury College, just prior to Popper's arrival, numbered around 15,000 volumes.[27] (It is striking, in this connection, that Popper's father's library, housed in the apartment in which Popper grew up, numbered some 14,000 volumes.[28]) The ethos, too, was distinctive: the concern of the college was with teaching, and, as Popper has described, research was discouraged, regarded as time stolen from this activity. To say the least, research was not supported: Popper had to pay for his own typing paper. This might not have seemed a problem, except that there was considerable inflation over the war period. Popper had been concerned as to what would happen to his wife, and had taken out insurance policies on his life (which, I might mention, matured when I was working with him in the 1970s, at which point they were almost worthless). The result was that their situation became dire, and they ended up living to a significant extent on rice and home-grown vegetables, with ice cream as an occasional treat.[29] A major drain on their finances was expenses connected with *The Open Society and Its Enemies*, as I will describe.

Popper was responsible for all the teaching in philosophy. He was in a two-person department, the head of which was responsible for teaching in psychology. Things were difficult; not least as the head of the department started to express concerns in public about Popper's political loyalty, and to make life very awkward for him. It appears that the head was suffering from some form of mental disturbance, but that it took some time for this to become generally apparent. Popper, in addition to his heavy teaching duties, also undertook a course of WEA lectures, and participated actively in local intellectual life; for example, in a number of broadcasts on the local radio.[30] In New Zealand, he undertook work on a variety of projects. On the one side, he continued his work on probability theory; on the other, he was engaged in some projects concerning political philosophy, his decision to write on which was, he tells us, taken when he received news in March 1938 of Hitler's occupation of Austria.[31]

The first of these was 'The Poverty of Historicism'. The situation here seems to have been as follows. In New Zealand, he became involved in discussion about problems of methodology in the social sciences with an economist, Harold Larsen. Larsen encouraged him to dictate an outline of a paper to his departmental typist, and Larsen then revised it. Popper then used this as the basis for a further version, which was completed by about the end of 1938. (Popper has also mentioned that, by that time, he had also written about twenty pages of a history of historicist ideas, from Plato to Marx.) A version of the paper was submitted to, but rejected by, *Mind*. In December 1943, *Economica* (in the person of its editor, Hayek) offered to publish a (by then expanded) 'Poverty of Historicism', which, however, had to be cut. Popper has written about this: 'The first part I left in the form it was ultimately in [in] 1938, but the second and third part[s] I had to re-write in the light of what I had learned in the years in which I had been working on the book [*The Open Society*].'[32]

The second of his projects was 'What is Dialectic?', and the third became *The Open Society and Its Enemies.* If these three pieces of work are put together, their broad lines are clear. 'What is Dialectic?' (which Popper had initially intended to be an appendix to *The Open Society*[33]) offers a critical reinterpretation of Hegelian and Marxian dialectic, in terms of Popper's theory of knowledge. 'The Poverty of Historicism' contains a wide-ranging discussion of issues in the methodology of the social sciences. Its key concern, however, is with the criticism of certain broad approaches to social theory; in particular, of those that see there as being a direction to history, the task of which it is the concern of the social scientist to grasp. (Popper seems to have introduced the term 'historicism' because he wanted to use something that allowed him to discuss elements which seemed to him common between Fascism and Communism.) *The Open Society* offers a controversial reading of Plato[34] and Marx as enemies of the *The Open Society* (one which, typically, was welcomed on Marx by Platonists and on Plato by Marxists). It also offers a positive account of liberal democracy, in terms which are informed by Popper's epistemology, and his ideas about 'piecemeal social engineering' (of which more later). It has typically been taken, along with Hayek's work and that of Aron and Berlin, as a version of cold war liberalism.[35] But this seems to me a misinterpretation.

First, Popper's work is strongly social democratic in its sentiment. Some aspects of his reading of Heraclitus and of Plato, in volume 1, might almost be called vulgar Marxist, in the sense that considerable emphasis is placed upon their social origins and setting, and the unprogressive character of their politics is treated as being a key to their intellectual ideas. Popper expresses genuine sympathy with the Austrian workers' movement, although he has some intellectual criticism of the Marxist theories by which they were influenced. And he is scathing about the proponents of conservative, organic theories of society, and about those who favour *laissez-faire.*

Second, there is a strong fallibilist and almost pragmatist concern for actual improvement in social affairs (though Popper is elsewhere a consistent critic of the anti-theoretical strain in pragmatism). His concern is that where there are problems, these should be identified and addressed in a practical manner, bearing in mind the fallibility of human knowledge. In this connection, he stresses the way in which those who initiate such measures are in need of feedback from all citizens. He may be seen as having offered a reinterpretation of democratic theory in the light of his epistemology, as well as stressing the importance of being able to get rid of governments through the ballot box, rather than by force.

Third, his preference for practical improvement is complemented by his criticism of those who would approach politics by way of profound diagnoses of the meaning of history. Here, he is critical both of views which see there as being any inherent meaning to history – which, for him, has been a story of morally unlovely power politics – and of those who are pretentious in the way in which they address political and ethical issues. More generally, he is sceptical as to the correctness of large-scale theories, and is particularly concerned if their proponents put their devotion to these before the things about which there could be agreement that practical improvements are needed. Popper is highly critical of pretentiousness in philosophy generally, and in moral philosophy in particular. Indeed, this seems to me a significant sentiment held in common by Popper and Wittgenstein.

At the same time, Popper himself has strong ethical concerns. In the realm of public policy, he commends to us what has been called negative utilitarianism: a concern for the remedy of avoidable suffering. This, however, is not the only strand to his ethical thought: he is clearly concerned for the freedom and well-being of the individual, and with the protection of the vulnerable. Beyond that, there is a strand of explicitly ethical argument in his work, which interrelates his ideas in epistemology and morality, and in which he offers an epistemologically based reinterpretation of the Kantian categorical imperative. I will not discuss this idea here in any detail, as we will consider it in Chapter 4.[36] But, briefly, Popper develops an argument for the 'rational unity of mankind', in which everyone is considered to be of value, and on a par with each other from an ethical point of view, because of their role as sources of possible criticism.

All this, in turn, relates to Popper's own ideas about history. History, for Popper, does not have an intrinsic meaning. Rather, in his view, it is open to us to try to give history an ethical significance, by way of political initiatives.[37] These initiatives are to proceed by means of what he calls piecemeal social engineering, in which we try to impress our ethical concerns onto what might otherwise be seen as amorphous social material. The enterprise is democratic, in the sense described above. Its piecemeal character is related not to political timidity, but to Popper's insistence on our fallibilism, and thus to the idea that we cannot be sure that a particular measure will accomplish what we desire. As we will see, later, Popper is not averse to experimentation of a quite radical kind, provided that its spirit is genuinely tentative.

THE PLACING OF *THE OPEN SOCIETY*

Popper wrote *The Open Society* in New Zealand. He wrote it, deliberately, as a political book – he has described it as his war effort. He took particular care to write informally and in an unpretentious manner, and, as I mentioned in the 'Introduction', to downplay the scholarship that went into it.[38] This and the book problem in New Zealand seem to me of importance in connection with the critical appraisal of the work: one is not, here, dealing with something written for academics, though Popper clearly took a great deal of care to document and to argue his points. At the same time, the idiosyncrasy of some of Popper's sources clearly relates to the limitations of the library facilities available to him at the time. Popper completed the book in difficult circumstances, and – as was still typical of his work when I assisted him many years later – after the production of many different versions of the manuscript. The problem was to publish it.

Concerning Popper's attempts to do this, there is a long and sad story to be told. In both the USA and Britain, there was rationing of paper. Popper thought that the iconoclastic character of the book would mean that established authorities would not like its tone.[39] He had only a few contacts with people whom he felt able to approach, but in the event he was able to send copies of the manuscript to the United States and the UK. Things did not go well in the United States. Popper felt that the issue was urgent, not least as he believed that the book had important things to contribute to the discussion of post-war reconstruction, and he also had his own firm ideas about how the friend, to whom the manuscript had been entrusted, should proceed. The friend took a rather different view of the matter, and Popper felt frustrated, as he could not discover what – if anything – was happening, and very unhappy, when, after many expensive cables, he did find out. . . .[40]

In the UK, the manuscript was in the care of Ernst Gombrich, who gave it to a number of publishers. Progress was very slow and disappointing; but there was one happy by-product: one of the referees used by a publisher (who, in the end, was not able to publish the book) was Harold Laski, who liked the book very much. This, in turn, had the consequence that when Popper was later mooted as a candidate for a readership in scientific method at the LSE, he had support from both Laski and Hayek. In the end, Routledge took the volume; a result that was considerably helped by Hayek's taking an interest in the publication, and by the enthusiasm of Herbert Read, who was then on Routledge's staff. (Popper had been reluctant that Routledge should be approached, because Mannheim, of whom he was strongly critical, edited a major series with them.) The whole process – which, because it was undertaken from New Zealand under wartime conditions, is amply documented in the Hoover Archives – is fascinating, both in personal terms, and also because of what is revealed about Popper's intentions with regard to the book.

One interesting feature that emerges from this material concerns Popper's relations with Hayek. As I have already indicated, prior to Popper's move to New Zealand his contacts with Hayek were limited. However, Popper had read those of Hayek's publications that were available in New Zealand, and made some references to them in *The Open Society*. Hayek's work was later to make some impact on Popper's social philosophy, notably in respect of his ideas about the importance of institutional procedures as opposed to individual discretion in government.[41] At the same time, it seems to me that while in New Zealand he did not, and did not subsequently, pay much attention to Hayek's argument concerning economic calculation under socialism – an argument which, in my view, is crucial for the shaping of Hayek's social theory.[42]

Popper was, however, somewhat disconcerted, when, on obtaining a copy of Hayek's *The Road to Serfdom*, he found the extent to which they had come to similar conclusions. Indeed, he wrote to Gombrich to ask him to insert into the manuscript of *The Open Society* an indication of when the manuscript had been completed, lest it seemed as if he had borrowed, unacknowledged, from Hayek.[43] In a letter to Carnap[44] Popper stressed that he did not know of Hayek's *The Road to Serfdom* prior to writing *The Open Society*, and that 'all he knew' at the time was Hayek's *Freedom and the Economic System*.[45] In his letter to Carnap,[46] Popper explains his reference to Hayek in the 'acknowledgement' to *The Open Society* in terms of Hayek's practical assistance, rather than his intellectual influence; although Popper then continues by saying that he has, since, read not only Hayek's *The Road to Serfdom*, and 'has learned a *very* great deal from it', but also 'several excellent articles'.

The reference to practical assistance related to the fact that Hayek read the manuscript of *The Open Society* and offered to assist Gombrich in placing it with a publisher. This leads to a point of some interest, politically. Gombrich gives an account of a meeting with Hayek at the Reform Club, and, in this connection, he refers to the pink and angular faces that he noticed there. Indeed, while Hayek was sympathetic to *The Open Society*, Gombrich and Popper seemed to feel that Hayek was not at one with them politically, and the 'pink and angular faces' theme is used by them as a kind of marker of that from which they distance themselves politically.[47] Popper seemed concerned that Hayek was sympathetic to conservatism, and, more specifically, to a *laissez-faire* approach within economics. Accordingly, while Popper is fulsome in his praise of Hayek's work, and is struck by the way in which its conclusions seem close to his own (suggesting at one point that *The Road to Serfdom* might be seen as a kind of third volume of *The Open Society*),[48] and hopeful that Hayek might be closer to him, politically, than he perhaps was, Popper is also somewhat critical.

In writing to Hayek about *The Road to Serfdom*, Popper stressed, as a practical point, that it seemed to him vital to acknowledge the importance of helping the poor, and to address the issue of unemployment. These were things which Popper himself thought should be on the agenda for government action, on moral grounds. But he wished to stress to Hayek that, in his judgement, if Hayek did not address them, he would lose the *political* argument.[49] More generally, Popper wished to argue against the political possibility of *laissez-faire*, and to champion, against Hayek, his own ideas about 'protectionism'. I discuss the respective views of Popper and Hayek in more detail below,[50] but it is important at this point to note one significant contrast between them. For Popper, central to politics were, in effect, substantive political judgements about which there was consensus, and which the state would undertake to implement. Popper doubted not only the political but also the moral acceptability of the kinds of view that Hayek favoured. He also took issue with Hayek's criticism of the ideal of social justice, in similar terms: in Popper's view, there was – *pace* Hayek – an intelligible and morally significant aspect to the idea.[51]

It is striking that, in what seem to be Popper's notes for a letter to Hayek of 28 May 1944, Popper expresses somewhat stronger misgivings, commenting that: 'although the free market is certainly irreplaceable for safeguarding freedom, it does not suffice to protect weak individuals'. Popper is thus concerned with 'protecting the vulnerable' (to use the title of Goodin's well-known book) in a way that Hayek is perhaps not, despite his endorsement of a welfare safety net. At the same time, it is understandable that Popper was somewhat ambiguous in his reaction to Hayek. At a purely human level, he had every reason to be profoundly grateful to Hayek in respect of *The Open Society*. Hayek was also taking 'The Poverty of Historicism' in *Economica*. (In this connection, it seems to me that one should be careful of reading too much into Popper's discussion of Hayek in the final parts of *The Poverty of Historicism*, which were being rewritten for Hayek's journal.) Hayek also subsequently played an important role in helping Popper to obtain a position at the LSE.

More significant from an intellectual perspective, there is a genuine sense in which the reader of *The Road to Serfdom* might be unclear just where Hayek stands. For there is much in that work which is compatible with *values* which are much more socialist-inclined than one would today associate with Hayek. The possible compatibility between Hayek's views and the concerns – if not the social theory – of those on the Left was stressed by Popper in his correspondence with Carnap. Hayek himself also expressed sympathy with socialist sentiments – in the sense of feeling the attraction of socialist values, if not then thinking that they could be realized – even *after* the publication of *The Road to Serfdom*.

The crucial difference between Popper and Hayek, however, is that while they both make use of epistemological argument for a broadly liberal position, Popper's views centre on the fallibility of scientific knowledge, while Hayek is concerned not with scientific knowledge but with political lessons which might be extracted from what could be called the social division of information. Further to this, central to Popper's vision of politics is the political imposition of a shared ethical agenda, through a process of trial and error: of piecemeal social engineering. What is central for Hayek are markets and their associated institutions which, on his account, form a kind of skeleton for a free society – one which, at the same time, enables us to make cooperative use of socially divided knowledge, and to enjoy a broadly 'negative' conception of individual freedom.

AFTER *THE OPEN SOCIETY*

As I have just indicated, *The Road to Serfdom* is somewhat ambiguous as to exactly where Hayek's political sympathies lie. Much the same might be said about Popper: it is striking that *The Open Society* has found a friendly reception at various different points on the political spectrum. In the United Kingdom, he has found champions from such politically diverse figures as Ian Gilmour and Bryan Magee (and, indeed, even from the one-time British Fascist leader, Sir Oswald Mosley[52]), while at one point Popper was being heralded as a kind of patron saint by both of West Germany's major political parties. But where did Popper himself stand, and how, politically, is *The Open Society* to be read? Some suggestions about this may be ventured, in the light of his ideas in the period immediately after *The Open Society*.

One immediate indication is given by his response to an invitation from Hayek to join what became the Mont Pelerin Society.[53] Popper's response was friendly, but he urged Hayek that he needed to invite some socialists to join. (His suggestions were: Barbara Wootton, Bertrand Russell, Victor Gollancz, George Orwell, G.D.H. Cole, Henry Dickinson, Abba Lerner, Evan Durbin, Reinhold Niebuhr, Lord Lindsay, Herbert Read and Lord Chorley.) This might seem a strange reaction, but it is understandable in the light of what, to Popper, was the key issue of the immediate post-war period: the need to forge and preserve an alliance between liberals and socialists, as distinct from those who were not concerned with freedom.[54]

There are, in fact, two aspects to this judgement of Popper's. On the one hand, he is concerned, lest a political gulf open between liberals and democratic socialists, which would drive the latter into the hands of those who were not democrats and who were not concerned with freedom. Second, there is the issue of Popper's own substantive views. This was raised in an interesting manner, in correspondence with Rudolf Carnap. Carnap, who had been a leading figure in the Vienna Circle, was then teaching in the United States. He was a socialist, and had known Popper in Vienna as a socialist. He had read – and, it appears, had liked – *The Poverty of Historicism*. But, he wondered, where did Popper now stand, politically? It was all very well to advocate discussion between liberals and socialists, but which of the two was Popper? And where did he stand on the crucial issue of the socialization of the means of production? Don't we, as Carnap suggested, need to transfer at least the bulk of the means of production from private into public hands?[55] And was this compatible with Popper's ideas about piecemeal social engineering?

Popper, in his response to Carnap,[56] gave an informative outline of his views. In some respects, he was in agreement with socialism. He favoured the idea that there should be much greater equality in incomes than currently existed anywhere, and bold but *critical* experiments in the political and economic spheres. This, he said, could include the socialization of the means of production, provided that the dangers of doing this were squarely faced, and that one did not regard it as a cure-all. He was also concerned about the way in which business interests might interfere in politics, and thought that it was vital that this should be curbed, including, possibly, by means of socialization. He was also concerned that action be taken against the power of monopolies.

All this might seem to place him squarely with the democratic socialists. But in this connection it is important to note some other points. First, Popper commenced his letter by saying that he thought that neither socialism nor liberalism was a term which could characterize a 'serious and responsible political position', and later in the letter he also explained that he held some views in respect of which he disagreed with socialists. He stressed that he did not believe in the existence of a 'cure-all' in politics – which, from the context, was clearly a reference to socialization. In addition, he stressed that, within a socialist economy, it was possible that there could be greater differences in income than existed currently, and greater possibilities for the abuse of economic power, because socialization involves the accumulation of economic power. Further, he was concerned that there could be greater interference in politics by those with economic power than was the case at present, and also the danger of the control of thought. Popper's overall approach was, he wished to stress, an undogmatic one: socialization might make things better, or it might make things worse; his concern was that socialists did not seem willing to see – and to address – its dangers.

At the same time, Popper combined this criticism with a re-emphasis on concerns – rather than measures – which might seem socialist in temper. He suggested that we are now rich enough 'to guarantee everybody a decent income (out of income taxes)'; something that, he believed, would eliminate exploitation based on the threat of starvation. This, he recognized, would involve state interference in the economic realm, and perhaps the socialization of monopolies. He criticized what he saw as the utopian – and almost religious – streak, which he thought was present in both socialism and liberalism. And he concluded by indicating that while he shared the conviction of liberals that 'freedom is the most important thing in the political field', he took the view that 'freedom cannot be saved without improving distributive justice, i.e. without increasing economic equality'.

It is worth noting that Popper's own attachment to freedom is not based upon consequentialist argument, or upon a kind of historicist triumphalism of his own. To take one example from many, in a lecture 'Freedom: A Balance Sheet', delivered originally in Switzerland and revised in October 1965, Popper concluded his discussion by stressing four points. First, that in his view Western democracies are the best of which we have knowledge. By this, he explained, he meant that: 'Never before was there a society in which common men were so much respected as in ours; in which there were so few who are downtrodden and insulted . . . never before were so many anxious to make sacrifices, in order to relieve those who are less fortunate than themselves.'[57] (Although he also stresses the imperfections of such societies and the importance of criticism.) More significant for our purposes are his subsequent points. Second, he stressed that 'we must not expect that freedom [or democracy] will deliver the goods', in the sense of their necessarily producing prosperity or happiness. Third, he emphasized that freedom is 'a . . . value in itself, irreducible to material values'; and finally that, 'if we choose freedom, we must be prepared to perish with it': there is no guarantee that it will triumph.[58]

As to Popper's own views about freedom, his reactions to Isaiah Berlin's Inaugural Lecture are not without interest.[59] Popper, in a letter to Berlin, compliments him on his treatment of positive freedom, but then goes on to discuss whether there may not be a notion of positive freedom that is compatible with negative freedom. Popper raises the idea that one may wish 'to spend one's life as well as one can; experimenting; trying to realize in one's own way, and with full respect to others (and their different valuations) what one values most'. He asks whether the search for truth may not be 'part of a positive idea of self-liberation', and suggests that such an idea is anti-authoritarian in spirit. He concludes by writing; 'only those who have, more or less, adopted the Socratic way of life can fully understand such ideas as the idea of negative freedom. Only they can expound it – as you have done so well.' This seems to me interesting, not only for the information that it gives us about Popper's personal views, but also in relation to contemporary discussion as to why negative liberty should be valued.[60]

It is also a theme that is echoed by Popper in a letter that he sent to Hayek on 24 October 1964,[61] in which he discussed some themes from Hayek's *The Constitution of Liberty*, including what Hayek had to say about freedom and coercion. Popper refers to Hayek's discussion of 'inner freedom',[62] – with which Hayek indicates that he will not be concerned – and Popper suggests that it may for some purposes be necessary to distinguish between this and what Popper terms 'Socratic freedom', which Popper relates to Hayek's own idea of 'inner strength' (compare *The Constitution of Liberty*, p. 138). Popper then continues: 'It is related to your concept of freedom because with zero inner strength all kinds of action would be [coercive] which do not coerce a man of average inner strength; so that one way of increasing one's freedom [from] coercion is, clearly, the increase of one's inner strength; which was the ideal of . . . Socrates.'

If, to this, the objection was raised that this means that Popper does not have a purely negative conception of freedom, then the answer is, surely, that that is indeed the case. When Popper, in *The Open Society*, discusses the protection of freedom, his concern is by no means to be understood in terms of non-interference. Rather, Popper, while sympathetic to the concerns of the theorists of a 'negative' interpretation of freedom, also takes the view that the state should have a positive role, not only in protecting people from economic exploitation, but also, for example, in providing access to higher education.

Let us now return to issues raised in Popper's letter to Carnap. It is important to bear in mind that, in addition to wishing to reconcile liberals and (democratic) socialists, Popper at the time had some very specific views of his own. In a paper, 'Public and Private Values',[63] he argues that socialists and liberals should shelve their disagreements in favour of a limited agenda for social reform, on the basis of that upon which they can agree. More specifically, Popper argued that liberals and socialists each had Utopian dreams – of, respectively, a society in which 'Spontaneously, without law, faith and right prevail', or of a state that 'looks after its citizens in the manner of a mother looking after her children' (p. 5). Popper argued that such dreams should be recognized for what they are, and offered instead his own agenda. His proposal was, in effect, for the socialization of misery – in the sense that its relief should be put on the public agenda. However, he argued that if liberals would accept this, then their own concerns about possible threats to freedom from state action, when they were specific, should be taken seriously by everyone. The liberals, by contrast, should be allowed to win in the field of positive or private values, where 'public policy should be confined to the protection of freedom, to the encouragement of free competition and of the freedom of choice' (p. 8). This agenda clearly relates closely to his ideas in *The Open Society* about negative utilitarianism (although it is important that we do not interpret 'utilitarianism' here in any narrow sense: Popper's agenda, in this paper, includes the relief of 'starvation, pain, humiliation, injustice, exploitation' (p. 1).

Popper's proposal would, presumably, be objected to by those socialists who insisted upon the socialization of the means of production as a precondition for significant social change. But it was against such a view that Popper had argued, in his criticism of Marx in *The Open Society*: surely, he argued, political initiatives could lead to reforms, and he suggested that this was shown by the fact that capitalism had changed from the time at which Marx was writing. Similarly, they would be rejected by those liberals who, like Hayek, wished to give priority to a specific institutional framework, and might be concerned about reforms of the kind advocated by Popper as being steps on *The Road to Serfdom*. But Popper, here, again had a response. As he had argued to Hayek in a letter,[64] *laissez-faire* was not a viable option (and indeed, Hayek was himself a *critic* of *laissez-faire*). But, argued Popper, once this is agreed, the issue then becomes what *form* of interventionism is to be pursued; and once this is accepted as the agenda for political debate, one has the *possibility* for agreement between liberals and democratic socialists. One might, indeed, take Hayek's dedication of *The Road to Serfdom* to 'socialists of all parties', and the interventionist strands within it, as signalling a measure of sympathy with this approach.

Popper and Hayek remained friends; they had some interesting exchanges over issues relating to Hayek's *The Sensory Order*,[65] and Popper was a particularly appreciative reader of the first volume of Hayek's *Law, Legislation and Liberty*.[66] At the same time, there were real differences between them. Popper offered an important argument against the view – to which Hayek sometimes seemed inclined – that institutions that had grown organically were beyond rational criticism, by pointing out that natural languages, which were among Hayek's prize examples, allowed for the formation of paradoxes and thus, in some areas, that they may be in urgent need of critical improvement.[67] He also (as I have previously mentioned) stressed, in writing to Hayek, that they were not in agreement over Hayek's criticism of social justice. For Popper, when people used this term, they meant something that was comprehensible and morally significant, and which Hayek would also disregard at his political peril.[68] Hayek, for his part, took the view that Popper remained too much of an economic interventionist.[69]

Finally, it is worth noting the view of socialism that Popper was to express later, in his intellectual autobiography *Unended Quest*:[70]

> if there could be such a thing as socialism combined with individual liberty, I would be a socialist still. For nothing could be better than living a modest, simple and free life in an egalitarian society. It took some time before I recognized this as no more than a beautiful dream; that freedom is more important than equality; that the attempt to realize equality endangers freedom; and that, if freedom is lost, there will not even be equality among the unfree.

This is a striking sentiment; but a critic might say that while Popper here suggests an interesting line of argument, he does not explain what he would have said to his younger self, and, in particular, what his view would now be about the (sociological) relation between the maintenance of freedom and equality.

All that I can here offer is a comment that Popper made in an address delivered on 29 October 1984, on receiving an award from the Fondation Tocqueville. In the course of his brief address, Popper discusses some issues in which he now judges that Tocqueville – whose work he did not know, when writing *The Open Society* – had anticipated him. Popper's final point is one in which, he judges, a knowledge of Tocqueville would have led him to improve upon his analysis; especially concerning what he says about 'the paradoxes of freedom'. In particular, Popper suggests that Tocqueville has seen that citizens' wish for equality can be 'a danger to freedom'. And Popper continues:[71]

> For equality of the citizens by necessity tends to strengthen the central government [presumably, because its power is needed, to bring about such equality; and if] that strong government should fall into the hands of bureaucrats, or if it should be usurped by a strong man [or, indeed, we may now well add, woman] the people may lose their freedom. They may even surrender it willingly.

However, one must not be too quick to conclude that Popper had moved into the ranks of classical liberalism. For in an (unsent) letter which he wrote in March 1974 to Bryan Magee, a friend of many years, who wrote the *Modern Masters* volume on his work, and who had just been elected a Labour MP,[72] Popper discusses nationalization. He is critical of the idea that there should be 100 per cent nationalization. But he suggests that the state should take a controlling interest – 51 per cent – of all public companies. However: (a) the companies should not be interfered with in general but 'only if the situation warrants it'; (b) government should initially take only 40 per cent of the companies' income – equivalent to the then-prevalent rate of company taxation; and (c) there should be some institution – such as a court – to which the state would have to go if it wished to make use of its 51 per cent share to control the company.

All this – just five years before Mrs Thatcher came to power in Britain – should, I think, give pause to those who want to see Popper as having something to do with the New Right (although in my personal view, the logic of his own argument should have led him in this direction). It also poses an interesting problem as to how the different strands in Popper's work are to be reconciled; one which I will try to address in later chapters in this volume.

2

THE OPEN SOCIETY AND *THE POVERTY OF HISTORICISM*

POPPER CONTEXTUALIZED

The Open Society, The Poverty of Historicism and 'What is Dialectic' are usefully seen together and as pieces in which Popper defends his own ideas in political philosophy against what he took to be widely favoured alternatives. In these works, Popper offers an account of the approach to politics and society that he wishes to commend, and arguments against views which he sees as incompatible with it. As indicated in Chapter 1, I will not, here, discuss his critical reinterpretations of the views of other political philosophers. His prime task in that analysis, however, would seem to me best understood not as a purely historical exercise, but as a critique of ideas that he believed to be widely influential in intellectual life and in the politics of his day; and also as part of an argument that was making space for his own approach, in a setting in which it seemed, as it were, to be crowded out.

Popper's discussions of Plato and Marx have been criticized, but they are serious if consciously controversial attempts to offer a critical account of the ideas of major thinkers. Popper was clearly willing to defend his views as historical interpretations. But it would seem to me a mistake to see a concern for this – and for the views of specific intellectual figures – as having pride of place in his work. For its underlying thrust is, rather, the advocacy of a particular approach to politics, and the criticism of what he considered to be widespread views which were incompatible with it. Popper's concerns were strongly practical. Indeed, his entire approach to social science depicts it as the handmaid of social reform. And, interested as Popper was in the more purely intellectual issues which he discusses, his concern was even more strongly with their effects upon people's practical conduct and with what seemed to him urgent issues such as the protection of the weak and the remedying of avoidable suffering.

The time at which Popper was writing was, in a significant sense, not ours. To us, his overriding concern with what he called 'historicism' may seem strange. But then, the period during which he was writing may itself also seem very distant from us. Today, many serious people are Marxists. But they are hardly communists in the sense of people who are willing to alienate their judgement to a political party. And while some people today still play with symbols drawn from Fascism and National Socialism, these very movements, too, seem grotesque; not just because of their consequences and the sentiments that informed them, but in their very character. Indeed, there is a sense in which it is only those who remained democrats and ethical individualists during that period – whether their politics were conservative, socialist or liberal – who seem to be dealing with problems, and to have sensibilities, which are anything like our own. But as a result, we may be too ready to treat them as our contemporaries, and thus to disregard the extent to which the problems that they were facing – and thus also that in opposition to which they developed their views – were different from ours.

In making this plea for contextualization – and thus endorsing an argument that has been made particularly powerfully by Hacohen – I am not wishing to argue that contextualization should supplant critical assessment. But I think that we should follow Collingwood – and Popper himself – in seeking to understand what the problems were to which people were reacting, in order to understand, and then to evaluate, their theories. I believe that we should take Popper's concern with what he called historicism at its face value; namely, as representing his understanding of something which was influential not only among many of those on the Left who were his contemporaries, but also among many on the Right. What he is combating is, in my view, best understood in terms of its denial of what he wished to advocate – namely, the possibility of a programme of humanitarian social reform, under-taken through a process of trial and error, and with respect for the liberty of the individual.

Historicism, for Popper, seems to me primarily to have been a view which suggested that there was a direction to history, to which we must accommodate ourselves. Many of Popper's contemporaries did clearly think in such terms. Consider the widespread view that the First World War and its aftermath were to be understood as marking the end of an old era. Consider, further, the attitudes towards communism which were widely held through that period by those who were sympathetic to it, as documented, for example, in *The God that Failed,* or, say, in Louis Althusser's discussion of his relations with the French communist party in the period after the Second World War, in his autobiography.[1] It is striking, also, to read of the impact made by translations of Popper's work into Polish, as late as the 1980s.[2]

The ideas of which Popper was critical may in some ways seem so foreign to us that Popper's own concern for their criticism, by way of the criticism of ideas which gave them support in the work of such figures as Plato and Marx, has been understood simply as a strange and illegitimately politicized way of treating of the work of these figures. Insofar as Popper was concerned with the interpretation of their work (and this is clearly something that Popper took seriously), his views can usefully be discussed as such. But we should not lose sight of the way in which Popper was responding to views which were current at the time he was writing.[3]

Our sense of distance may be compounded by the fact that today there are few around who are defending the kind of views of which Popper was critical. Those who now interpret Marxism typically offer interpretations to which Popper's strictures would not apply as easily, and would themselves often agree with his criticism of earlier interpretations of Marx's work. At the same time, there is a sense in which views like those of which Popper was critical are to be found quite widely today; not only in that notorious refuge of the intellectually vapid, the liberal interpretation of religion, but also among some of those who favour 'new social movements' and post-modernism. I have in mind the idea that certain ideas are to be rejected *because* they are dated, or in some sense against the spirit of the age, rather than on the basis of a critical discussion of their merits.[4] In making this point, I do not mean to deny that there may be ways in which the ideas that inform such views could be reinterpreted in ways that would escape this criticism, and indeed, that there may be something of value in them. But for this to happen itself requires that their proponents come to terms with Popper's criticism.

There is, however, also a sense in which Popper's own substantive views in *The Open Society* and *The Poverty of Historicism* are distant from our own. Indeed, as I have already mentioned in the Introduction to this volume, I was struck by the extent to which ideas are to be found in those texts that came as a shock to my own sensibilities, developed, as they were, by close contact with the older Popper. Popper's own arguments against historicism and moral futurism counsel that one must not uncritically take later for better. One of the tasks of this volume will be concerned with the critical assessment of some of the differences between Popper's earlier and later ideas. But it does, nonetheless, seem to me important that we do not uncritically treat these early works of Popper's as if they could speak to us directly; rather, it would be desirable if we could treat them as objects distant from ourselves, in order to understand them, and then to assess them critically.

A proper attempt at this would, as Hacohen has argued, involve their contextualization, in the sense of placing them within the ongoing debates in which Popper was a participant in Vienna, and in the context of his own intellectual development. This is not a task that I can here undertake, and I must restrict myself, instead, largely to an attempt at the reconstruction of his argument as it speaks to us from his writings, and I await with interest the research of such writers as Hacohen and Caldwell on the context to this material. My reconstruction, however, must be understood as something that will surely be open to significant correction, in the light of a fuller contextualization.[5] At the same time, it nonetheless seems to me that a critical discussion of Popper's own ideas is also of considerable current significance. Not only are his own views close to those of certain important contemporary writers,[6] but their critical discussion leads us into a host of issues which seem to me of pressing importance for current debate.

BETWEEN SCYLLA AND CHARYBDIS

I have indicated, above, that *The Poverty of Historicism* and *The Open Society* include Popper's attempt to make space for his own views, against two alternatives which he sees as widespread, and of which he was critical. The views in question were what he called 'historicism' and 'utopian social engineering'. Let us consider these in turn.

There is a danger that historicism, for Popper, becomes simply a repository for a whole range of ideas that he does not like. But there is a unity to his discussion; one which is provided by its contrast with his ideas about piecemeal social reform. Historicism, for Popper, may be seen as the theory that history has an intrinsic direction, to which, if we are rational, we can only accommodate ourselves. It denies, in a fundamental way, our own responsibility for what occurs in politics and in history, in that this direction to history is seen as being something that stands independently of our will and our evaluations.

Popper's term 'historicism' is very much of a portmanteau, within the body of which many different ideas are discussed. That he proceeds in this manner might be seen as exhibiting a feature akin to a Platonic realism within his own approach, in that he seems to suggest that he is dealing with something that is shared by many *prima facie* different ideas. There are, to be sure, some historical links between the ideas which he is criticizing – in the sense that there is a clear relationship between Hegel's ideas and later and vaguer ideas about the periodization of history, and also with the forms of 'scientific' Marxism with which Popper engaged. There is also a similar relationship between Platonic and, subsequently, 'civic humanist' ideas about cycles of corruption and decline in history and views which were current at the time at which he was writing. Historicism, in his view, clearly underlay the popular political movements of his day to which he was opposed. One might also look at the unity of 'historicism' in terms of its functional role: of serving to call into question, by a variety of arguments, Popper's own favoured approach to politics. In Popper's various works, he combats these ideas in many different fields, including the philosophy of the social sciences and social theory, the theory of explanation, and also in moral philosophy and aesthetics, in which connection he is critical of both moral and aesthetic futurism.[7]

Very broadly, Popper argued that historicist social theory was mistaken, in that it drew on incorrect analogies with the physical sciences, in which, he argued, nothing akin to laws of social development were to be found. Popper also argued – making use of his own theory of explanation – that scientific explanations were conditional, in that they involved both universal laws and initial conditions. While, to be sure, in the presence of instantiated initial conditions one could make forecasts akin to those of the historicists, the knowledge required for this was typically not available to us in respect of long-term predictions.[8] The idea that

41

we might have, in the social sciences, something akin to the kind of prophetic knowledge that we have in respect of the seasons or the movements of the solar system was, he argued, mistaken; not least, because the large-scale regularities which we experienced there, and whose behaviour we were able to forecast, depended upon the physical systems in question being relatively isolated. In the fields of morality and aesthetics, Popper argued that moral and aesthetic historicism – the idea that what was right or aesthetically good was what would be realized in the future – was intellectually unacceptable, and pernicious in its practical consequences.

All this served as the basis for an argument that what occurred in the political and social realms, and in the realm of aesthetics, was, squarely, our responsibility. In this respect – as in much else in Popper's work – there are strong Kantian resonances, in that what we are dealing with here amounts to a powerful repudiation of heteronomy. There is, however, as we will see, a certain ambiguity in Popper's work as to what results from all this. Before discussing this – and Popper's own substantive ideas – we need also to look at the other view against which Popper wished to defend his approach: the Charybdis of utopian social engineering.

What Popper meant by this was a certain conception of large-scale social change, akin to that with which Hayek took issue in his writings against the engineering mentality and large-scale social planning,[9] and which is perhaps most easily understood in terms of Popper's arguments against it. At the heart of this view, to which Popper was opposed, is the idea that social reform should involve the cleaning of the social slate, so that a new and ideal society could be imposed in place of the imperfect institutions which existed before. Against this, Popper advances a battery of arguments.

First, he argues that for such an exercise to be undertaken, there must be a single, unchanging social ideal which is to be realized. But this, he argues, we do not have: there is disagreement with respect to social ideals, which there is no rational way of settling. And this, he suggests, means that if a single ideal is needed, it will have to be imposed by force.[10] He also argues that there is a danger that the success of the plan may become tied up with the prestige of powerful political interests, who cannot allow for the admission of failure.

Second, he argues that we do not possess knowledge appropriate to such a task. He warns, in this context, that we are apt to over-rate the value of our theoretical knowledge. And he suggests that, if we take the analogy with actual engineering seriously, we do not have the kind of practical, experience-based know-how which would be needed for such a task. Actual engineering always calls for practical adjustments, not the simple application of a blueprint. He further argues that we will typically wish to modify our aims, once we have started to implement them, and that this contrasts with the style of 'utopian social engineering', and also with the idea that we may demand, morally, present sacrifices to be made by others, for the future achievement of this end or goal.

Indeed, this leads us to his third argument. This is that the approach which he is criticizing involves a form of aestheticism. Against this, Popper argues that moral priority should be given to the alleviation of suffering and the putting right of injustice, rather than the realization of some grand social vision. In addition, he argues for each person's right to model his or her own life, rather than being a means to an end in someone else's grand design, and he also argues strongly against the morality of trading off the concerns of one generation against the supposed benefits to others (a point in respect to which his fallibilism is also of course highly relevant).

Popper was also, later, to advance an additional argument against utopian social engineering.[11] It is perhaps best expressed by way of a brief quotation:[12]

> a revolution always destroys the institutional and traditional framework of society. It must thereby endanger the very set of values for the realization of which it has been undertaken. Indeed, a set of values can have social significance only insofar as there exists a social tradition which upholds them.

This, however, introduces a theme in Popper's work, relating to the importance of tradition, which seems to me to contrast with the approach of *The Open Society*, and which I will therefore discuss in a later chapter.[13]

Some comments are, perhaps, worth adding about all this.

The first relates to utopian social engineering, and to the contrast between it and Popper's own favoured idea of 'piecemeal social engineering'. It is important to note that the contrast is not one either of scale or of type. Popper stresses that he does 'not suggest that piecemeal social engineering cannot be bold';[14] and from his correspondence with Rudolf Carnap, it is clear that it could include socialization of the means of production, provided that this was undertaken in a tentative and piecemeal spirit.[15] Indeed, in a sense, what lies at the heart of his picture of utopian social engineering is Popper's objection to the assumption, on the part of its practitioners, that they have knowledge which does not stand in need of testing through trial and error, and critical feedback.

My other comments relate to distinctive features of Popper's views about the social sciences at the time at which he wrote *The Open Society*. The first concerns his repudiation of 'essentialism'. This he develops in the course of a criticism of Aristotle's ideas about scientific knowledge and definitions; but the idea runs much deeper than that (if I can so express it). Popper repudiates the idea that science should be aiming for essential definitions which are known for certain through intellectual intuition. In *The Open Society*, he endorses the view that science aims at description, which is counterpoised to a knowledge of what things (essentially) are. For example, in an exposition of views which he favours, and to which he refers as 'methodological nominalism', he writes:[16]

> Instead of aiming at finding out what a thing really is, and at defining its true nature, methodological nominalism sees the aim of science in the description of the things and events of our experience, and in an 'explanation' of these events, i.e. their description with the help of universal laws.

Popper also notes Berkeley as having held the 'methodological nominalism' which he favours;[17] and he also discusses him as having held the view that 'science should *describe* rather than *explain* by essential or necessary connections'.[18] This view Popper describes as having 'become one of the main characteristics of positivism', but then goes on to argue that it 'loses its point if [Popper's] theory of causal explanation is adopted'.[19]

The term 'essentialism' is used in *The Open Society*, however, not only in respect of Aristotle's theory of definitions, but also to mark any view in which – as in Marx – a contrast is drawn between appearance and essence. However, in the light of Popper's own later ideas, this seems to me to risk drawing too sharp a contrast; in particular, one which does not allow for the possibility of a (conjectural) knowledge of structures which may serve to explain the appearances of things, and offer a degree of 'depth' in explanation, which goes beyond the discovery of universally true regularities. Such ideas, I will argue,[20] are to be found in Popper's own later work;[21] but the fact that he did not hold them at the time at which he wrote *The Open Society* seems to me to leave its mark upon that work. In particular, Popper's repudiation of essentialism and of historicism has the consequence that certain ideas – for example, as that a certain way of ordering our affairs (i.e. a particular form of economic organization) has certain systematic consequences, such that, to remedy those consequences requires that change be made to that way of ordering things (which is a way in which the concerns of economists as different as Marx and Hayek might be read) – would seem to stand condemned on methodological grounds. By way of contrast, social laws seem to have been thought of by Popper in terms of universal regularities.

An issue in some ways related to Popper's repudiation of essentialism concerns the pragmatic character of his view of social science. In *The Poverty of Historicism*, Popper quotes Hayek to the effect that:[22]

> economic analysis has never been the product of detached intellectual curiosity about the why of social phenomena, but of an intense urge to reconstruct a world which gives rise to profound dissatisfaction.

Popper accepts that sociology, say, is 'a theoretical discipline', the task of which is to 'explain and predict events'.[23] But he commends to us, as an account of its aims, what he describes as 'technological social science'.[24] He urges a concern with practical problems upon those social sciences that have not (yet) made this the focus of their attention, stating that those that have not 'show by the barrenness of their results how urgently their speculations are in need of practical checks'. Popper also comments that 'many of the followers of historicism' wish to transform 'the social sciences into a powerful instrument in the hands of the politician', and Popper is willing to take this 'practical task of the social sciences' as 'common ground for discussion between the historicists and some of their opponents'.[25]

While I would not wish to over-stress the point, all this serves to give Popper's account of the social sciences an atheoretical character; something that is complemented by his stress upon an absence of *practical* experience in institutional design which we noted in connection with his arguments against utopian social engineering, where he also counselled against the over-rating of our knowledge of causes. There is, however, more to it even than this. For example, he is critical, in the course of championing 'an engineering approach to the problem of peace', of approaches which focus upon the task of discovering the *causes* of war, arguing also in more general terms that 'the method of removing causes of some undesirable event is applicable only if we know a short list of necessary conditions'.[26]

Popper may well be right in particular cases. And there would seem to me every reason that research should be undertaken with an eye to the solving of practical problems. But there is a danger in his approach, if it is taken as co-extensive with the social sciences. For complex relationships may exist between different factors of a kind that will be disclosed only through theoretical investigation, the orientation of which is concerned with explanation and understanding rather than social engineering. Indeed, it is striking in this connection that while Hayek argues that theoretical economics *started* from a concern with practical problems, in his view it did not remain there, yet knowledge that he believes to be the product of more purely theoretical enquiry turns out to be highly relevant to practical tasks of exactly the kind with which Popper is concerned.[27] We will return to this issue in Chapter 5.

My final point relates to historicism. Popper is surely right about the poverty of historical teleology, and also that, at a fundamental level, our fate is in our own hands. Yet there is a risk that he is throwing the baby out with the bath water.[28] For it would seem plausible that certain kinds of human action, in particular institutional settings, do have systematic consequences of which we can have knowledge of exactly the kind of which Popper seems to be critical. Ideas such as, say, Adam Smith's understanding of 'commercial society', or contemporary notions about the development of a global market economy, are not part of a historical teleology. It is also clearly the case that the transition into, or the development of, such arrangements are within human control in the sense that there are actions which it would be possible for people to take, which would halt them. It is important not to over-rate our theoretical knowledge of such arrangements, or the firmness of the constraints that they impose upon us. Yet it would also seem plausible that developments within them some-times have an inevitability about them, of a character that could be explained in terms of Popper's favoured ideas about the logic of the situation of those who are acting within them. There is always a danger about such ideas, in that our theoretical ideas about them, or about that upon which any particular effect depends, may well be incorrect. And there is a further danger of turning human history into a grand saga in which speculations about such ideas are given much more attention than they are worth. Yet, at the same time, Popper's own treatment seems to me, through his concentration upon social technology and on voluntarism, to under-rate what we can genuinely hope for from explanatory social theory.

My argument here is not that Popper is necessarily incorrect in his substantive views, as this would depend on what, in the end, should turn out to be a tenable theory. My doubts concern the strength of his more general and methodological argument as to how it is plausible to approach these issues.

THE POLITICAL PHILOSOPHY OF *THE OPEN SOCIETY*

What were Popper's own ideas in this period? In the rest of this chapter, I offer a brief guided tour, under four heads: his ideas about values; his programme of 'protectionism'; his ideas about democratic politics; and his views about history. Some of the themes introduced in this chapter will be pursued at greater length later in the volume.

Values

Popper's views are reasonably clear cut (we will discuss what underlies them, and problems about them, in more detail in Chapter 4). Let us begin with two themes. On the one hand, there is a liberal universalism which has a decidedly Kantian flavour, in that all people are treated by Popper as ends in themselves, not to be sacrificed to the general well-being, or to the well-being of the state. On the other, there is what may be described as a 'negative utilitarianism': it is the view that the proper agenda of public policy is the alleviation of suffering. The promotion of positive ideas about the good life, is, in his view, something for one's friends – a relationship which can be terminated if their concerns for one's positive well-being become too onerous.

Such an account, however, is in some ways perhaps a little misleading. First, to emphasize the alleviation of suffering, as

Popper himself does sometimes, is to paint much too narrow a picture of his concerns within the sphere of public policy. For when, at various points, he writes about what is comprised by this, it includes the alleviation of injustice and the assistance to people to acquire a higher education; there should also be equity in respect of the restrictions on liberty that are required by social life. Second, there is an oddity about Popper's view, in the sense that he offers us both a substantive account of what the agenda of public policy should be, and also a procedural account of how such an agenda should be determined, in terms of that in respect of which he thinks there could be a social consensus. Here, his view is that people should consider what calls out for remedy, and that, if they are willing to put to one side their visions of the good life, and also their more grandiose theories about what social arrangements would realize the good life, then a fair degree of consensus could be achieved. His own substantive account is, presumably, to be regarded as his anticipation of what he hopes that reasonable people would be able to agree needs to be tackled, and with what order of urgency.

Given that we are involved, here, with a largely negative agenda, the idea is attractive, and it certainly does not look quite as unrealistic as it might, if people were asked to form a consensus about their ideas concerning the good life. Yet, on the face of it, there would seem to me to be several problems about it. First, it assumes that people are willing to take an impartial perspective between the needs of citizens, if not of the inhabitants of the world, more generally. On this, Popper writes that:[29]

> I hold, with Kant, that it must be the principle of all morality that no man should consider himself more valuable than any other person.

This sentiment is both noble and attractive; but, as a matter of brute fact, it is not clear to what extent it is shared. And while Popper often suggests that it is intellectuals – the foes of democracy and cosmopolitanism – who bear a special responsibility for undermining such views, on the face of it, a tendency towards moral tribalism is hardly just a fault of the educated. Clearly, much will depend on whether Popper can furnish arguments that might be telling to those not initially inclined to share his universalistic perspective.

Second, there is a problem that relates to the fact that his ideas are offered by Popper as an agenda for public policy. There is, indeed, a sense in which it might seem outrageous for a public official to be discriminating between persons, in the pursuit of such concerns. But this is, by contrast, not something that we would expect of people in their private lives – to the point where we would find their conduct unreasonable, if they were to do so.[30] To this, Popper might respond that he has discussed the difference between the agenda of public policy, and the pursuit of visions of the good life, which, as we have seen, he places within the private sphere. But, to me, this does not seem adequate to the issue. For on the face of it, if we are concerned with someone acting in a private capacity, we *would* expect that person to exercise partiality with respect to the relief of suffering, by here giving preference to considerations of the well-being of those with whom he or she has personal or family relationships, over the relief of suffering on the part of other people. The very character of those personal relationships, and the character of our moral life, depend upon it. It would also seem monumentally implausible to suggest that, in our personal lives, we should pursue a utilitarian agenda of any systematic kind (although clearly, considerations of the general well-being of others may be of *some* moment).

All this, however, poses the problem: on what basis should we be asked to go along with a shift of resources from the private to the public sphere? For this, clearly, has significant consequences for what can be done. If, say, I should choose to relieve the (unpressing) need of a nephew, or to buy a book for a friend, on what basis are these resources to be shifted to the public realm, in which they are, instead, to be given over to the relief of suffering upon – presumably – a basis that is judged most urgent, in impersonal terms? While it is desirable that suffering be relieved, it is not clear that it is morally pressing that I should direct myself to its relief, or even that a concern with it should triumph over the smaller obligations of our day-to-day lives.

A further question concerns what constitutes the public,[31] in the sense of the agenda of public policy. As a matter of fact, political action with regard to welfare issues is (still) largely restricted to the sphere of national politics.[32] Yet if we were to take Popper's Kantian argument literally, there would seem no good reason for this whatever – such that, say, most of those in receipt of welfare in Western countries would not figure among the needy, on an international basis.

Finally, even if one could get agreement upon the earlier points, there are two further difficulties. First, although, as I have indicated, agreement upon what calls out for remedy is likely to be easier than agreement about the good, I wonder to what extent one could get agreement as to *relative* priorities, even among people who accept an impartial, Kantian perspective. Second, I wonder to what extent theoretical disagreement really can be banished. Consider, say, two such Kantians, concerned about the relief of poverty, one of whom is impressed by neo-classical economics, the other by features of Marx's work. I am not clear what Popper is here really suggesting – that their theoretical disagreements as to the likely outcomes of different possible measures can be settled, or that they be put to one side, while we undertake practical experimentation. In fact, Popper's approach is not as systematically atheoretical as some of his arguments might lead one to suspect. For he ventures what must be understood as his own conjecture about the understanding of the trade cycle.[33] And he seems happy enough to interpret Hayek's ideas about the knowledge-related problems of economic calculation under socialism in terms of knowledge which should inform the activities of his social engineer.[34]

This, however, brings us to our next set of problems: ones which pertain to how the agenda for public policy is to be pursued.

The democratic state and protectionism

Popper is insistent on the importance of democratic government, which, he argues, we should understand in terms of the ability of the population to change its government by means of a vote, as opposed to force. Such a government, he argues, renders citizens themselves responsible for what government does – such that, in the event of their being unhappy with the results, they should blame themselves, rather than democracy. He is also insistent, against Marxism, on the significance of such a 'formal' democracy, and on its ability to make real changes. (A case which he argues in part by taking issue with historicism and essentialism; and in part by arguing that real changes, of ethical significance, have taken place since Marx wrote – changes, however, which he seems to me to assume, a little too readily, took place because of ethically inspired political intervention.) And he argues for the importance of not resorting to violence, unless it is against a tyranny which cannot be changed to a democratic form of government, other than by force. Popper also elaborates what might be described as an activist theory of the state, which he discusses under the term 'protectionism'. In Popper's view, there is an important ethical agenda, involving not only the protection of people's liberty, as this might be understood by a theorist of 'negative' liberty, but also, more generally, the protection of people from oppression, including economic exploitation. In this connection, he is strongly critical of what, in the first edition of *The Open Society*, he referred to as *laissez-faire*.

'Protectionism' is initially introduced by Popper by way of a discussion of the idea that 'what I demand from the state is protection; not only for myself, but for others too'.[35] He suggests that 'any kind of freedom is clearly impossible unless it is guaranteed by the state',[36] and distinguishes between his view, which he takes to be liberal, and a policy of *laissez-faire*. He argues against the latter in two ways.

First, he claims that 'Unlimited freedom means that a strong man is free to bully one who is weak, and to rob him of his freedom' – and thus that freedom requires limitation, and also protection by the state.[37] Popper suggests that this is, in fact, to be seen as an example of a more general idea that he discusses: of the paradox of freedom. This he introduces in connection with his discussion of Plato, who, he suggests, implicitly introduces the following idea:[38]

> What if it is the will of the people that they should not rule, but a tyrant instead? The free man, Plato suggests, may exercise his absolute freedom, first by defying the laws and ultimately by defying freedom itself and by clamouring for a tyrant

Popper elaborates on this idea, in the following terms:[39]

> The . . . paradox of freedom is the argument that freedom in the sense of absence of any restraining control must lead to very great restraint, since it makes the bully free to enslave the meek.

And he argues that a policy of *laissez-faire*, or of non-interference, is paradoxical,[40] suggesting that: 'If the state does not interfere, then other semi-political organizations such as monopolies, trusts, etc., may interfere, reducing the freedom of the market to a fiction.'[41]

The second strand of his argument is different. In this, he embarks upon a hard-hitting moral tirade against proponents of *laissez-faire*. Here, he takes Marx's account in *Capital* as a broadly correct descriptive account of social conditions during the period about which Marx was writing,[42] and which Popper identifies as the products of the economic non-interventionism of which he is critical,[43] but which he thinks no longer pertained at the time he was writing. Against the defenders of *laissez-faire*, Popper writes of:[44]

> shameless and cruel exploitation . . . cynically defended by hypocritical apologists who appeal to the principle of human freedom, to the right of man to determine his own fate, and to enter freely into any contract he considers favourable to his interests.

And he continues by arguing for a programme of political interventionism – the complement to his ideas about protectionism – which will protect not only individual freedom, but also people's freedom from economic exploitation. That is to say, Popper argues not only that[45] 'Nobody should be at the *mercy* of others, but all should have a *right* to be protected by the state', and that these ideas should be extended to the economic realm. He argues that it is unacceptable that 'the economically strong is . . . free to bully one who is economically weak, and to rob him of his freedom' or to 'force those who are starving into a "freely" accepted servitude, without using violence'.

Popper's response – which he describes as 'the most central point of our analysis' – is the demand that:[46]

> We must construct social institutions, enforced by the power of the state, for the protection of the economically weak from the economically strong. The state must see to it that nobody need enter into an inequitable arrangement out of fear of starvation, or economic ruin . . . We must demand that unrestrained capitalism give way to an economic interventionism.

Popper then cashes this out, in terms of limits to the working day, insurance for all citizens against 'disability, unemployment and old age', and a guarantee 'by law [of] a livelihood to everybody willing to work'. And he argues, further, that 'economic power must not be permitted to dominate political power; if necessary, it must be fought and brought under control by political power'.[47]

Popper has, in latter years, been seen as part of the 'New Right'. In a later chapter, I will suggest that this is, in a certain interpretation, a view that can legitimately be drawn from some of the underlying arguments within his work. But it should be clear enough that this is not the view that he held himself; and that he would probably have had scathing things to say against such an interpretation of views. It is striking, for example, that the material that we have just been discussing concludes with a criticism even of 'equality of opportunity', on the grounds that it 'does not protect those who are less gifted, or less ruthless, or less lucky, from becoming objects of exploitation'. Further, Popper argues that the 'mere formal freedom' that Marxists have disparaged 'becomes the basis of everything else'. But Popper glosses this statement by identifying this 'freedom' with 'democracy', in the sense of 'the right of the people to judge and to dismiss their government' which, he claims, is 'the only known device by which we can try to protect ourselves against the misrule of political power', and which he describes as 'the only means for the control of economic power by the ruled'.[48]

What all this amounts to is a programme within which various ideals and institutions (including aspects of free markets: he favours, for example, the absence of trade barriers and the protection of consumer choice[49]) are commended to the citizens of a democracy as being things for the realization of which institutions should be designed by, or with the use of the power of, the state.

In the course of his criticism of Plato, Popper places considerable emphasis on the importance of the construction of 'impersonal institutions', rather than on the selection of political leaders. While he admits that 'Institutions are like fortresses. They must be well designed *and* manned', he argues that 'All long-term politics is institutional'.[50] In later editions of *The Open Society*, these ideas are developed, under the influence of Hayek,[51] into a theory of the way in which government should act in the economic sphere. Popper offers a contrast between action via the design of a legal framework, or by means of empowering the organs of the state to bring about some specific result. He favours the former 'wherever this is possible', arguing that it has the advantage of stability – both as an object upon which piecemeal improvements can be made (making allowances for those who had made their plans on the basis of earlier arrangements), and also because it 'can be known and understood by the individual citizen'.[52] Popper's concerns here seem to me to mark a significant strengthening of his position: something of real significance in the light of his concern for the liberty of the individual. But at the same time, they would suggest to me a difficulty at which I hinted in the Introduction to this volume – namely, that if politics is conducted in institutional terms in this fashion, we may not be able to achieve certain goals which, *prima facie*, we might think desirable, just because individuals can, as it were, step around institutions which have this character.

Before moving on to the next section of this discussion, it might be useful to make a few comments about the ideas which we have met here. In particular, I would like to suggest that Popper's discussion of *laissez-faire* is not as strong as it might at first appear. There are two aspects to this, relating to the two different strands to his discussion.

The first of these concerns the allegedly self-contradictory character of the doctrine. This seems to me a strange line of argument, in that all proponents of such a view known to me argue in terms of a theory of natural rights,[53] or its conventional equivalent (i.e. that people will, by custom or explicit agreement, agree to accord to one another such rights). These serve to limit people's freedom of action, and – as in Locke's, in this respect, classic discussion – will accord executive powers to other people, for their enforcement, in the event of people infringing them. Typically, in the face of problems about the enforcement of such rights, the state – seen in terms of what, today, we might refer to in Weberian terms as holding a monopoly of legitimate force – was seen as the agency to which the provision of institutions for assuring the impartiality of the administration of these rights, and their enforcement, was to be entrusted. But Locke, significantly, took the view that the state might well behave unjustly, and allowed that there might be legitimate revolt, on the basis of something like a consensual judgement that there had been a serious breach of its responsibilities, by the political community, interpreted as an extra-institutional body.

The typical views of theorists of *laissez-faire* thus differ from Popper's in two respects. First, they focus on what, in their view, is the content of the views on which reasonable people should agree, conceptualized in terms of the rights of the individual. Second, they take a different view from Popper as to what should be treated as people's legitimate *mandatory* moral call upon others.

In respect of the first of these, a reader might wonder if there is, in fact, really a difference; for Popper is also strong on what he thinks is morally incumbent upon us. However, one difficulty in his position is that, in institutional terms, he is committed to democratic decision-taking, yet says little about the relationship between what he is commending to us and the decisions that democracies can be expected to take (other than that we may get things wrong, and that this is our responsibility). And while he refers to the problem of the exploitation of a minority by a majority, he does not say anything about how it is to be addressed, other than in terms of the powers of *rulers* being limited.[54] His discussion of checks and balances, for example, is typically in terms of the control of rulers in a setting in which this is most obviously to be understood in terms of their acting against the judgement of a majority of citizens. Yet the problem may lie with the judgement of that majority.

Is there any procedural difference between Popper's views and those of, say, an individualist rights theorist?[55] One might say that, in both cases, the bottom line is a judgement by the majority of people – or, at least, those capable of political action – as to whether certain things are acceptable. Here, however, it seems to me that the rights theorist has the advantage.[56] In my view, this is not in terms of the rights theorist's ability to give his or her claims some kind of philosophical justification, but, rather, because of the way in which he or she asks us to think about such matters. For we are directed to the question: what is it reasonable for us to accord to one another, and in what circumstances? In this connection, it is not enough that some people should consider something desirable, or something that they would like others to accord to them or to other people. They need, rather, to explicate what is involved in particular individuals' bringing it about, and to submit the claim that these people should be obliged do this under scrutiny and criticism. Popper's approach similarly rests on an appeal to certain things as being reasonable. But it does not seem to involve the same kind of argumentative structure: the things which Popper commends to us come over, rather, as a somewhat varied wish-list for action by the state, in which the different elements have a somewhat heterogeneous character,[57] and in his analysis of which he does not consider the relation between the accomplishment of such goals and the actions of individual moral agents. But Popper's approach, it seems to me, makes argument about such things somewhat difficult; not least because it does not discriminate between things which we would find attractive, if they occurred, and things which we have a positive obligation to bring about.

This brings me to the second issue: to what should constitute our moral responsibilities towards one another. I have already, earlier in this chapter, made the point that Popper's discussion seems to me not to address the differences between public and private obligations, and the problem of how they are interrelated. Further, Popper seems to me to run the risk of failing to make important discriminations with the public sphere. We are all, clearly, moved by poverty, misery, and so on, in the sense that it is difficult to imagine any sane person not wishing that these things did not occur. But it is not clear that it should, just from this, be assumed that we have an obligation to act in respect of them. What is legitimately a charge upon us would seem to depend upon our, and others', circumstances; upon our own legitimate agendas – moral and otherwise – and also upon what is responsible for the phenomena in question. All this, in turn, requires recourse to both moral and social theory, in order to clarify what is, and what is not, a legitimate call upon us.

In some of the cases of exploitation that Popper discusses – such as a particular example of his, drawn from Marx, of the exploitation of children[58] – there would seem no question that things were wrong. But in other cases of possibly remediable avoidable suffering – say, as to whether we should be responsible for picking up the consequences of others' actions, in circumstances where we have strongly advised them against the course of action in question – it seems to me a moot point whether there is any *obligation* there at all, although, clearly, it may be open to us to respond to their plight with generosity. In still other cases – for example, with regard to whether there are obligations upon those who are more affluent to assist those who are relatively disadvantaged – it is surely a matter for detailed argument, in terms which relate both to rights and to the likely consequences of different courses of action. Popper's approach seems to me to put all these things into one basket. If a defender of *laissez-faire* were to respond in terms similar to those which Popper used against that position, he might say that Popper makes his point through the cynical manipulation of examples which tell, emotionally, in favour of his approach, and that his views only look plausible because of the crudity in terms of which he discusses these issues.

I should stress, however, that this is not my final response to this material. We will return to these issues in the course of a consideration of Popper's ideas about reason and values in Chapter 4, and I will offer a response to them of my own in Chapter 5.

Piecemeal social engineering, and the role of social science

It is in the context of the ideas discussed in the two previous sections that we can usefully understand Popper's ideas about 'piecemeal social engineering', and the task that he accords to the social sciences. The ideas which we have just been discussing are, for Popper, to constitute an agenda for politics, which is to be implemented by means of piecemeal social engineering. In this connection, the social sciences have the role of:[59]

> the discovery and explanation of the less obvious dependencies within the social sphere . . . the discovery of the difficulties which stand in the way of social action – the study, as it were, of the unwieldiness, the resilience or the brittleness of the social stuff, of its resistance to our attempts to mould it and to work with it.

As noted earlier (see text to note 34 on p. 50), the ideas involved would include claims, such as Hayek's, about problems concerning the centralization of our knowledge. Such ideas would seem to be thought of, by Popper, in terms of tentative claims about what can and what cannot be accomplished, and as constituting 'a social technology . . . whose results can be tested by piecemeal social engineering'.[60] He discusses the way in which the construction of social institutions requires 'some knowledge of social regularities which impose limitations upon what can be achieved by such institutions',[61] and *The Open Society* has scattered through it various – obviously tentative – examples of such social laws.

Now, one of the features of historicism, of which Popper was critical in *The Poverty of Historicism,* was the idea that social laws are limited in their validity to particular historical periods, in a way in which this is not the case in the natural sciences. In this connection, Popper offers three lines of argument. First, in an attempt to take the wind out of the historicists' sails, he argues that it may indeed be the case that specific generalizations do not hold good outside of some specific historical period or location, but he notes that this is the case with regard to the natural sciences, too.

Second, he argues, similarly, that in neither case should we assume that we have reliable knowledge. And, third, he argues that – as in the natural sciences – there are good methodological reasons for searching for universal laws.[62]

However, it seems to me that Popper's discussion here is highly problematic for reasons that, in a sense, relate to his anti-essentialism. For when Popper is discussing these matters, his concern is with social regularities, and it seems to me that he does not ask – as I believe that he should – on what these may depend. Popper himself at one point does mention, in passing, that the functioning of institutions 'depends largely on the observance of norms'.[63] While I would not wish to use that terminology,[64] it is surely plausible that most social regularities depend on specific behaviour and institutions, and ones which, in principle, it would be open to us to change (though in many cases this is not something that we would necessarily wish to do). Popper, when discussing critically the idea of psychologism, also mentions that 'typical social regularities, or sociological laws, must have existed prior to what some people are pleased to call "human nature"'.[65] This seems to me true enough; but I do not see why *the same* regularities or sociological laws should have been in operation then as they are now: why could these not change with our institutions and practices? It is, after all, striking that even pieces of macro-economic 'social technology', such as what became known as 'Keynesian' economics, seemed to become ineffective for reasons that their critics have related to just such dependencies.[66]

What lies behind my argument here is the view that we may be able to gain access to what lies behind such regularities, and that it is important that we do this, if we can. In order to make this argument, I do not need to canvass the view that there is a single, specific theory which will be adequate in this respect. But for what it is worth, my own view is that, in part, we may need to look at considerations about meaning and socialization; in part, at the consequences of self-interested action; and, in part, at structural constraints (for example, as they have been described by Robert Nozick in his criticism of methodological individualism[67]). The significant point is that there seems every reason to suppose that social regularities are dependent upon such things, and that an understanding of such dependencies may be of vital importance to us. (Indeed, it is striking that Popper himself at times offers – without much real argument – his own more restrictive account of what should be the basis of explanation in the social sciences: methodological individualism and the rationality principle;[68] yet he does not, as far as I know, explicitly qualify his earlier accounts, which give pride of place to social laws, in the light of these ideas, or discuss the implications of such changes.[69]) I will argue later, however, that if the ideas which I have canvassed in this paragraph are admitted, they have significant implications for Popper's ideas about 'social engineering' and, as a result, for his political philosophy.

Be all this as it may, what Popper seemed to envisage was a process of the following kind. Various political demands – like those in *The Open Society* – are accepted within a particular society and voiced into the decision-making process through democratic elections. Those in positions of political power then have the task of designing, or altering, institutions so as better to realize those demands. They – or, more realistically, civil servants – make use of knowledge from the social sciences in the design of such institutions. But, because of the fallibility of such knowledge, because of the dependence of such 'social engineering' on practical experience, and because of the need to be open to problems as they are discovered and to possible changes in our aims, there should be a process of critical feedback involved. Indeed, Popper's interpretation of democracy has two main aspects: the significance of our ability to get rid of our rulers without violence, and this theme of critical feedback and rational assessment from citizens, as indicated in a quotation that he makes from Pericles' funeral oration: 'although only a few may originate a policy, we are all able to judge it'.[70] Popper places considerable emphasis on the need for careful institutional design, and for what one might term democratic vigilance, when he stresses that:[71]

> without democratic control, there can be no earthly reason why any government should not use its political and economic power for purposes very different from the protection of the freedom of its citizens

On reading Popper's work on this topic, however, one reaction that the reader might have concerns how the institutions that Popper is discussing are supposed to function. For example, after quoting Karl Krauss to the effect that politics consists in choosing the lesser evil, Popper writes that:[72]

politicians should be zealous in the search for the evils their actions must necessarily produce instead of concealing them, since a proper evaluation of competing evils must otherwise become impossible.

This, while it would seem desirable enough, might be considered to be a beginning rather than an end of political theory, in the sense that Popper does not discuss how political institutions will – or, indeed, whether political institutions could – function in such a way. In making such a point, I am not offering an argument against Popper, for it would be churlish to expect that he could have addressed such issues, over and above writing what he did. But it is, I think, important to stress that this is an issue which needs to be addressed, so that one could either show how Popper's ideas could be realized or, alternatively, develop a criticism of his work, by showing that they could not. I will discuss this issue further in Chapter 5.

I do not, however, wish to suggest that Popper's attitude was Pollyanna-ish. For he was acutely aware that the measures he was suggesting would increase the power of the state, and considered this to be problematic. Indeed, Popper wrote:[73]

> it is not enough to say that our solution [to problems that require state planning] should be a minimum solution; that we should be watchful; and that we should not give more power to the state than is necessary for the protection of freedom. These remarks may raise problems, but they do not show a way to a solution. It is even conceivable that there is no solution; that the acquisition of new economic powers by the state – whose powers, as compared to those of its citizens, are always dangerously great – will make it irresistible.

Popper did, to be sure, offer a possible solution to the problem which he raised, in terms of the differentiation between intervention by means of a legal framework, and on a discretionary basis, which we have discussed earlier. However, not only does the passage that I have quoted indicate that Popper took the problem seriously. But he returned to it later in his book. Popper there wrote:[74]

> It is undoubtedly the greatest danger of any interventionism – especially of any direct intervention – that it leads to an increase in state power and in bureaucracy. Most interventionists do not mind this, or they close their eyes to it, which increases the danger.

Popper's passage again continues on a more optimistic note: he suggests that once the danger is recognized, 'it should be possible to master it', and says that it is 'merely a problem of social technology and of social piecemeal engineering'.[75] But he does not suggest anything specific by way of a solution.

Giving meaning to history

Popper is a critic of the idea that there is a teleology operative in history, that there are laws of historical development, or that we should take history as our judge, in the sense of basing our moral judgements on what will, or what we believe will, come to pass in the future. As we have seen, he is also insistent that human affairs are our responsibility. Together, these ideas amount to the view that while history has no intrinsic meaning, it is open to us to try to give it an ethical significance, in the sense of trying to shape what will happen on the basis of our ethical concerns. Things are, however, a little more complex than this, and it will be useful to conclude this (highly selective) guide to some of the themes of *The Open Society* by considering further Popper's views about history.

A useful starting point is with his ideas about epistemology more generally. Popper rejects induction as an account of both the acquisition of knowledge and of the justification of knowledge claims. As against traditional empiricism, Popper offers an adaptation of Kantian ideas, in which we are understood as attempting, actively but fallibly, to make sense of the world. He has offered a simplified contrast between his approach and empiricist accounts of the acquisition of knowledge, by making use of a distinction between the 'bucket' and the 'searchlight' theories of the mind.[76] Empiricism, on this account, depicts our mind as open to the world – with information coming in, as it were, through the different senses – and knowledge as being a kind of product of what gets in by this means. By way of contrast, when discussing the searchlight theory Popper stresses the role of our expectations and ideas in selecting, highlighting and forming what we are experiencing – although, as contrasted with a Kantian view, there is no guarantee that such expectations (even the most fundamental) will be correct, and it is possible for us to *choose* to proceed in such a way that we may learn if they are wrong.[77]

All this is of some significance in relation to his ideas about history. Popper argues that in both the natural sciences and in history we must select and shape our material – that we bring to it a point of view. This is of significance for two reasons. First, Popper argues that while there is selection in both areas, there is also a difference: in historical interpretation there are not, typically, testable theories involved in the same way as there are in the natural sciences.[78] Popper does argue that universal laws are used in historical explanation;[79] but he also argues that these are, for the most part, trivial and not things in which the historian has any interest.[80] A major selective role is played, on his account, both by our current concerns, and also by what he calls historical interpretations. In some cases, these will be testable theories; in others, they will be things about which some degree of argument may be possible. He stresses, however, that there will always be several, perhaps incompatible, interpretations which may be given to historical events.[81] This arises for three reasons: in part, because what is involved is simply selection and interpretation from a particular historical situation or value perspective; in part because of the relatively low testability of (many of) the theories in question; and in part, because of what might, if one may here use decidedly non-Popperian terminology, be called distinctive problems of the under-determination of theory choice by evidence. For, as distinct from universal theories in the sciences which can, in principle, be tested anywhere, there may be only limited evidence available on the basis of which general interpretations of history could be tested, and this evidence itself may have been pre-selected to fit a particular perspective on the events in question.[82] Popper argues that one consequence of all this is that while general interpretations of history or interpretations of specific events may in some cases be testable in ways that are close to the kind of testability one has in the natural sciences, more typically this will not be the case. While he argues that not every interpretation is as good as any other, he stresses that we will always be faced with a plurality of possible interpretations.[83]

The result is that Popper offers a view of history which is in some ways close to that of Weber.[84] In each case, there is a repudiation of the Hegelian view that there is an objective meaning to history. Popper rejects the idea that there is a meaning intrinsic to history, on the ground that history, as it is written, involves selection: 'the realm of facts is infinitely rich, and that there must be selection'.[85] In fact, Hegel's own view of history and of its objective significance was highly selective. But in his account, much of what happened in history was objectively unimportant.[86] Indeed, if one contrasts the views of Popper and Weber with those of Hegel and Marx, it is worth noting that what is being objected to is an account which combines the ideas that, first, there are some issues that are of overwhelming objective explanatory significance, and which lie behind the phenomena of history; and, second, that these are also of paramount ethical significance. In the case of both Weber and Popper, one has a disagreement with the first of these claims (albeit for what would seem different reasons[87]), but the heart of what is distinctive about their views would seem to lie in the role that they each give to (subjective) values in the constitution of history (as it is written).

Here, their common view would seem to be that, in each case, various different value orientations are possible towards the subject-matter of history, and that these serve to constitute different topics for study. However, this does not in itself affect the objectivity of historical writing, in the sense of its being open to inter-subjective scrutiny – subject, in Popper's case, to the limitations about historical interpretation, to which I referred earlier.

One might add, however, that insofar as objectivity depends on inter-subjective scrutiny,[88] there may be reasons why certain kinds of strongly value-based history are not objective in this sense of Popper's. If they are written largely by people who share the values in question, and if those who do not share them, or are antipathetic to them, are not attracted to work upon this subject-matter, then there is every reason to suppose that bias would not be removed as a product of criticism, in the way in which it might in other fields. The very fact that different values may constitute different historical subject-matters has the consequence that those not favourable to certain particular values may simply choose to work on other topics.

There is, though, what seems to me one distinctive – and, I believe, surprising – feature to Popper's approach. It is that, after he has written about historical interpretations and value-based points of view, he then goes on to defend the idea that:[89]

> since each generation has its own troubles and problems, and therefore its own interests and its own point of view, it follows that each generation has a right to look on and re-interpret history in its own way, which is complementary to that of previous generations.

I do not wish to contest that each generation *could* do this; but given Popper's analysis, I do not see the point. Or, rather, there is a sense in which there is *a* point to such an activity, which is akin, say, to the person who is extremely interested in Manx cats also being interested in their history. Such a person may read, and even write, such a history; it is open to correction by anybody – for example, by those who loathe Manx cats, or, say, by those who are indifferent about them, but are suddenly struck by what seems to them bad history. But Popper clearly seems to have something more in mind, in that he refers to such things as someone's writing a history as a history of progress, and I would think from the context that he would also apply this kind of analysis to his own work. His own view of the status of his interpretation of history in his own work would, thus, have to be understood in these same terms.

However, in such cases, the value of the work would seem to me to depend on the extent to which both the interpretation and its value basis could be made inter-subjectively compelling. For the point of producing such work would surely be to encourage one in viewing the world in this way, and perhaps even in acting on the basis of the perspective in question. But to this, the admission of the possibility of pluralism – the admission, as it were, that some-one could equally write a story interpreting history as a story of human decline, or of the 'Organic Society and Its Enemies', which would be just as good – would seem to me to render the exercise pointless.

Clearly, there is nothing to stop someone from doing the political equivalent of writing history like the history of Manx cats. And I am not claiming that there is a single explanatory thread to history, or even to the history of specific academic subject-matter.[90] But what people do, when they write about *The Open Society and Its Enemies* seems to me very different, and to be under-mined by the pluralism about history and the subjectivism about values, that at times seem to me to be found in Popper's text. However, everything is not lost; for his work also contains ideas about objectivity and inter-subjective acceptability which seem to me to offer a better approach to these issues. These will be discussed in Chapter 4.

3

AFTER *THE OPEN SOCIETY*

INTRODUCTION

In this chapter, I will discuss three issues relating to Popper's writings on political philosophy after *The Open Society*: his ideas about epistemological optimism, his ideas about tradition, and a wider issue that this latter material opens up, and which has been raised recently by Geoff Stokes[1] – his assumptions about psychology, human nature, and what Popper was to call 'world 3'. These issues are very much a selection; one which I have made with an eye to the more general argument that I am developing in this volume. I am well aware that other, and interesting, issues are also raised in Popper's later discussions of political topics;[2] some of which I plan to address on another occasion.

The material with which we will be concerned, however, does have both a significance and a kind of unity. The significance is that, in some important ways, it serves to mark changes in Popper's views; ones which, it seems to me, he did not stop to take account of in, say, revisions of *The Open Society*. The unity is that it involves a discussion of the interrelations between his epistemology and his politics, and of some issues posed by developments within his epistemology for his views on politics. To these issues we will also have recourse, in the discussion of his work in Chapters 4 and 5.

The themes which we will be discussing might, together, be interpreted as marking a shift in Popper's political thought, in a slightly less radical direction. They certainly seem to me to have this implication. I am not sure, however, that to interpret them in this way would serve as a useful way of understanding the development of Popper's own political thought. For while there is, certainly, a shift away from socialism in his work,[3] and while the ideas which we will be discussing do, in some ways, have more conservative consequences, it is not clear to me that Popper had himself consciously shifted his understanding of own views in the manner which this interpretation of his work would suggest; and he certainly did not seem to have systematically re-thought his views, in the light of these later developments.[4]

EPISTEMOLOGICAL OPTIMISM

Our first theme is developed in Popper's writings on both epistemology and politics, subsequent to *The Open Society*. It relates to his discussion, and repudiation, of the view that the truth is manifest.

What is involved may usefully be introduced by way of his paper 'Epistemology and Industrialization'.[5] In this, Popper offers a sketch of what is, in effect, a competing account to those of Marx and Weber, concerning the characteristics of 'Western' society, and its development. To write in such terms may run the risk of over-rating a brief and modest piece of work. But this essay seems to me of some significance, nonetheless.

Popper's general thesis is in some ways neither startling nor original. He argues for the historical significance of ideas and their consequences, and, in this connection, invokes such writers as Heine, J.S. Mill and Hayek,[6] as among those who have stressed the significant role played, in history, by ideas. Further, what he specifically singles out as important might seem almost a commonplace from the ideas of the Enlightenment, and of those earlier thinkers whom the thinkers of the Enlightenment saw as their precursors. However, what is distinctive about Popper's account is his characterization of the ideas that he singles out for attention, and especially his attitude towards them. For while Popper is broadly sympathetic towards what he calls 'epistemological optimism', he is also critical of it, and especially of some of the ideas which were responsible for the historical developments with which he is concerned.

In order to understand what Popper means by 'epistemological optimism', and also the respects in which he distances himself from it, it would be useful for us to look at another essay of his: 'On the Sources of Knowledge and of Ignorance'. This is a critical discussion of epistemological ideas which, however, also has important ramifications for Popper's views about politics. In it, Popper takes issue with a view – which he attributes to both Bacon and Descartes – that 'truth is manifest'. Popper is himself a defender of the Enlightenment, of the significance of scientific knowledge, and of the idea of 'self-emancipation through knowledge'. But he argues that the founders of both empiricism and intellectualism shared a view which seems to him incorrect; one which they bequeathed to the currents of thought with which Popper himself broadly identifies. It is the idea that, provided that one follows the appropriate initial procedures, and also that one frees one's mind from prejudice, the truth is manifest: one cannot but have correct views.

These ideas, in Popper's judgement, were of great significance. On the one hand, they led to an immense optimism concerning the possibilities of human knowledge: truth, it was believed, was accessible to mankind. Further, it was anticipated that this would have important practical consequences. Bacon, for example, had a vision of the way in which knowledge would give mankind power over nature, which would lead to the possibility of transforming the human situation. On the other hand, Popper felt that there was much wrong with them.

First, there was their radical anti-traditionalism: the errors of the past were to be swept away and replaced with new knowledge. Second, their proponents suggested that, if only the correct procedures were followed, we would have knowledge, in the sense of certain truth. Indeed, one had only to be guided by one's senses, or reason, to get at this truth. This, however, led to the consequence that, assuming that you had accomplished this task, if others did not agree with you they were either perverse or had been misled – either by people who themselves were perverse or by people who had a sinister interest in the perpetuation of error. As a result, one was led to a kind of conspiracy theory of error – both to explain why it was that, in the past, mankind had not managed to reach the truth, and also in the face of their continued failings. There must, as it were, be something or someone responsible for why things had gone wrong; something that *might* call out for political remedy. Finally, Popper was highly critical of Bacon's linking of knowledge and power. For Popper, by way of contrast, the advance of knowledge continually revealed new aspects of our ignorance; and he argued that it was vital that we be aware of our fallibility, in respect of both our theoretical knowledge and its application.

These ideas are of importance in placing Popper in relation to the Enlightenment and, more generally, to the intellectual movement which looks to the growth of scientific knowledge as a source for human self-emancipation, and the improvement of our physical and social conditions. On the one hand, he identifies strongly with it. He sees such ideas – which he would identify with rationalism – as of immense importance, but also as fragile. And he is relentlessly critical not only of those who are opposed to this tradition, but also of those who, in his view, put it at risk through their lack of intellectual modesty, and their unwillingness to address those who have views that differ from their own in the simplest and clearest ways possible. On the other hand, Popper is critical of the substantive views of most of those who are in the same camp as he is. He is critical of the theme that the truth is manifest from Bacon and Descartes down to the empiricists of his own day. And he is concerned also about undesirable consequences that follow from such views.

All this means that Popper's views cut across what are often today seen as the alternatives that are available to us. This is true in respect of both social theory and epistemology. Here, Popper has been a consistent critic of the idea that uninterpreted data is available to us. By way of contrast, he stresses not only the role of theories in the description of even the simplest of facts, but also that we cannot but bring to our understanding of the world a host of unjustified presuppositions. At the same time, Popper argues that it is possible for us to learn from others and from our interactions with the world, if we wish to do so, and if we conduct ourselves in appropriate ways – although these, on his account, are also fallible. What he offers is a theory of knowledge which is not foundationalist in its character, but which nonetheless offers us the hope of progress, and of learning from one another.

It is in this connection that Popper's concern for truth takes on a character that is politically distinctive. On the one hand, he is in agreement with the Enlightenment that established authorities – whether moral or intellectual – must be opened to challenge. Yet at the same time, his own fallibilism has the consequence that those who do the challenging cannot set up as infallible authorities themselves. Their very aspiration for truth means, by contrast, that they open themselves to the need for criticism from other people, in respect of both their claims about the world, and their political actions. Indeed, perhaps the most striking aspect of Popper's epistemology is its anti-authoritarianism: there are simply no authorities which are beyond criticism, and this goes not only for human beings and institutions, but also for what may seem self-evident to us, or to be the plain evidence of our senses. At the same time, the fact that there are not sources of reliable knowledge also introduces a more conservative aspect to his work. First, nothing is to be rejected simply because it cannot be justified – for *nothing* can be justified in a way that puts it beyond the need for possible future critical scrutiny. Second, it is important to discover where things are wrong. But, at the same time, just because we have discovered that something is defective does not, in itself, tell us how to make an improvement upon it. Popper's concern for progress, in both knowledge and politics, leads us to a concern for what would constitute an improvement on what we have at the moment, and for a concern that we achieve progress in that sense.

These ideas lead Popper to take a distinctive view of modern history, too. For he argues in 'Epistemology and Industrialization' that it is epistemological optimism, including those aspects of that view of which he is *critical,* which has played a crucial role in the development of the West. In Popper's view, what played a key role was not only optimism about the possibility of knowledge, but also the view that it would give mankind power to transform its situation. This underlies not only the epistemological self-confidence of the West, but also its distinctive feature of industrialization. Yet, in Popper's view, epistemological optimism is flawed, not only because of his misgivings about power and its link with knowledge, but also because of the arrogance which can go with the idea that one has the truth in one's pocket. In addition, the view that truth is manifest – that anyone can see the truth, if they are willing to look at things without prejudice – leads to a terrible attitude towards those with whom one is in disagreement. For, as I have suggested, it means that they are perverse, or that they have been misled, or that they are acting in bad faith. Popper was critical of such views – and he was also concerned about their consequences (for example, he saw such ideas as playing a significant role in the problems of the 'cold war'[7]). It is also important to see just the extent to which his own views differed from them. His fallibilism puts a premium upon criticism. While his view that the truth is not manifest indicates both that we may have a lot to learn from others, even in respect of those things about which we feel most secure, and also that our pursuit of the aim of reaching truth may not be an easy task, or one in which we reach consensus.[8]

'TOWARDS A RATIONAL THEORY OF TRADITION'

While Popper does not discuss the point explicitly, there is a sense in which the ideas which we have just discussed might be seen as in tension with the approach of *The Open Society*. In claiming this, I do not mean that there are significant differences in respect to his substantive views between the ideas upon which I have reported, above, and the views which inform that work. But there nonetheless seems to me a point of tension with what is perhaps a streak of over-optimistic rationalism in *The Open Society*. I have in mind what seems to me Popper's assumption there that if we concentrate upon what is wrong, we should be able to agree, and then to design institutions which, if we all work hard at it, will enable us to improve things. I do not wish to make too much of this point. But, despite the fact that *The Open Society* is informed by Popper's own distinctive epistemological views and is strongly fallibilistic, it seems to me that at times one catches sight of ideas that are too close for comfort to the ideas of which he was critical in the material which we have just been studying.

This contrast is even more marked in respect of Popper's 'Towards a Rational Theory of Tradition'. This striking essay may be interpreted as involving a significant re-thinking of Popper's attitudes towards tradition, made – or so it would appear – under the impact of Michael Oakeshott's 'Rationalism in Politics'.[9] In some ways it is a rather strange piece of work. For in it, Popper develops views which differ, in some significant respects, from those in *The Open Society*, and which also pose some difficult problems for the approach advocated in that book. In doing this, Popper at the same time returns to ideas about the significance of an interplay between dogmatism and criticism which played an important role in his intellectual development prior to *The Logic of Scientific Discovery*, and which thus, historically, come before *The Open Society*. This poses an interesting problem as to why one does not find these ideas in *The Open Society* – which has a more rationalistic flavour than it might have done, if these ideas had been taken into account. 'Towards a Rational Theory of Tradition' also contains views of which one might have expected the author of *The Open Society* to be critical. It is at times psychologistic in more or less the way of which Popper had been (justly) critical in *The Open Society*. It even, at one point, exhibits a concern for the (true) function of institutions in a manner which seems not only naive, but which *The Open Society* had explicitly criticized. As a piece of social theory, it seems to me in some ways very badly flawed. But I will argue that it nonetheless contains a theme which is of very great importance for Popper's political views. As I have indicated in the Introduction, it seems to me to open up a problem for Popper's work which one can only cope with if one makes a significant departure from Popper's own preferred approach to politics.

What are we to make of the essay itself? I believe that we should understand it as an exercise – which Popper went through on several occasions[10] – in which he goes back to material of which he has been critical, to see if something might be said in its favour, nonetheless.[11] (It is significant, in this context, that 'Towards a Rational Theory of Tradition' was delivered at the conference of the Rationalist Press Association, which in Popper's view would have been a particularly suitable audience for such a reconsideration.) Popper also seems to have been genuinely struck by the fact that Oakeshott has raised questions to which he – and rationalists, more generally – had not furnished answers. There is also *possibly* another, and more political, aspect to the issue. In *The Open Society*, Popper is consistently scathing about conservatives and conservatism. Here, under the prompting of Oakeshott's article, he is willing to take more seriously what both Burke and Oakeshott are saying. In *The Open Society* he was also strongly critical of an explanatory appeal to matters psychological, when discussing and expressing a good measure of admiration for Marx's ideas about methodology. Given that it is around this same period when Popper confronts Stalinist versions of Marxism,[12] and was clearly open to some influence from Hayek (e.g. on his emphasis on institutional rather than discretionary processes in the implementation of policy), one might conjecture that there could be a political aspect to his selection of intellectual concerns here, albeit perhaps at the level of an unconscious elective affinity. Be all this as it may, it is striking that, in exploring ideas to do with tradition, he is looking at a theme that he clearly associated with epistemological *pessimism*,[13] and thus with views of which he had been much more critical than he was of epistemological optimism.

What is Popper's *argument* in 'Towards a Rational Theory of

Tradition'? His starting point is with the claim that Burke has 'never been properly answered by rationalists'.[14] He also refers to Oakeshott's invocation of tradition as part of an argument against rationalism, in his 'Rationalism in Politics'. Popper indicates that while he disagrees with Oakeshott, he thinks that, at the time at which Oakeshott wrote, 'there was not much in the rationalist literature which could be considered an adequate answer to his arguments'.[15] Popper tells us that he does not set out to advance 'anything like a full theory' of tradition, but instead aims at illustrating 'the kind of question which a theory of tradition would have to answer', as well as offering a few suggestions as to how such a theory might be developed.[16]

Popper's paper contains, broadly speaking, four themes. First, there are some remarks on the value of some traditions, and on the idea that they cannot be transferred or conjured up, *ex nihilo*. I have discussed this theme briefly in my introduction, and I will return to it at the end of this section. Second, Popper suggests that while he does not 'think that we could ever free ourselves entirely from the bonds of tradition',[17] it is possible to understand the function and the significance of a tradition, and to submit it to criticism. This he proceeds to do, by way of an example: the critical discussion of some themes from what he refers to as the rationalist tradition.

It is useful here to supplement what Popper writes in this paper with what he has written elsewhere on the theme of criticism. In the final part of this chapter, we will look at some of Popper's ideas about objective knowledge, and about what he calls 'world 3'. Just because of his emphasis, in this material, on the importance of the linguistic formulation of knowledge, and upon its critical appraisal, it is important that we do not overlook what Popper has written about the tacit aspects of knowledge, and about what he has called our 'horizon of expectations'. For Popper, expectations are there, prior to observation. Indeed, in his view, specific expectations are biologically preformed in us, and we are also biologically predisposed to try to interpret the world in certain ways (e.g. in terms of causality). At any one point, we have much more knowledge – in the sense of implicit theories about the world – than we can be aware of consciously. We may also only discover that we had certain expectations when, suddenly, those expectations are refuted. At that point, they will typically become objects of our critical attention – but, at the same time, other things will move out of our conscious attention. Further, when we are consciously attending to some problem – e.g. of identifying and submitting to scrutiny our unsuccessful expectation – we must, at the same time, take countless other things for granted.[18] What is distinctive about Popper's view is that while, on his account, we have such expectations, and take all kinds of things for granted, he stresses that we have no reason to believe that they are correct. It is important that items of our knowledge be made the objects of our criticism. But we can do this only in a piecemeal manner. At the same time, there is no single element in our knowledge which cannot be made the object of critical scrutiny – provided that we understand that this implies that there are other objects of our knowledge which cannot be submitted to criticism at the same time.[19]

All this, it seems to me, applies also with regard to our knowledge of, and participation in, the social world, and thus to what Popper wrote about tradition. While his plea for a self-conscious critical awareness is important, we should interpret it in the terms that I have indicated above – and thus understand that Popper is not suggesting that we can come, at the same time, to a fully self-conscious understanding of what is involved in any particular tradition. Indeed, as Popper has written:[20]

all social criticism, and all social betterment, must refer to a framework of social traditions, of which some are criticized with the help of others, just as all progress in science must proceed within a framework of scientific theories, some of which are criticized in the light of others.

In his paper, Popper moves to the discussion of two other themes. The first of these is the rationalist tradition, something that he sees as going back to the Greek reaction to the experience of culture clash, and to the institution, by the pre-Socratics, of a second-order tradition of the criticism of received explanations.[21]

The second, with which we will be concerned more fully, relates to the social function of tradition. Popper suggests that we should understand traditionalism in the light of a human need for order, in the sense that people become anxious – and, indeed, terrified – if they cannot predict what will happen,[22] arguing further that:[23] 'institutions and traditions . . . may give people a clear idea of what to expect and how to proceed.' He further suggests that:[24]

We should be anxious and terrified, and frustrated, and we could not live in the social world, did it not contain a considerable amount of order, a great number of regularities to which we can adjust ourselves. The mere existence of these regularities is perhaps more important than their peculiar merits or demerits. They are needed as regularities, and therefore handed on as traditions, whether or not they are in other respects rational or necessary or good or beautiful.

Popper argues that people cling to traditions (and to myths) because they offer uniformity, which they value, and also because they wish to reassure others that they are rational. The idea that traditions may play this psychological role is related by Popper to what he describes as 'the emotional intolerance . . . characteristic of . . . traditionalism'.[25] Popper, however, also discusses the way in which traditions not only create an 'order or something like a social structure', but also give us something upon which we can work critically, and change and improve.[26] (There is a parallel here with his discussion of institutional versus discretional forms of action in *The Open Society*.) From this, he moves to a criticism of rationalism's traditional anti-traditionalism, and to the idea that what rationalists should call for, instead, is 'a new tradition – the tradition of tolerance'.[27]

Two points are, I believe, worth exploring concerning this material. The first relates to its connections with Popper's ideas about epistemology, and to the relation between this, in turn, and the anti-psychologism of *The Open Society*. The second relates to some problems about criticism and toleration, given what he has written about traditions.

In *The Open Society*, as we have noted, we find Popper arguing strongly against psychologism, with acknowledgement to Marx. Instead, he suggests that we should give explanatory priority to the social, and that it is of importance even in respect of the understanding of *prima facie* psychological ideas, such as his notion of the 'strains of civilization'. By way of contrast with this, and as Stokes has emphasized,[28] one finds in the material which we have been discussing, and also in Popper's discussion of human cognition, an account which gives pride of place to certain psychological expectations; for example, concerning causality.[29]

If one applied Popper's ideas from *The Open Society* to this material, one might be led to pose questions concerning the possibly social constitution of these things, or at least – by way of a parallel with Popper's discussion of the 'strains of civilization' – to consider the possibility that they may have a particular role to play, in certain distinctive social situations. I have no specific axe to grind here, and I am certainly not wishing to suggest that Popper's epistemology should be relativized to some historical teleology or, indeed, turned into a form of relativism. But it does seem to me that the openness of Popper's work towards such approaches should be noted; not least because of the dichotomy that Lakatos was to build up between his Popper-derived approach, and anything that smacked of the sociology of knowledge.[30] In addition, as I have argued elsewhere,[31] it suggests that we might usefully take an epistemologically informed approach towards issues in the social organization of knowledge. This would involve, on the one side, understanding the ways in which participation in various different institutional arrangements has the consequence of making people behave as if they are behaving in accord with one or other set of methodological rules. And, beyond that, it would suggest that we should discuss what institutional arrangements we should choose, in order to generate the kind of epistemological product that we wish for.

Popper's own later discussions have taken a somewhat different direction, in that, while he persisted with his anti-psychologism, in his later work he placed emphasis upon the priority of the logical over the psychological, and also suggested that this idea has been of long-standing importance in his work.[32] I have nothing against such a suggestion. But I do not see why, in developing it, we should give up on his earlier ideas – the parentage of which, as I will discuss later, is usefully to be seen as stemming from what for me also happens to be the politically more acceptable source of Adam Smith!

The second – and rather different – issue relates to the criticism of traditions, and to Popper's plea for toleration. I would fully agree with what he says about the importance of criticism. But it seems to me that there is a problem about his argument which *might* lead us to have some reservations about his ideas concerning toleration. The problem relates to a disanalogy between knowledge and social practices.

In the case of scientific knowledge, the people concerned will clearly have a concern for the replacement of theories with ones which are better, and in this context individuals' ideas about what is wrong with currently accepted theories, and their ideas about what should replace them, may be submitted to inter-subjective scrutiny, and where appropriate to experimental testing. By way of contrast with this, in the social sphere, received conditions and customs are typically open to the scrutiny of each individual on, as it were, a disaggregated basis. And while there are some pressures towards social conformity, it is not clear that these have anything much to do with the *merits* of the behaviour in question, and especially with how they operate in anything like a systematic manner.

In social affairs, however, we face certain problems, as indicated by Popper's point that it is sometimes the mere existence of regularity which may be important (see the text to note 24, above). Thus, while in one sense it may be extremely important that existing traditions, codes of conduct, forms of behaviour, and so on, are subjected to criticism, this does not, of itself, generate a new, and better, *shared* code of conduct. Instead, it may result simply in the breakdown of a convention into a sea of variants and individual innovations. And this may, in turn, result in unhappiness and confusion in respect of social interactions with people who are (relative) strangers. For while it may have been made clear how they should *not* behave, people may feel genuinely in the dark as to what, positively, they should now do. While attempts to address this problem within specific institutions – say, by means of the provision of codes of conduct for behaviour in universities – have often had an air of authoritarianism or unreality about them.[33] I should stress that I am *not* here offering an argument against such criticism. But I would suggest that there may be a problem concerning toleration, if this results in unco-ordinated diversity in situations in which we have need of shared conventions. At the very least, there seems to me a difficulty here; one to which I will return in Chapter 5.

To conclude this section, I would like to discuss one other issue raised by this essay of Popper's. It relates to the consequences that Popper draws from this material for social theory. He first distinguishes between institutions and traditions,[34] suggesting that the former may be seen as a 'changing body of people who observe a certain set of norms of fulfil certain *prima facie* social functions . . . which serve certain *prima facie* social purposes', while he explicates the latter as:[35] 'a uniformity of people's attitudes or ways of behaviour, or aims of values or tastes'. Popper then poses the problem that social institutions may:[36] 'function in a way which strikingly contrasts with [their] *prima facie* or "proper" function'.

This terminology is strange, given Popper's earlier insistence, in *The Open Society*, that we should not discuss social institutions in terms of their essential role.[37] But let us put this to one side, and interpret Popper's concern as being with a contrast between how an institution currently behaves and the functions it is widely expected to perform. The nub of Popper's argument is that an institution's ability to perform its 'proper function' may depend on traditions, which he believes, because of their less instrumental character, are less open to certain kinds of corruption than are institutions themselves. I do not here wish to endorse Popper's analysis, but I have examined it because it leads up to the following statement:[38]

> It may be said, perhaps, that the long-term 'proper' function-ing of institutions depends mainly upon such traditions. It is tradition which gives the persons (who come and go) that background and that certainty of purpose which resist corruption. A tradition is, as it were, capable of extending something of the personal attitude of its founder far beyond his personal life.

I will offer two comments about this.

The first is that this argument might seem to provide a new lease of life for those conservatives of whom Popper was so critical in *The Open Society*. For it might on the face of it seem to be the case that certain institutions could play exactly this role, while being based on a particular kind of anti-democratic exclusion. That is to say, one could well imagine certain genuinely desirable forms of social conduct being maintained in such a manner. For example, it might indeed be the case that certain people could be depended upon not to behave corruptly because they were part of a tradition in which such conduct was considered ungentleman-like; yet this tradition may depend, for its very character, on particular forms of social and sexual exclusion. (Of course, there are also many examples of such traditions in which the exclusion is clear enough, but the social benefits are not so clear.)

A second and more significant issue is this. As I suggested in the Introduction to this volume, once the role of tradition – or some-thing like it – is acknowledged, the programme of *The Open Society* becomes much more complex. For involved in the creation of social institutions to serve a particular process is, also, the problem of tradition, and of the behaviour of those involved in manning and monitoring the performance of the institutions, more generally. The institution has to be seen as comprising those people, rather than as consisting of an amorphous social stuff, onto which we can simply impose our will.[39] But insofar as social engineering also involves us in the moulding of the behaviour of these people, we start to get into some very deep water, and to be involved in problems that Popper may not have seen, and which he certainly does not address.

POLITICS AND 'WORLD 3'

In Popper's later years, he developed his theory of 'world 3'. As is well known, he suggested that we need to recognize the existence of three different 'worlds' – the physical world, the world of mental states, and a third world, the contents of which he wrote of at various times as comprising cultural objects and logical objects. The distinctions that Popper made were rough and ready, and he was also willing to recognize the existence of objects of an intermediate or mixed character – as in, say, the case of a book which instantiates an abstract object in a physical form, or, say, an intentional object, as when someone is thinking about a particular theorem. Popper did not even set out to offer a systematic theory concerning these things (e.g. to elaborate just what fitted into what category, to sort out the status of such things as numbers, and so on). His initial concern was, rather, to highlight some problems about reduction, and to argue that if one brings in world 3, then in various respects the task of reduction to the physical becomes more difficult than if one simply considered relations between the mental and the physical. Popper's approach to the question whether reduction could eventually be accomplished seems to have been undogmatic.[40] But in the course of his various discussions, he raised issues which seem to me of importance for our present concerns, in that this material is of considerable importance in relation to the anti-romantic strand in Popper's political thought. The central theme, here, is of humans being able, together, to create a culture that is greater than themselves, and through interaction with which they may be reshaped and transformed. As Popper wrote already in *The Open Society*:[41]

Man has created new worlds – of language, of music, of poetry, of science; and the most important of these is the world of moral demands, for equality, for freedom, and for helping the weak.

As ideas of this kind are elaborated in Popper's later work, several themes relating to them are developed.

First, and most simple, is Popper's stress on the significance of the articulation – and, better still, the writing down – of ideas. These make of preconceptions, and so on, objects upon which we can work: objects which we can improve, through criticism. Of crucial importance, in this context, are Popper's ideas about language and reason. Concerning language, Popper has, on many occasions, elaborated on some ideas of one of his teachers, Karl Buehler. Buehler had discussed language as having different functions, which he described as constituting a hierarchy, running through expression to signalling and, finally, to description. Popper added a further function to this: that of argument.[42] All this, in turn, is related to Popper's views about reason. This, for Popper, is seen not as a faculty possessed by the individual, but as an inter-subjective process. In making a claim that something is true (or, by extension, that something is morally valid, or that it is a good solution to some practical or artistic problem), one is making a claim that is in principle public, and open to inter-subjective appraisal. Objectivity, on Popper's account, is to be understood in terms of openness to such inter-subjective scrutiny (so that there is a fallibility to any claim to objectivity, in the sense that it may always be open to later challenge by others). And insofar as one wishes to refer to an individual as rational or as objective, it will be in terms of their openness to such criticism,[43] or to them as having internalized its products and standards. It is as a result of this that Popper's account is also one that can be applied to the artist or the composer, working in isolation. Popper depicts them as engaged in a process of problem solving, and of thus working by trial and error within material which, while a human creation, creates its own autonomous problems.[44]

This brings us to our second theme: that of autonomy. Popper stressed the way in which our products do not remain under our control, as they have a content which may be full of surprises to its originator. He developed this idea especially in connection with the logical consequences of a theory.[45] But he stresses it, also, in connection with works of art; for example, with reference to the story of Hayden who, Popper writes: 'when listening to the first chorus of his Creation, broke into tears and said:[46] "I have not written this".'

In this way, the autonomy of 'world 3' objects plays a role both in relation to our fallibility and to our ability to create things which go beyond what we intentionally put into them. There is a sense in which this may be understood as involving a downplaying of the importance of the self; certainly as compared to approaches towards ourselves and to human culture which stress the importance of self-expression. But there is also a sense in which these ideas of Popper's are also, in his view, of considerable importance for how we understand the self.

We have already noted how, in his discussion of the relation between mind and body, Popper thought that it was ideas about world 3 which raised particularly difficult problems for reductionism. (Popper reports, in his autobiography, on David Miller's quip that Popper had 'called in world 3 to redress the balance between worlds 1 and 2';[47] we will discuss the substance of what is involved in this a little later in this chapter.) World 3, in Popper's account, also has a key role to play in relation to the self. For, as Popper says at the end of his autobiography:[48]

Admitting that world 3 originates with us, I stress its considerable autonomy and its immeasurable repercussions on us. Our minds, our selves, cannot exist without it; they are anchored in world 3. We owe to the interaction with world 3 our rationality, the practice of critical and self-critical thinking and acting. We owe to it our mental growth. And we owe to it our relation to our task, to our work, and its repercussions on ourselves . . . we grow, and become ourselves, only in interaction with world 3.

Popper elaborates on these ideas in his discussion of the self in his contributions to *The Self and Its Brain*. There are, it seems to me, three elements to his discussion. The first is that he takes the development of the self to be an inter-subjective process: we are born, he conjectures, with an expectation that we will be surrounded by persons, who will play a crucial role in the development of our self.[49] As Popper suggests:[50] 'a human child growing up in social isolation will fail to attain a full consciousness of self'. This idea has an interesting parallel with some of the ideas of Adam Smith, and also with some recent work on the child's development of language.[51]

Second, there is the idea that the self is also an object upon which we can work, critically. World 3 and human language, Popper argues, make 'it possible for us to be not only subjects, centres of action, but also objects of our own critical thought, of our own critical judgement'.[52] Third, there is a sense in which the self is 'anchored in world 3'.[53] That is to say, on Popper's account, becoming a self involves developing theories about ourselves,[54] including a theoretical orientation in space and time.[55] Further, we ourselves are, Popper suggests, world 3 objects, in the sense of being theoretical constructions. By this he means not only that we are 'the products of other minds' and of the world 3 objects upon which we work, but also of our having 'a (changing) plan, or set of theories and preferences', which, as Popper says, may allow us to 'transcend ourselves – that is to say, transcend our instinctive desires and inclinations'.[56]

All this, in turn, relates to Popper's view of human freedom and of creativity. This is not the place for an extended discussion of Popper's ideas about human freedom. But it may be useful to say the following. In Popper's view, our starting point in philosophy should, quite generally, be with commonsensical ideas, in the sense that the burden of argument is, as it were, upon those who wish to challenge them.[57]

It is in this connection that the kind of determinism involved in Newtonian physics seemed so much of a challenge to our commonsensical ideas about the significance of human action and our personal responsibility for what we do and do not do. For if an account like that of Laplace were correct,[58] his 'demon' could predict the future movement of physical bodies on the basis of a knowledge of natural laws, and of the state of the physical world at some point in the past. On such an account, our goals and plans, and our concerns for such things as human freedom and the relief of suffering, would seem to be an irrelevance, in that anything that occurred in the physical world – including the movement of our bodies – could have been predicted on the basis of an account of the state of the world prior to the existence of human beings, or life in any form, and on a basis which did not refer to such objects of our concern.[59]

It was, thus, against the tenability of such a view that Popper argued – in his 'Indeterminism in Quantum Physics and in Classical Physics', and in a variety of subsequent publications.[60] Popper initially developed an argument against the predictability of the future of even a deterministic system, once knowledge was admitted into the picture. Popper was also subsequently to argue for emergence, and not only for the indeterminacy of the physical world, but also for its causal openness to consciousness and, through that, to his world 3.[61] (He also suggests, in the course of his reply to Watkins in *The Library of Living Philosophers*, that one might say, if one had a taste for such jargon, 'that the world, in becoming conscious of itself, becomes necessarily open and incompletable'.[62])

I will not discuss the details of his argument here, but will instead consider the view of human creativity to which all of this leads. Popper stresses, first of all, what he called the blindness of the trials that we make, to the solution of our problems:[63]

> It is not from the trial but only from the critical method, the method of error elimination, that we find, *after* the trial . . . whether or not it was a lucky guess.

As we have seen, this critical method is, for Popper, inter-subjective in its character. At the same time, Popper has also stressed the way in which, in working on a problem, we may come to understand it:[64]

> in the sense that we know what kind of guess or conjecture or hypothesis will not do at all, because it simply misses the point of the problem, and what kind of requirements would have to be met by any serious attempt to solve it.

Creativity, on his account, has two elements. First, aside from an intense interest in, and knowledge of, a problem, there is what Popper has called 'critical imagination', in the sense of an 'ability to break through the limits of the range – or to vary the range – from which a less creative thinker selects his trials',[65] something that Popper also describes as breaking with an implicit conjecture, held by others, as to the range of all possible trials,[66] and which, historically, he notes may be the product of culture clash. Second, Popper stresses the role played by dogmatic restrictions, in giving us a framework within which to work. In the course of a discussion of the historical role, in the development of music, of 'the canonization of Gregorian melodies', Popper comments that this:[67]

> piece of dogmatism . . . provided the necessary scaffolding for us to build a new world . . . the dogma providing us with the frame of coordinates needed for exploring the order of

this new unknown and possibly even chaotic world, and also for creating order where order is missing.

He is then led into a wide-ranging comparison between creativity in science and in music:[68]

> musical and scientific creation seem to have this much in common: the use of dogma, or myth, as a man-made path along which we move into the unknown, exploring the world, both creating regularities or rules and probing for existing regularities.

Popper is also explicitly critical of the person who aims at being original, or works with the intention to express their personality – something which, he suggests, will 'interfere with . . . the integrity of a work of art'. By contrast, Popper writes:[69]

> In a great work of art the artist does not try to impose his little personal ambitions on the work, but uses them to *serve* his work. In this way he may grow as a person, through interaction with what he does.

By this point, the reader may well wonder: interesting as all this might be, what does it have to do with issues of social and political philosophy? The answer is that it all goes to underpin the strong strand of anti-romanticism, which plays an important role in *The Open Society*, but for which he does not there advance many arguments. For his approach to the self and to creativity means that, while Popper is, strongly, an ethical individualist, his views are almost the antithesis of an approach that places individual self-expression at the centre of things, or which demands that society, culture or politics should be remoulded so as to fit the instinctive concerns of the individual. Reason, on which Popper places so much stress, is on his account to be understood as an inter-subjective process, which acts as a retrospective check upon what we produce. This, and the sense in which the self, for Popper, is also an achievement of this inter-subjective culture, means that we can well expect there to be tensions between what comes to us, instinctively, and these things. Further, as the earlier passage about Gregorian melodies suggested, what is involved in such a culture, and in creativity, more generally, may include what are *correctly* experienced by ourselves as dogmatic restrictions.

Popper has also frequently argued that we may have much to learn from culture-clash, and from interactions with those who take views of things, and follow customs and conventions, which are radically different from our own. Such experiences, while they may be very fruitful, may by no means always be easy or pleasant. (In *The Myth of the Framework*, Popper refers to the story from Herodotus, of Darius forcing an encounter between Greeks within his empire who burned their dead, and Callatians who ate theirs – something which, while doubtless both groups *may* have learned from it, both equally well might have wished to do without.[70]) More generally, the business of discovering that our individual preconceptions are false, or that what the group of whom we are a member had taken as necessary or universal is, in fact, merely conventional and local, may be unsettling.

Popper has argued that it *is* possible for us to learn from others: that differences in 'frameworks' need not be insuperable barriers. But two things are worth noting about this. The first is that, as I have suggested, such learning may not come easily or naturally to us. It will typically require an act of determination, on our part, to hold our views in forms that are open to criticism; to relate them to a 'public' world within which they can be evaluated; and to avoid the use of terminology, or of other approaches, which will close our views off to the access of other people.[71] It cannot be stressed enough that, on Popper's account, all of these things are the result of submitting ourselves to certain conventions, which we may experience as being cumbersome or 'unnatural'. Second, there is a point that Popper made in the course of a lecture on toleration.[72] It is that, while we may gain greatly from such exchanges, we should not expect that they will lead to unanimity or consensus, and judge that they have been unfruitful unless this is the result (or, still worse, unless one of the parties to the argument brings the other round to their initial point of view). In his lecture, Popper discusses the extended disagreement between Einstein and Niels Bohr. This, he argues, was extremely productive, although neither of them convinced the other. By way of contrast, one might stress just how restricted, in Popper's view, are the matters in respect of which he thinks that consensus can be reached. These are basic statements in the sciences, which consist of claims about the behaviour of publicly accessible objects, such as pointer-readings; and – although we have had occasion to criticize even this, as *over*-optimistic – an agenda for public policy, based on the idea of what avoidable suffering (and related issues) are most urgently in need of remedy.

It should not be thought, however, that Popper is urging on us a kind of secular gospel of self-renunciation. For he urges that we should find personal significance in our own work, and in our decisions about what our purpose in life should be.[73] As we noted in Chapter 1, it is in this connection that Popper suggested, to Isaiah Berlin, that negative freedom should be valued.[74] It is also worth noting Popper's concluding comment in his autobiography that,[75] 'in struggling with ideas he has found more happiness than he could ever deserve'. One might question the extent to which, under current social arrangements, the things to which Popper points are opportunities that are open to more than a small fraction of the population. However, academics should not underestimate the extent to which entrepreneurial activity within a market economy, on however small a scale, may also provide opportunities for such things.

Be this as it may, there is a sense in which, if Popper's approach is correct, we can expect life in an open society to be an unsettling business. For while we may come to enjoy the consolations of which Popper speaks, it is nonetheless the case that the openness of an open society will often be found unsettling. While we may gain from critical scrutiny and from the unsettling discovery that what we had thought correct, natural or an achievement is false, a parochial convention or something from the failures of which, at best, others might learn something, it is not clear how much we will *enjoy* it.

Popper argued, in *The Open Society*, that an open society would also be expected to have some problematic features of its own. He referred, in this connection, to its 'abstract' character – to the way in which, within it, social relations may be de-personalized.[76] In addition, he made much of the idea – which we have had occasion to mention before – of the strains of civilization. This Popper describes as:[77]

> the strain created by the effect which life in an open and partially abstract society continually demands from us . . . the endeavour to be rational, to forgo at least some of our emotional social needs, to look after ourselves, and to accept responsibility.

He relates it also to a breakdown in what had been experienced as 'natural' class relations, and to the security of membership of a tribe or an organic community.[78]

Popper's specific discussion of this is related to developments in Athens, and to the background to the work of Heraclitus and Plato. But he also discusses it in relation to the behaviour of the individual, more generally.[79] And, in the light of the key, but unannounced, theme of his whole book – the parallel between Hitler and Plato[80] – it is clear that he is dealing with a phenomenon he believed to be experienced at specific historical junctures, and which seemed to him illuminating not only in respect of classical Greece, but also in respect of the society in which he had grown up.

There is one additional and related theme in Popper's work which deserves to be brought out explicitly, and this is his critique of nationalism, and his clear but critical preference for multi-national regimes.[81] Popper saw nationalism as related to a wish to return to a community of a kind which was called into question by population growth, and the development of commerce and an open society.[82] In Popper's view, the aim is misconceived. For what people are reacting against is a necessary and unavoidable feature of an open society. Further, their chosen vehicle is hopeless, in the sense that, given the intermingling of actual populations, the ideal of a nation state is unrealizable, and the attempt to realize it a source of disaster.[83]

In the light of the attention paid, today, to the supposedly moral principle of national self-determination, and in the light of the revival of nationalism in Eastern Europe and what were Yugoslavia and the Soviet Union, Popper's criticism seems to me, alas, highly topical, and very much to the point. While the idea of nationalism may seem appealing, the fact that virtually any nation state will contain minorities, and that any definition of nationality will rest on arbitrary decisions,[84] its adoption will lead to a multiplication of problems. For the fact that the nation state is supposed to give particular recognition to the nation in question – and thus to its language, religion, culture, and so on – produces genuine grounds for resentment on the part of those who end up living within it but are not members of the nation in question, on the grounds that their language, culture and so on will be treated worse than, say, would be possible within a multi-national state. Those who are not nationals, under the favoured definition of nationality, are typically treated as second-class citizens, if they are accorded citizenship at all. The emphasis placed, by nationalists, on the idea of national self-determination conjures up a totally spurious picture of emotional satisfactions to be obtained from life in a *Volksgemeinschaft*. While it is also somehow suggested that if we govern ourselves – by which is actually meant that we are governed by people who share with us some distinguishing characteristic[85] – the result should be satisfactory, which is a complete red herring with regard to *all* the real problems of good government.

Popper's own approach is worth considering, just because of its contrast with what is, today, customary. While he was critical of some of the aspects of its policy towards its neighbours, he was broadly in favour of Athenian imperialism, not least because of its cosmopolitan character.[86] Indeed, he suggested, in the classical Greek context, that 'tribalist exclusiveness and self-sufficiency could be superseded only by some form of imperialism'.[87] Popper also, in the course of a criticism of Masaryk, argued for the preferability of an international federation in the Danube basin rather than a division into nation states.[88] Hacohen has mentioned, in the course of his discussion of Popper's views, that it is striking that it was the institution of the Austro-Hungarian empire and, more specifically, the emperor, that in the end was a significant force for the toleration and the protection of its Jewish citizens, against growing nationalist forces.[89]

In our contemporary context, it would seem to me that there is something to be learned from Popper's argument, over and above his criticism of nationalism. It is that we should interpret the idea of multiculturalism – in the sense of the toleration and, so far as we can manage it, the welcoming of social diversity – in individualistic terms, rather than in the form of giving political status to quasi-nationalistic bodies within a wider liberal state. Further, we need to realize that the toleration of diversity will not necessarily come naturally to us. We may, from time to time, find aspects of it difficult to take, and it may well require a degree of deliberation and explicit discussion as to what we are doing, why it is valuable, and as to how genuine problems to which it gives rise (for example, by way of diversity which people may find unsettling in social life) are to be handled. This in turn, however, indicates that we must think of multiculturalism, in this sense, as a kind of artefact, which is part of the wider culture within which individual cultural diversity is situated, rather than something which we can expect to be a 'natural' part of each of the diverse cultures within such a community. The culture of a multi-national empire is, here, a useful image; not least because of the way in which, if we value the liberal ideal of toleration, we must recognize that it, and the liberal culture of which it is a part, must be accorded priority over the different individual cultures the toleration of which are valued within it. There is also a further dimension to Popper's opposition to nationalism, in that he argued, strongly, for an[90] 'international organization which has legislative, administrative and judicial functions as well as an armed executive which is prepared to act', arguing also that it is *individual* human beings, not states or nations, which 'must be the ultimate concern even of international organizations'.[91]

If we were to accept these suggestions of Popper, the proper concern of politics would be with the remedying of avoidable suffering, which would include the oppression of others on the basis of their national origin, and so on. Popper himself put the matter, in the course of an (unpublished) interview,[92] by saying that what is to be demanded is the *protection of minorities*, wherever they live, rather than political independence. In this connection, there would – as in Popper's approach to politics generally – have to be public discussion as to just what the problem was, and something like consensual agreement as to its character; a clear statement as to how it was proposed that the problem should be remedied, and then evaluation as to how, in fact, the 'remedy' performed, and as to undesirable unintended consequences that may have arisen from the attempt to remedy it. All this might seem a far cry from politics today – both in terms of our willingness to treat others on a par with ourselves, and also to address the practicalities of the remedy of suffering and oppression in such an unromantic manner. But it is this that indicates the moral and organizational challenge of Popper's approach to politics.

There is, however, a problem raised for Popper's own views, by his ideas about world 3 and the social constitution of the self. For, as I indicated in the Introduction, they add a further strand to the problems that we raised earlier about 'social engineering', in connection with Popper's 'Towards a Rational Theory of Tradition'. We will return to these issues in Chapter 5.

4

VALUES AND REASON*

MORAL THEORY

The Open Society and Its Enemies is heavily influenced by Popper's ideas in the theory of knowledge, and at many points his moral and political ideas follow, closely, the pattern of argument developed in his work on more general philosophical issues. As Popper has written, both *The Poverty of Historicism* and *The Open Society*:[1]

> grew out of the theory of knowledge of [*Logik der Forschung*] and out of [the] conviction that our often unconscious views on the theory of knowledge and its central problems . . . are decisive for our attitude towards ourselves and towards politics.

In this chapter, we will be concerned not only with Popper's ideas about reason and values, but also with some respects in which Popper seems to me less than consistent in the parallels which he draws between these different fields. I will here argue that the parallels should be applied more consistently than Popper himself seemed willing to do. The consequences of this seem to me interesting. On the one side, Popper's views are drawn closer to those of the classical liberalism about which he said such scathing things in *The Open Society*. Yet, on the other, his views then also turn out to have certain striking similarities to some aspects of the later views of Juergen Habermas, something that may relate to a common Kantian influence. . . .

Our starting point is with Popper's discussion of values in the text of *The Open Society*. The key theme there is his emphasis on the distinction between facts and decisions, and his insistence on the individual's responsibility for his or her or own moral decisions. Popper also stresses that our standards are 'of our making in the sense that our decision in favour of them is our own decision'.[2] What does this amount to? In chapter 24 of *The Open Society*, section III, Popper discusses 'the rational and imaginative analysis of the consequences of a moral theory'. He suggests that:[3]

> wherever we are faced with a moral decision of a more abstract kind, it is helpful to analyse carefully the consequences which are likely to result from the alternatives between which we have to choose. For only if we can visualize the consequences in a concrete and practical way, do we really know what our decision is about.

Popper illustrates this with a striking example from Shaw's *St Joan*, in which a figure who had urged the execution of St Joan breaks down when he sees what the consequences of his demands are, as she is burned to death. Popper compares this analysis of an action's consequences to 'scientific method', arguing that 'in science, too, we do not accept an abstract theory because it is convincing in itself; we rather decide to accept or reject it after we have investigated those concrete and practical consequences which can be more directly tested by experiment'.[4] However, Popper then says that there is a fundamental difference:[5]

> In the case of a scientific theory, our decision depends upon the results of experiments. But in the case of a moral theory, we can only confront its consequences. And while the verdict of experiments does not depend on ourselves, the verdict of our conscience does.

There is more in his work on broadly the same theme. For example, Popper is critical of the project of 'scientific ethics' on the grounds that, *inter alia*, 'if it could be achieved, it would destroy all personal responsibility and therefore all ethics'.[6] In the same context, he also criticizes 'moral judgements . . . i.e. judgements involving such terms as "good" or "bad"', as 'irrelevant', stating that 'Only a scandal-monger is interested in judging people or their actions'.[7] His discussion continues with a critique of the views of moral philosophers who have addressed the issue of how we ought to act by reference either to human nature or to 'the nature of "the good"', suggesting that, in one way or other, these approaches are barren.[8]

In the face of all this, together with similar comments elsewhere in the volume – a critique of natural law theory as confused[9] – Popper's stress that[10] 'it is impossible to derive a sentence stating a norm or a decision or, say, a proposal for a policy from a sentence stating a fact', and his emphasis on the idea that 'norms are man-made . . . in the sense that the responsibility for them is entirely ours',[11] it might seem reasonable to conclude that Popper is an ethical subjectivist.

This, however, is not the case. For Popper also tells us[12] that he does 'not mean that . . . [moral conventions] must be arbitrary'; and he writes of it being 'our business to improve them as much as we can'. The reader, however, might understandably be puzzled. For Popper does not discuss that by which our moral judgements (if we are allowed to speak in such terms) are *morally* constrained. He thus seems to have left unexplained that in terms of which moral conventions are not arbitrary, or in what their improvement may consist. What is more, Popper might seem to have criticized all the more obvious alternative answers to this question. This includes even Kant, with whose views Popper elsewhere exhibits considerable sympathy, and even on this topic, in that Kant's recourse to 'human reason' is explicitly criticized along with other appeals to human nature.[13]

I here wish to suggest – somewhat timidly, in view of the extent to which *The Open Society* was rewritten, in attempt to put his views both clearly and effectively – that Popper's presentation of his ideas is badly misleading, and that what may come over as a form of subjectivism is, in fact, best understood as an espousal of the autonomy of ethics. I wish, further, to suggest that Popper's views are best interpreted as a form of ethical realism, in which the epistemological approach developed in his more general writings may be applied, also, to ethical judgements. (Although one must here take note of his point that 'there may be different systems of norms, between which there is not much to choose'.[14]) I will argue that there is much in *The Open Society* itself which may be interpreted in this way, and that it is also supported by ideas to be found in some of Popper's other writings. If this interpretation is accepted, however, it would be necessary to reinterpret, in the light of it, some of what Popper says about the significance of individual decisions. In addition, my interpretation is clearly at odds with some of the material in the notes to *The Open Society*, to which I have referred above. But this seems to me in order, in that, if the ideas in these notes are retained, it is simply not clear in what terms Popper could explain how individuals' moral judgements are non-arbitrary.

My argument will start with some discussion of the thrust of Popper's argument in *The Open Society*. I will suggest that what Popper is doing, fundamentally, is defending the autonomy of ethics, against various forms of heteronomy.

First, it is striking that at one point Popper actually says as much. For he says the following concerning the dualism of facts and decisions about which he had just been writing: 'so much concerning the dualism of facts and decisions, or the doctrine of the autonomy of ethics'.[15] Second, consider what most of Popper's argument is directed *against*. It is directed against various forms of moral positivism, including the idea that ethical decisions should be determined by non-moral facts; by forms of sociological positivism, or forms of moral futurism. As Popper himself says, in one of his notes, of the text of *The Open Society*: 'our considerations in the text . . . are concerned solely with the impossibility of deriving norms from psychological or sociological or similar . . . facts'.[16]

The note from which I have just quoted is, however, of further significance for our purposes. For in it, Popper refers to Tarski's semantics, and to his definition of truth. This Popper explains briefly, and then argues:[17]

> there is no reason why we should not proceed in an exactly analogous fashion in the realm of norms. We might then introduce, in correspondence to the concept of truth, the concept of the validity or rightness of a norm.

Popper then adds – which, indeed, represents the whole point of *his* discussion of this material – that this would have the consequence that 'if we use the term "fact" in such a wide sense that we speak about the fact that a norm is valid or right, then we could even derive norms from facts'. It was from such facts that he distinguishes what he describes as the 'non-semantical' facts, in the material on which I quoted him in the text to note 16, above. Popper does not himself discuss that in virtue of what a norm would itself be understood to be valid or right. In my personal view, the best account of such matters has been offered in the work on non-naturalistic ethical realism by some recent British writers.[18] As I will explain below, I think that a useful account of the methodology of such a view is, in fact, offered by a distinctive reading of Adam Smith's *Theory of Moral Sentiments*. These issues, however, are ones into which Popper himself, possibly wisely, does not venture.

The broad interpretation of Popper's views which I am offering here can draw some support from his 'Addendum: Facts, Standards and Truth: A Further Criticism of Relativism' to *The Open Society*, of 1961. Popper there suggested that both truth and the idea of absolute moral standards could serve as regulative principles, and also that there are parallels between what we hope to be our epistemological progress towards truth, and progress in the realm of standards.[19] Popper also there stressed *The Open Society*'s concern for 'Kant's idea of autonomy, as opposed to heteronomy'.[20] He suggests – in parallel with his ideas about truth – that there is no criterion of absolute rightness, but that – again, in parallel with his ideas about science – we can nonetheless 'make progress in this realm', and he gives what he calls some 'elementary' but 'extremely important' examples of discoveries in the realm of standards:[21]

> That cruelty is always 'bad'; that it should always be avoided where possible; that the golden rule is a good standard which can perhaps even be improved by doing unto others, wherever possible, as *they* would be done by. . . .

What Popper says here may seem unexciting; but I suspect that this reflects his own impatience with wordy meta-ethical discussion. At the same time, his notion that there are absolute moral standards of which we may fall short – which suggests the possibility of the application of his fallibilist epistemology to ethics – is an idea that *is* of interest to someone concerned with the problems that preoccupy us here. It is also of some wider significance, just because non-naturalistic ethical realism is usually identified with forms of *non*-fallibilistic intuitionism, so that Popper's approach opens up something distinctive – even if he shows no sign of pursuing it himself.

Popper's discussion concludes with some material that might seem to diminish from the force of his argument. For he raises the possible objection that he does not *establish* any absolute moral standards, and that 'at best [his arguments] show that the idea of an absolute moral standard is a regulative idea of use . . . to those . . . who are already eager to learn about, and search for, true or valid or good moral standards'.[22]

To this, however, Popper responds that it would do no good even if one could demonstrate the existence of some absolute moral standard even on the basis of pure logic (which is here, clearly, to be taken not as suggesting that one might accomplish this, but as a reference to what Popper took to be the highest standards of proof that are available). For one's interlocutor may take no interest, 'or else might reply "I am not in the least interested in your 'ought', in your moral rules – no more so than in your logical proofs, or, say, in your higher mathematics".' Popper goes on to say:[23]

> Thus even a logical proof cannot alter the fundamental situation that only he who is prepared to take these things seriously and to learn about them will be impressed by ethical (or any other) arguments. You cannot force anybody by arguments to take arguments seriously, or to respect his own reason.

This argument relates to one of Popper's underlying concerns about the limitations of reason, which we will discuss at the end of this chapter. It is, perhaps, worth indicating at once that I do not think that *this* problem needs to be taken as seriously as Popper seems willing to take it.

Let me, however, sum up the state of the argument so far. I have suggested that what might seem to be the subjectivism with regard to ethics of Popper's ethical 'decisionism' in *The Open Society* is not to be interpreted as such. Indeed, and despite one or two of the things that Popper says, his underlying view would seem to be an ethical objectivism, in which there are close methodological analogies with his theory of knowledge. At the same time, we have not yet looked at anything which might pertain, so to say, to the ontology or methodology of ethics. With regard to the first of these, I do not think that Popper says anything much – except that the remarks with which we started this chapter would clearly seem to indicate that ethics have what Popper would later call a 'world 3' status. At the same time it should not surprise us that Popper does not discuss this issue, as he displayed no real interest in the discussion of ontology in general.[24] Accordingly, much as we may regret it, I would be surprised if anything of significance could be found in his work on this topic.

With regard to methodology, there is something to be found which seems to me of some real interest. Our starting point here is with what Popper says about the idea of the 'rational unity of mankind' in *The Open Society*. In the course of a characterization of what he calls the rationalist attitude, Popper writes:[25]

the fact that the rationalist attitude considers the argument rather than the person arguing, is of far-reaching importance. It leads to the view that we must recognize everybody with whom we communicate as a potential source of argument and of reasonable information; it thus establishes what may be described as the 'rational unity of mankind'.

He also writes, a little later:[26]

Rationalism is ... bound up with the idea that the other fellow has a right to be heard, and to defend his arguments. It implies the recognition of the claim to tolerance. ... One does not kill a man when one adopts the attitude of first listening to his arguments. (Kant was right when he based the 'Golden Rule' on the idea of reason. ...)

In the light of the explicit link that is made here between this approach and Kant, I would like to refer to an unpublished typescript in the Popper Archives, which is grouped together with material from Popper's New Zealand period, and which discusses this same theme.[27] It is not at all clear that this is Popper's own work. But in the present context, this does not matter, for its interest here is that it contains the argument that ethics shares with science the use of reason in an interpersonal sense, and that if one wished to justify the categorical imperative, this would involve one in[28] 'a desire to overcome one's partiality and prejudices by taking serious account of the conflicting beliefs of other people'. But this, in turn, it is suggested, means trying to be impartial between oneself and others – which is itself described as 'the content of Kant's categorical imperative, in its best formulation'.[29] It is subsequently suggested that:[30]

[suppose] someone is only willing to accept [the categorical imperative] as an ultimate moral principle if we can justify it. We can then tell him that he already accepts it tacitly, because the desire for justification implies the desire to treat the problem rationally, and rationality implies impartiality, and that this is what the categorical imperative requires.

I have referred to this material, not because I think that the argument is all that telling in the form in which it is advanced,[31] but because of the parallel not only with the argument in *The Open Society* but also with points raised by some of Popper's 'hermeneutical' critics is so striking.[32]

95

Popper's account of his argument in *The Open Society* is brief. But it seems to me that we may give it more substance if we explore another line of argument – one which links together Popper, Kant, and also the theme of communication which occurs in the material quoted at note 25, above. Our starting point here is with the link that Popper makes between rational procedures in science and ethics. At the same time – and as we mentioned earlier, in connection with the material from Shaw's *St Joan* – Popper seemed reluctant to take the parallel too far, stressing, in the end, the individual's responsibility for his or her own moral judgements. I will argue here that there is room for a greater parallel than Popper allows between the foundations of ethics and Popper's view of the foundations of scientific knowledge.

In sections 8 and 29–30 of *The Logic of Scientific Discovery*, Popper emphasized the way in which objectivity is best secured through inter-subjective testability. This notion was there developed with an emphasis of two kinds: (i) on objective test results, envisaged as statements about such things as publicly observable pointer-readings; (ii) on the foundations of our knowledge as consisting of a revisable, open-ended consensus as to what is the case. Now the first of these, especially if it is understood physicalistically, would not seem directly applicable to the foundations of moral judgement. But I believe that the second is. It is here worth noting that Popper, in *The Self and Its Brain*, applied this latter approach to psychological illusions, and argued (with reference to the techniques of the Wuerzburg School) that there is no necessary methodological objection to introspective psychology, just because inter-subjective tests are possible in this field, if the appropriate methods are used.[33] This example indicates that the idea of inter-subjective testability can be taken beyond the realm of tests that are conducted with such publicly observable objects as pointers.[34]

Now Popper, when developing his ideas about the 'empirical basis', referred to a passage in Kant's *Critique of Pure Reason*, which I would here like to quote:[35]

> The holding of a thing to be true is an occurrence in our understanding which, though it may rest upon objective grounds, also requires subjective causes in the mind of the individual who makes the judgement. If the judgement is valid for everyone, provided only he is in possession of reason, its ground is objectively sufficient, and the holding

of it to be true is entitled conviction ... truth depends upon agreement with the object, and in respect of it the judgements of each and every understanding must therefore be in agreement with each other. ... The touchstone whereby we decide whether our holding a thing to be true is a conviction or mere persuasion is therefore external, namely, the possibility of communicating it and of finding it to be valid for all human reason. For there is then at least a presumption that the ground of the agreement of all judgements with each other notwithstanding the differing characters of individuals, rests upon the common ground, namely, upon the object, and that it is for this reason that they are all in agreement with the object – the truth of the judgement being thereby proved.

My suggestion is that it is to this approach (albeit with the theme of 'proof' revised in the light of Popper's fallibilism) which we might look, as a common background for Popper's epistemology and for his meta-ethics; a meta-ethics, however, from which – as I will argue later – some limited but substantive ethical consequences can also be drawn.[36]

One might ask, however, what ethical argument might actually look like from such a perspective. I do not wish to discuss this issue here at length. But it does seem to me that a model of this is, in fact, to be found in Adam Smith's *Theory of Moral Sentiments.* Or, at least, it is to be found if one does not pay too much attention to the ideas with which Smith starts the book, in which he discusses sympathy as involving a kind of re-experiencing of an emotion that others are feeling,[37] but instead moves, as does Smith himself, to a concern simply with approval or disapproval of actions. This approach also gives pride of place to the ethically particular: ethical principles would be evaluated on the basis of an open-ended consensus concerning the moral character of particular actions. (There is obviously a parallel here with Popper's ideas about 'basic statements'.[38]) The moral character of our actions is discovered through the judgements made upon them by others. At the same time, we may conjecture that particular judgements made by particular people on particular occasions are poor: they are fallible, and open to correction. Indeed, we as actors will be concerned with how our actions would be evaluated by an impartial spectator (understood, here, as the bearer of judgements with which well-informed spectators would agree), and we may refine and internalize such judgements, as our conscience. There is again, in all this, a strong parallel with Popper's ideas about the objectivity of science, and rationality. (Although it is at odds with Popper's critical remarks about moral judgements, to which we referred earlier.)

In the development of such ideas, Popper's point – which we noted earlier – concerning the plurality of moral systems would need to be taken into account. But so also, I believe, must Smith's own ideas about the relativity of moral judgements to what he referred as the 'mode of subsistence'.[39] All this does not imply a moral relativism, but, rather, the need to have recourse to explanatory theory, and to meta-ethics, as well as to directly consensus-seeking discussion, when we try to move towards agreement from positions which may initially seem radically at odds with one another.

Such an approach can also secure the ethical responsibility of the individual, about which Popper was so concerned. For if we claim that what we are doing is right – as contrasted, say, with our claiming that it is a pure matter of taste – we are claiming that in principle it could withstand the scrutiny of others, much as, say, if we were making a claim about the outcome of an experimental observation. And while, clearly, human fallibility, limited time and the fact that most of our actions are of little import will mean that neither we nor anyone else is likely or well advised to take these matters too seriously on a day-to-day basis, it is striking that such a rigorous standard of evaluation is, in principle, available to us. It allows for autonomy, in the sense that it is up to us to decide what we wish to claim is right; and a view such as this is perfectly compatible with our acting in the face of actual disapproval from those around us. But there is a striking notion of moral responsibility involved, in the sense that, in so doing, we are claiming that we are acting in a manner in which all well-informed moral agents would judge to be the action that should be taken in those circumstances.

I will spare the reader any further speculations concerning this theme of a reconciliation of Popper with a (distinctive) reading of Smith's *Theory of Moral Sentiments* and about moral realism. But I do need to make one point explicit. At the level of *meta*-ethics, the programme is universalistic. After the manner of our quotation from Kant, objectivity is to be understood in terms of *universal* agreement (although, as we noted, there is the possibility of the correction of faulty individual judgements, as well as other forms of adjustment). But – and it is here that I take issue with the archive paper on the categorical imperative – the actions upon which there is such moral agreement do not themselves need to be made on the basis of principles which are universalistic, in the sense of treating all rational beings as on a par. For an approach such as the one sketched here would seem to be compatible with an objective ethics in which there was agreement that it was morally appropriate to be partial – say, as between friends and strangers, those related to us by kinship or identity, and those with whom we have no such connection.

All this, however, raises a problem: what of Popper's own moral universalism?

MORAL UNIVERSALISM AND NEGATIVE UTILITARIANISM

One of the more striking themes in *The Open Society* is Popper's emphasis on what he describes as 'moral egalitarianism'. This is the idea that there should be moral equality between all members of mankind, and also a more specific kind of moral equality between citizens. Let us treat each of these in turn.

First, against those who favour some notion of moral inequality, Popper states that:[40]

> I hold, with Kant, that it must be the principle of all morality that no man should consider himself more valuable than any other person.

And he follows this up by quoting from Rousseau's *Origins of Inequality*, a reference that is striking because of Popper's more general dislike of Rousseau's romanticism. Popper also offers extended argument concerning the existence, in Athens, of moral universalism,[41] and to the effect that it is not shared by Plato.[42] Popper champions the Kantian theme that 'every individual is an end in himself'.[43] He discusses this in connection with his ideas about the public character of reason, which we have explored earlier (compare the passage from Popper quoted at note 25 (p. 95)). And he also argues – against those who would stress the importance of love or of emotion – that it is 'reason, supported by imagination, [which] enables us to understand that men who are far away, whom we shall never see, are like ourselves'.[44]

Popper's claims about equality, it should be stressed, are moral rather than factual, in the sense that he urges that we should 'treat men, especially in political issues, as equals . . . that is to say, as possessing equal rights and equal claims to equal treatment',[45] while at the same time frequently saying that it is a moral demand, which can be pursued in the face of empirical differences between people. With regard to citizenship, Popper argues for the equal distribution of the burdens of citizenship, for equal treatment before the law, for laws that are impartial between citizens, groups and classes, and that all citizens should have an equal share in the advantages that follow from membership of a state.[46] He stresses, further, that citizens should be treated impartially; he argues for the importance of ethical individualism; and he insists that it is the task of the state to protect the freedom of its citizens.[47]

Two questions may be raised about all this.

The first relates to Popper's moral universalism. I personally find his argument against what one might call the claims of moral aristocracy telling, both rationally and emotionally. The idea that anyone should claim that he or she is intrinsically more important, morally, than anyone else seems simply risible. There does seem to me, however, another problem that faces Popper's view, which I am not sure can be disposed of so easily. It relates to people not as moral agents, but as moral patients. For suppose we grant Popper's first argument, we can still ask: can we expect moral universalism to arise, as a result of the moral actions which others take towards them in their day-to-day lives? Here, it seems to me, there is a problem, given that we can all quite reasonably – and in ways which, I believe, would withstand moral scrutiny, after the fashion of the kind of theory briefly sketched in the previous section – act in ways that are morally partial, in the sense of our moral lives being dominated by our interactions with, and obligations towards, those with whom we have various kinds of particular relationships. To be sure, it would not be in order for us to engage in an act of direct injustice towards strangers, by commission, so that the minimal demands of classical liberalism may be secure. And we may well regret that the consequences of our moral actions may be that people 'who are far away, whom we shall never see' lose out. But it is not clear that, in most circumstances, we have any positive duty to address this issue; not least because, in our particular situations, various particular moral responsibilities will, quite properly, be experienced as more morally pressing.

Historically, one problem about moral universalism is that it seems to have been thought compelling largely on religious grounds, for which there is no obvious secular substitute. Indeed, one striking lesson from eighteenth-century moral philosophy would seem to have been the collapse of attempts to offer a non-religious basis for just this feature of what was then understood as natural law.[48] There is, perhaps, a ghost of an argument for moral universalism in Popper's ideas about the rational unity of mankind: that insofar as I care about truth and about the validity of my moral judgements I have a concern for other people as bearers of such judgements, and thus a concern for their autonomy and well-being.[49] It would seem clear enough, however, that the force of this argument is limited; not least because the universalism involved is formal, where it needs to be substantive.

For the argument is, in fact, only as good as the *actual* contributions that others may make, by way, as it were, of critical moral feedback. But this gets us to something well short of universalism. We may well benefit from criticism from, say, people from a specific culture remote from our own, with whom we have no other relations. But what they are likely to be able to contribute will surely relate to their membership of that culture, and possibly to the specific role that they play within it. As a result, it is not likely that we will obtain anything more from another individual who shares those same characteristics.[50] Accordingly, if we are to draw additional arguments from Popper on the ethical importance of each individual, we must, I suspect, go elsewhere in his work.[51]

The second problem relates to what Popper says about the state. The objection that I wish to voice here is that it is not clear why, on Popper's premises, we should owe any special moral duty to others simply because of shared citizenship. Indeed, in the light of what Popper says about the unity of mankind, and against nationalism, there would seem to be no basis for distinctive *moral* obligations of citizenship – i.e. ones which we would not owe to non-citizens. Clearly, this would not affect an argument for rights of citizenship which saw them as something like the products of membership of a mutual insurance association. But these are not the terms in which Popper addresses these issues. I do not regard this consequence as a weakness of Popper's position, in that the idea that citizenship has some special moral significance, while it is widespread, seems to me insupportable.[52] But I would like to register that there does seem to be a tension between what Popper writes about the state, and what he has arguments for.

The force of his argument, rather, seems to me to be carried by his negative utilitarianism and 'protectionism'. But I would argue that these cannot – other than pragmatically[53] – be interpreted in terms of citizenship. I have referred to Popper's 'protectionism', and to his ideas about negative utilitarianism, earlier in this volume. Briefly, his concern is that the role of the state should be the protection of the liberty of citizens – including liberty from economic exploitation – and the relief of avoidable suffering. The latter is to be understood in fairly generous terms – including the provision of access to higher education, and the remedying of injustice – while the specific agenda for action would be set through a process of consensual decision-taking. These ideas have an obvious appeal. But I am here going to criticize them.

My first line of criticism is that, despite their advantages over traditional utilitarianism,[54] they share in a range of broad defects of utilitarianism. These concern the relation of the goals of utilitarianism to the actions of individual citizens. While no reasonable person could not wish that avoidable suffering be avoided, and that those who suffer from unavoidable suffering be given succour, it is not clear to what extent we can take it to be their moral responsibility to bring these consequences about. There are several issues involved here.

Popper is strongly critical of what he sees as the moral collectivism of Plato's work: of the way in which the individual is sacrificed for the sake of (what is claimed to be) the well-being of the whole. At one point, however, Popper refers to this as Plato's 'principle of collective utility'.[55] This seems to me significant, just because the features of Plato's work which so disturb Popper here would seem as much related to his utilitarianism as to his distinctive organic theory of society. It is *utilitarianism* that is no respecter of persons. But does not the same problem – that individuals become a means to some collective end – arise also in respect of Popper's 'negative utilitarianism'?

To this, Popper could well respond that negative utilitarianism's concern for the relief of suffering, injustice, and so on, at least means that one individual is not to be sacrificed casually to meet the pleasures of others. And as to the relief of others' suffering, and the possibility that this might become an end for which the individual is sacrificed, Popper could stress his protectionism – his concern with the liberty of each citizen (which, in the light of his universalism, and his remarks made in connection with international organization, we must surely interpret in terms of each *individual*).

The problem here, however, is that Popper seems to me to have introduced two different ideas, negative utilitarianism and individual autonomy, which are in at least potential conflict with one another, without giving us any indication as to how we are to handle their mutual interrelations. In the light of the strong strand of ethical individualism, and the Kantian pedigree, of Popper's moral thought, we must, I think, give priority to 'protectionism' in the sense of a concern for the liberty of the individual, widely interpreted. I am not sure, though, that this really solves our problem. For Popper developed his ideas about protectionism and negative utilitarianism in terms of an agenda for public policy without – as far as I can see – discussing its interrelationship with the exercise of individual freedom, and individual moral responsibility, which he is so concerned to protect.

The simplest way to raise the problem with which we are here concerned relates to the actions of free, and morally conscientious, individuals. They will be concerned to live their lives decently and effectively. They will, *inter alia*, work in a reliable and conscientious manner, help out their neighbours, assist members of their families, engage in a variety of pursuits, including trying to interest their friends in what they believe to be the finer things of life, and so on. They will respect the rights of others, and abide by the law other than where this seems unduly cumbrous or unconscionable. They will also give to charity – to those who seem particularly unfortunate or are overcome by some unexpected disaster – or may promote various causes which seem to them to be worthwhile. By and large, they will expect that self-coordinating social mechanisms, legislation and the actions of the courts will take care of problems relating to the coordination of their actions with those of others, and with damaging unintended consequences of individual action. They will, doubtless, share Popper's concerns about the relief of suffering generally. But the weight that they give to its pursuit will depend on their judgement as to how it measures up, against the other priorities of their lives – including the moral obligations involved in their various special relationships. They may be moved to become involved in some form of extraordinary action – for example, by way of active participation

103

in a charitable organization, taking part in a boycott, or making some change in their patterns of consumption, because of the moral weight which they give to such activities. But its pursuit beyond a certain point, however worthy the cause, seems to me certainly not to be morally *obligatory*.

Now the problem that I wish to raise concerns the relationship between such actions and that aspect of Popper's protectionism that goes beyond the traditional concerns of classical liberalism, and also his negative utilitarianism. For these ideas of Popper are addressed as proposals concerning actions that *government* should take, governed by some form of social consensus. But those individuals with whose freedom Popper is concerned could surely say: we have our *own* agendas for action, concerning which we are already exercising our own conscientious moral preferences. It is simply not clear on what basis you wish to deprive us of resources which are already morally committed to pursuit of our agendas, in order to follow some other agendas, determined largely by other people.

Some items within these agendas could, of course, be justified: those which are prerequisites to the pursuit of those people's freedom to pursue their agendas, together with trade-offs that they may have to make with others so as to secure those prerequisites. One might also be able to justify action on the basis of those issues on Popper's agenda on which there was genuine unanimity (although, as I mentioned in Chapter 2, even this may be problematic). But it would seem to me that this would fall far short of Popper's own agenda. The heart of the problem, here, is that Popper's negative utilitarianism, and many aspects of his protectionism, would not seem to be sustainable on the basis of the moral autonomy which he is so concerned should be accorded to his citizens. One can reasonably expect them not to infringe upon the rights of other individuals, conceived after the fashion of negative liberty. But it would seem to me utterly *reasonable* that they should prefer, say, to spend the proceeds of a pay rise on a new bicycle for a nephew, or on a set of CDs of Beethoven symphonies for their own enjoyment and elevation, rather than on the relief of suffering, or the provision of some of what Popper wishes to include within his notion of protectionism (e.g. access to higher education for other people). By way of contrast, any theory which puts the pursuit of some general social good above such things would, if were really taken seriously, seem to me to make a nonsense of day-to-day human life.[56] I would argue, further, that our decisions to act as I have indicated above, would be seen as reasonable, if unheroic, by an impartial spectator. While moral heroism is something that can be demanded of us only in small and occasional doses, and which seems to me dangerous and sometimes *immoral* in its treatment of others, when it is pursued with too great an intensity, *however* worthy the overall goal might be.

It is not, in all this, that I am in any way denying Popper's Kantian appeal to our moral equality with others. I am, rather, arguing that in our capacity as moral agents, we each have our own lives to lead, with our own moral agenda; one which admits only limited room for positive duties towards people who are far away, and whom we shall never see. This, emphatically, does not mean that there should be no place in our lives for a concern for the well-being of others, and for the relief of suffering or, indeed, for large-scale changes in our institutions, made in the light of these concerns. But it seems to me that this has to be seen in the context of our lives as a whole, rather than being something that it is appropriate for some other body to impose upon us, on the basis of some moral agenda of its own, and against our own moral judgement.

There is, however, one line of argument that could be advanced against these conclusions, on the basis of Popper's arguments. It is that, in the argument that I have developed above, I was appealing to the moral validity of the judgements of the conscientious individual. But this, as I have argued earlier, contains an implicit reference to a form of inter-subjective validation. This, in turn, would seem to require not only that we get to hear what others think of what we are doing, but also that those other people themselves enjoy a reasonable degree of autonomy, and so on.[57] (For they can hardly exercise such a critical function if they are dependent upon us or upon others; and there is something grotesque about the idea that they should be asked to perform such a role, if they are starving.) Insofar as this argument has any clout (see, however, the text to note 50 (p. 101)), it might suggest a basis not only for the maintenance of a public forum in which our actions are held open for criticism, but also for a more extended view of our obligations towards others. The more general thrust of my suggestions here, however, is that once considerations such as those which have been advanced in this section are brought in, we have reason to limit Popper's moral interventionism to protection in something closer to the sense in which this was understood in the classical liberal tradition, together with those forms of welfare provision which flow from the moral agendas of various free individuals.

THE LIMITS OF RATIONALISM?

We have already had occasion to note, in this chapter, the way in which Popper places emphasis on the idea that 'you cannot force anybody by argument to take arguments seriously'.[58] This idea has greater significance in Popper's work than might at first appear to be the case. For it relates to a distinctive thread in his argument: that we have to make a morally based *commitment* to reason. In the first edition of *The Open Society*, Popper, after a criticism of that form of comprehensive rationalism which argues that all assumptions must be based on argument, champions what he calls 'critical rationalism'. He writes that 'whoever adopts the rationalist attitude does so because without reasoning he has adopted some decision, or belief, or habit, or behaviour, which therefore in its turn must be called irrational'.[59] He further writes of this as 'an irrational faith in reason'. Popper identifies his own view as a 'critical rationalism, which recognizes that the fundamental rationalist attitude is based upon an irrational decision, or upon faith in reason',[60] and then goes on to argue that what is involved is a moral decision.[61]

These ideas are deep-seated. As I indicated in Chapter 1, Bartley has argued that they may stem from the influence upon Popper of Kierkegaard, at a time when he was reacting against his youthful involvement with the Austrian communists.[62] Bartley comments that Popper reacted by taking a non-rational decision in favour of a Kantian ethics. It is striking that Popper has himself suggested that Kant's own idea of the primacy of the will 'may be interpreted as the primacy of an irrational decision'.[63]

There is, however, another and more practical side to Popper's view as well; one which he has explained in the introduction he wrote to *The Myth of the Framework*. Here, Popper refers to an encounter with a young member of the National Socialist Party, who was armed with 'a pistol' around 1933. Popper reports that this man said to him: 'What, you want to argue? I don't argue, I shoot.'[64]

Popper himself seems to have thought of these issues – the practical and the theoretical – as being interrelated.[65] But I believe this to be incorrect. First, as Bartley has argued at some length, to see rationalism as resting upon an irrational commitment depends upon our taking a view of rationality which identifies it with justification, which is against the broad spirit of Popper's own 'critical approach'.[66] As Bartley argues, a 'comprehensively critical rationalism' need make no such concession to irrationalism.

But what of Popper's Nazi? Popper is clearly right that one cannot, by means of argument, force someone to take argument seriously. But is this a problem for the rationalist? I do not think that it is, for reasons that we have discussed earlier in this chapter. For if we claim moral validity for what we are doing, we are implicitly appealing to the idea that our views will withstand inter-subjective critical scrutiny. It is open to us to reject such claims for the moral validity of our actions. But to do this renders the basis on which we are acting one which, as it were, is a matter of taste rather than of morality. And this, in turn, means that others have no reason to respect it, should it prove harmful to them.[67] Accordingly, while it is open to people to behave as did the Nazi, there is a moral cost to their so doing – for others will have no reason to respect their actions, as they would those of a moral agent. As I suggested earlier in this chapter, the result of all this is that the moral realist interpretation of Popper's ethics, for which I have argued earlier, enables us to resolve what would otherwise seem to be a problem in Popper's views; one for which he has been taken to task by Apel and by Habermas.

These issues are also, however, of some direct importance for the individual. For it is difficult to imagine people living their lives while treating all their actions as being taken simply on the basis of tastes. For good – or ill – we tend to take ourselves, and our projects, with a seriousness which belies understanding them in such a way. Popper, in *The Open Society*, advanced the view that while toleration was of great moral importance, it had significant limits. There was, he argued, no obligation upon us to tolerate the intolerant, although this is something upon which we would not necessarily need to act, if the intolerant can be otherwise socially controlled.[68] It would seem to me that Popper's argument could be extended, and that we should not have to accord the same degree of protection to actions that are taken simply on the basis of tastes, as we do to those the basis for which is made open to inter-subjective scrutiny.[69]

It is, however, important to raise one concluding point. For the reader might well have thought that there is something very wrong with the argument of this chapter. In it, I have stressed the importance of the individual's moral autonomy. My account of this, however, might have seemed to some both callous and complacent. At the very least, it might seem to have left one issue unresolved. For, over and above our concerns for those around us, for the formal rights of others, and for the misfortune of those who, say, suffer from the consequences of some social or physical disaster outwith their responsibility or control, we also have concerns for other things. Our moral preferences may range over the kind of life conditions in which we and others are living; things which, in Hayek's expression, taken over from Adam Ferguson, are the products of human action, but not of human design. Popper's work is acutely concerned with such matters. And at the time at which I write, we would typically add to his concern for the relief of suffering, a concern, say, for the quality of life in cities, and, more broadly, for the environment in which we live – matters for which we are responsible, but which are not the direct products of our actions. What, it might well be asked of me, is to be done about such matters? Are they, too, to be sacrificed to the complacencies of our day-to-day moral lives, and thus, say, a nephew's desire for a new bicycle. This is an issue that I will address in the next chapter.

5

POPPER, LIBERALISM AND
MODIFIED ESSENTIALISM

INTRODUCTION: LIBERALISM AND DEMOCRATIC
SOCIALISM IN *THE OPEN SOCIETY*

Let us start by pulling together some of the threads that we have
encountered earlier in this volume. In *The Open Society*, Popper,
while giving a powerful restatement – and reinterpretation for our
own day – of many of the themes of Kant's moral and political
philosophy,[1] displays a passionate, but at the same time rational
and critical commitment to liberal democracy. When Popper wrote
– during the Second World War – liberal democracy was hardly in
a strong position. To champion it then was to take up the defence
of a position already under siege. To defend that position without
fanaticism, and with a willingness to admit its intrinsic imperfections and open problems, was indeed remarkable and was itself
an impressive exemplification of the very approach that Popper
recommended to us in *The Open Society*.

While the book takes academic issues seriously,[2] Popper was
himself clearly concerned about practical issues. A constant
theme in that work is the bearing of philosophical ideas upon
the conduct of practical affairs. As Popper emphasized later:[3] 'our
often unconscious views on the theory of knowledge and its central
problems . . . are decisive for our attitude towards ourselves and
towards politics.' Again and again in his work this idea comes
through. It is hardly surprising that many of Popper's readers
are left not only challenged and inspired intellectually, but also
impressed with the desire to put some of Popper's ideas into
practice. The problem to be discussed in the present chapter
concerns the situation of someone who wishes to put Popper's
political ideas into practice: to a preference for what kind of
political order should Popper's ideas lead him?

My answer will be: a form of liberalism in the classical or 'old-fashioned' sense. This answer might seem unsurprising, as Popper has himself indicated that he is a liberal.[4] But it is more controversial than it may at first appear. Bryan Magee, in his book on Popper, while admitting that Popper 'would now describe himself . . . as a liberal in the old-fashioned sense of the word', has argued that 'the young Popper worked out . . . what the philosophical foundations of democratic socialism should be'.[5] In the final paragraphs of chapter 21 of *The Open Society*, in which Popper speculates as to what might have happened had Marx not 'discouraged research in social technology', Popper comes close to saying that the ideas of his own work would be exemplified by a 'socialism of a non-collectivist type'.[6] Popper also reaffirmed more recently that he still found democratic socialism an attractive – if now an impracticable – ideal.[7]

Magee, and others who are attracted by Popper as a theorist of democratic socialism, might put the change in Popper's views down to the frequent tendency for people to become more conservative as they grow older; and they could perhaps counter the suggestion that 'older' here means 'wiser', by referring to Popper's own criticisms of the gerontocratic aspects of Plato's political philosophy! But how might this issue be more seriously decided?

A first move might be to see what Popper says on these issues himself in *The Open Society*. If we pose this question, however, we are at once faced with a problem. It is related to the fact that Popper's approach to political philosophy is consciously opposed to system building. As Popper says:[8]

> Marx was the last of the great holistic system builders. We should take care to leave it at that, and not to replace his by another Great System. What we need is not holism, it is piecemeal social engineering.

This theme is reflected in Popper's writings by his making a series of 'proposals' and 'demands'. These are to be imposed onto a political world that is seen as not being intrinsically rational, or fully rationalizable, but which, Popper believes, we should try to rationalize as far as possible,[9] by concentrating upon the remedying of those ills or defects that are most urgent. But with what proposals or demands are we here concerned; how should we set about our task; and by what institutional means?

As we have seen, Popper is concerned with the freedom of the individual and with altruism. In connection with the former, he refers to Kant's idea of 'a constitution that achieves the greatest possible freedom of human individuals by framing the laws in such a way that the freedom of each can co-exist with that of all the others'.[10] In connection with the latter, he refers to 'Kant's central practical doctrine ("always recognize that human individuals are ends, and do not use them as mere means to your ends")'.[11] We have also seen that while Popper opposes the project of 'constructing a code of norms upon a scientific basis',[12] and emphasizes that 'it is impossible to prove the rightness of any ethical principle, or even to argue in its favour in just the manner in which we argue for a scientific statement',[13] he nonetheless suggests that 'Kant was right when he based the "Golden Rule" on the idea of reason'.[14] Popper's own discussion of what might be called the grounding of ethics, in chapter 24 of *The Open Society*, consists of a restatement of the Kantian connection between freedom and reason in terms of a discussion of the relation between Popper's own values of freedom and altruism and themes from his epistemology. Rationality, for Popper, is to be identified with openness to criticism; and each individual is to be valued as a source of possible criticism. Objectivity, rather than being regarded as the attribute of the particular, wise individual, is regarded as a social product – a product of critical discussion. Popper also writes of the role of 'social institutions to protect freedom of criticism, freedom of thought, and thus the freedom of man'.[15]

Popper regards misery and suffering as making a direct moral appeal to us: that they be alleviated; though he combats the idea that we have a similar obligation more positively to promote the happiness of others. Popper's epistemological fallibilism plays an important role here, too:[16]

> rationalism is closely linked up with the political demand for practical social engineering – piecemeal engineering, of course – in the humanitarian sense, with the demand for the rationalization of society, for planning for freedom, and for its control by reason; not by 'science', not by a Platonic, a pseudo-rational authority, but by that Socratic reason which is aware of its limitations, and which therefore respects the other man and does not aspire to coerce him – not even into happiness.

111

The *way* in which Popper suggests that we should set about our task relates closely to these same epistemological themes. In *The Open Society*, the central suggestion about how we should proceed has two aspects. First, we impose our demands for the rationalization of society by political means. Here, the social sciences are looked to, to provide us with an appropriate social technology. But our attempts at 'social engineering' must be of a character that enables them to be critically monitored, and their failures and unintended consequences attended to. This theme of monitoring, or critical scrutiny, represents the second part of that suggestion that Popper offers us; one that is linked to his epistemological fallibilism. It is also ably expressed in a passage that Popper quotes from Burke as a 'motto' to his book:[17]

> I have never yet seen any plan which has not been mended
> by the observations of those much inferior in understanding
> to the persons who took the lead in the business.

That is to say, all political measures would benefit from being open to the critical feedback of those whom they concern.

There is, however, one other theme in Popper's book that we must also take into consideration. It concerns Popper's reaction to 'unregulated capitalism'. Popper, in his discussion of Marx, shows himself to be to a considerable extent in agreement with him in the judgement that 'unregulated' liberalism – which, as we have seen, was identified by him in the first edition of the book as *laissez-faire* – is pernicious. Popper's agreement with that judgement rests on two main planks. Economic non-interventionism, as a programme, is considered problematic, because Popper considers that 'unregulated' liberalism would itself require that certain freedoms be protected by the state.[18] Second, Popper broadly endorses Marx's account of capitalism as a historically correct account of 'exploitation' which was taking place in the period about which he wrote. In the face of this 'exploitation',[19] Popper says that 'we must demand that unrestrained capitalism give way to an *economic interventionism*'.[20]

When Popper moves to discuss such intervention, however, he emphasizes strongly:[21] (i) that, in this, 'we should not give more power to the state than is necessary for the protection of freedom'; and – after the first edition of *The Open Society* – (ii) that economic intervention should be effected through the design of 'a "legal framework" of protective institutions', rather than through 'empowering organs of the state to act . . . as they consider necessary for achieving the ends laid down by the rulers' – a contrast which he also describes as being between '"institutional" or "indirect" intervention', and . . . '"personal" or "direct" intervention'. Now as we noted earlier, it is striking that, in *these* demands, Popper formulates points that stand at the very heart of the discussion of the actions of government in modern forms of 'classical liberalism' – for example, F.A. Hayek's *The Constitution of Liberty*.[22] In addition, while Popper demands intervention in the market 'to see to it that nobody need enter into an inequitable arrangement out of fear of starvation, or economic ruin',[23] he also emphasizes that, 'without a carefully protected free market, the whole economic system must cease to serve its only rational purpose, that is, to satisfy the demands of the consumer'.[24] And this latter demand is, again, a central theme of liberalism. Popper sums all this up by saying:[25]

> We are clearly faced with an important problem of social engineering: the market must be controlled, but in such a way that the control does not impede the free choice of the consumer and that it does not remove the need for producers to compete for the favour of the consumer.

Let us now consider the problem of the institutional exemplification of the 'Open Society' as discussed in Popper's own book. Some matters are clear. Popper emphasizes the idea that the state is to have an active, interventionist role. But, where it can take this form, its intervention is to take place in the spirit of the rule of law as this is envisaged in the liberal tradition. The state will be concerned, particularly, with the relief of suffering, on a negative utilitarian basis. (Popper points to the analogy between negative utilitarianism's 'formulation of our demands negatively' and the emphasis on the negative in his epistemology.[26]) Negative utilitarianism, however, is given a wide interpretation, to include the provision even of higher education,[27] but Popper also sets limits on what is to count as the relief of suffering, or 'protectionism':[28]

> The fight against suffering must be considered a duty, while the right to care for the happiness of others must be considered a privilege confined to the close circle of [our] friends. In their case, we may perhaps have a certain right to try to impose our scale of values – our preferences concerning music, for example. . . . This right of ours exists only if,

and because, they can get rid of us; because friendships can be ended. But the use of political means for imposing our scale of values upon others is a very different matter. Pain, suffering, injustice, and their prevention, these are the eternal problems of public morals, the 'agenda' of public policy. . . . The 'higher' values should very largely be considered as 'non-agenda', and should be left to the realm of *laissez-faire*.

With respect to government itself, Popper has written against theories of sovereignty, seeing them as leading to paradoxes, and as being the products of attempts to answer a question that is not well put: 'Who should rule?'[29] In the place of this question, Popper urges on us a concern with the institutional control of rulers, by way of a system of checks and balances. As a form of government, Popper favours democracy, on the grounds that 'only democracy provides an institutional framework that permits reform without violence, and so the use of reason in political matters',[30] considering democracy as 'a set of institutions . . . which permit public control of the rulers and their dismissal by the ruled, and which make it possible for the ruled to obtain reforms without using violence, even against the will of the rulers'.[31] In line with Popper's opposition to theories of sovereignty, his acceptance of democracy 'is not based upon the principle that the majority should rule; rather, the various equalitarian methods of democratic control, such as general elections and representative government, are to be considered as no more than well-tried and . . . reasonably effective institutional safeguards against tyranny'.[32] Popper further explains that one who accepts democracy in this sense is 'not bound to look upon the result of a democratic vote as an authoritative expression of what is right. Although he will accept a decision of the majority, for the sake of making the democratic institutions work, he will feel free to combat it by democratic means, and to work for its revision.'[33]

To try to sum all this up is not an easy task. Popper's own ideas about political organization in *The Open Society* are difficult to classify. They would seem to me to be incompatible with either liberalism or socialism in their traditional forms. They are, perhaps, closest to 'social democracy'; for example, in their emphasis on the political; on economic interventionism and democratic control; and in their combining this with an appreciation of the rule of law, and a recognition of the importance of individual liberty (including freedom from economic exploitation) together with consumer choice as expressed through a market economy. In his comments about political institutions, themes from Popper's epistemology are also very much in evidence; notably in the interplay between 'proposals' on the one hand, and Popper's emphasis on the need for the critical scrutiny of the results of trying to implement them. The very multiplicity of 'proposals' that are made in Popper's book makes it difficult to treat his work as suggesting, directly, any particular system of political institutions. I would therefore like to explore a somewhat different line of argument: one that starts from Popper's ideas, but which leads, gradually, in a direction different from that which Popper himself took in the *The Open Society*, and which ends, perhaps closer to – but a long way beyond – the views of the older Popper.

I will start from Popper's emphasis, in the *The Open Society*, on the importance of our active critical monitoring of the consequences of various political initiatives. It would seem to me useful to draw a parallel here with what might be called the 'activism' of Popper's epistemology. By this I mean the theme, in Popper's work, that the falsifiability of our theories, and the very possibility of our achieving objectivity and truth, depend on our actively choosing to impose upon ourselves certain distinctive methodological and strategic constraints, and procedures for criticizing and attempting to refute our theories: ways of behaving that may run counter to what comes to us naturally.[34]

In *The Open Society*, in accordance with his general stress, there, on the importance of institutions, Popper also discussed 'the social aspect of scientific method'[35] in a way that suggests[36] that we can look at various social institutions as serving as methodological and strategic constraints on human action: something which is, obviously, of the greatest importance when we consider actual human conduct. For the extent to which our behaviour can effectively be guided, especially against our natural inclinations, by methodological strategies or norms that we entertain in a self-conscious manner is obviously somewhat limited.

Our situation is more closely parallel to that of the man who, say, resolves to stop smoking. If he is wise, rather than just working on the basis of 'will power', he will attempt to bring into being various informal institutional changes, so that his behaviour will be influenced towards his new goal by changes in his situation and in the monitoring, by other people, to which he will be subject.

A comparable move, in the realm of epistemology, would be to consider, critically, the epistemological consequences of our current institutional practices, and how our institutions might be improved on, from this point of view (making use, here, of Popper's emphasis, in the philosophy of the social science, of a concern with the unintended consequences of human action). Beyond this, one could consider how, more positively, the methodological and strategic constraints and the demand for effective criticism, which I mentioned in the context of Popper's epistemology, might best be given an institutional exemplification, so as better to regulate our conduct.

I would suggest that the 'activism' of Popper's political philosophy be reinterpreted in the same way – i.e. as urging that we should actively scrutinize, reform and redesign our institutions, so that they will then best constrain us to achieve our goals. In *The Open Society*, Popper emphasized that we must not expect too much of institutions; and I am certainly not suggesting that they can enable us to dispense with personal dedication, and with an explicit commitment by individuals to holding their proposals and policies open to criticism. But our particular stress on institutions, here, leads naturally to a consideration of the different kinds of monitoring to which the individual will be subject within various different institutional arrangements, and on what may be expected to be the consequences, of these, on his conduct.

SOME REMARKS ABOUT MONITORING

I would like here, fairly briefly, to make a few remarks concerning institutions and monitoring,[37] which relate to some of the points at issue between the claims of social democracy and of liberalism to stand as institutional exemplifications of Popper's ideas. In both of these systems of institutional organization, there is a state. In liberalism, its role is largely limited to 'nightwatchman' functions (and, more generally, to the provision of such requirements as a market might need for its operation – which, indeed, might on some accounts involve an active line in economic policy); to the provision of external defence; to the protection of children from exploitation by their parents;[38] to the provision of a welfare safety net,[39] and other limited, paternalistic measures. The political realm is thus present; but its presence is regarded somewhat uneasily, both as a concentration of power and of influence and as something which, in its welfare and paternalistic roles, does not cohere too well with the principles of a liberal social order.[40] For the liberal, other goods and services are to be provided through the market. Their provision will thus be effected by entrepreneurs and, through time, it will take a changing pattern following the tastes – and the assets – of those who pay for this provision. What is provided will thus reflect the preferences that lie behind assets as they are distributed in the economy – though it is always possible for people to use lawful means to try to persuade others that their assets should be disposed of in different ways.

Now, there is a form of monitoring built into the liberal system, in the sense that entrepreneurs will only continue to receive money for their goods and services if their customers continue to find them satisfactory. Insofar as they will in the future depend on their reputation in order to make a living, there is also an incentive for entrepreneurs to behave in a reputable manner.[41] They will also have an incentive to monitor the activities of their competitors, actual or potential. Of course, the useful operation of such a system of monitoring depends, as has often been stressed, on avenues for making a profit *against* the interests of other people being closed off by the institutions of the law.[42]

This theme of the significance of different forms of monitoring merits slightly more extensive discussion. As we have already noted, Popper is of the view that our ideas are likely to be inadequate, and therefore that they will stand in need of criticism. He favours a pluralism of competing ideas. And he has been most emphatic about the way in which we should allow our ideas to die in our stead. That is to say, we should be willing to detach ideas from the personalities of their creators, and submit them to criticism, *without* this constituting an assault on the person who created them.

Let us now consider these ideas in relation to the choice between liberalism and social democracy as exemplifications of Popper's idea of a rational social order. One major contrast relates to the merits of political as against market accountability, and here the mechanisms of the market seem to me to have certain advantages.

First, they allow for the important dissociation between products and the personalities of their creators. In a market, products are appraised without concern for who produced them. And while in certain circumstances this may have undesirable consequences, with regard to our problem, it gives us just what we want. For in a market order, criticism is swift and telling and the producer cannot pretend that his product is acceptable if it is not; and it is in his interest to respond by producing something better. (Although, of course, it is open to the producer to use lawful means to convince us that what we *really* want is what he is producing.) In the political sphere, the politician is identified with his product to such an extent that if it is seriously defective, he is likely, politically, to die with it. Accordingly, the politician will be reluctant to be seen to accept criticism on any matter of importance. Should he change his views, this will be a constant source of political embarrassment, whereas the entrepreneur who changes from producing a poor to a good product is both successful and justly regarded as a wise man.

Second, in a market, competition is the norm, and it is possible for consumers to exercise fine discrimination, if they so wish, concerning what they will accept. In the political realm, however, competition is usually more limited, and consumers are faced with making rough choices between entire bundles of services.

Third, and most important, there is the issue of criticism and accountability. Here it seems to me that the market has the greatest of advantages. For the relationship between producer and consumer requires constant reaffirmation; whereas the politician is called to account infrequently,[43] and in a rather ineffectual manner. Indeed, the whole apparatus of *political* accountability appears to be intrinsically very weak, and to be such that, if attempts were made to strengthen it and to introduce really close monitoring – say, by the introduction of some system of recallable delegates – the result would be likely to be paralysis, or a shift of political power elsewhere. Liberalism has also the particular advantage that it has at least *some* sketch of a mechanism that would link the self-interest of entrepreneurial decision-takers to the interests of citizens. Whereas, while one could *perhaps* expect more genuine idealism in a system favoured by social democrats, controls over decision-takers in privileged political positions would seem comparatively weak.

Now these themes, long familiar from the history of liberal political thought, also have a counterpart if regarded from the point of view of knowledge. What I have in mind, here, is not so much Hayek's interesting view of the market as a system for the handling of information and the coordination of individuals' plans,[44] as his theme of the market as a forum within which discovery can take place by trial and error.[45] For we can look at the institutions of the market, as favoured by liberalism, as a system the rules of which (principally, the legal system, but also informal rules of conduct) function so as to allow ideas to be tried out, but try to minimize the coercive imposition, by one person, of his or her ideals or ideas on another. It is assumed that our position is, basically, one of ignorance, in that we do not know what the best system of institutions is, what the best style of life is, or what patterns of the provision of goods and services are the most desirable. And the market, as an institution, allows for hypotheses about these things to be tried out – and to fail and be discarded if they are unsuccessful. It is this theme in liberalism which seems to me to be particularly close to Popper's epistemological ideas.

A liberal must, obviously, admit that such a system of learning by trial and error may fall short of the ideal of rational social organization pictured by Popper in *The Open Society*, especially insofar as decisions are made on the basis of disposable wealth, rather than on the basis of each individual citizen being treated as equal in his rationality or in his capacity to express his opinions and criticisms. The liberal socio-economic system will also reward those who deliver what is in demand – which may mean that merit goes unrewarded, and greatness unrecognized. In addition, the liberal should, I think, admit that those who possess significant assets (whether this is understood as a few individuals with great wealth, or, more typically, many individuals each of whom only has a limited disposable income) may indeed, in practice, sometimes be able to impose his or her tastes and opinions on others. In addition, there may be problems about the shaping of our tastes – and especially the tastes of the young – by commercial interests, in circumstances in which it is difficult for what is going on to be subject to effective critical scrutiny, or for opposing voices to be heard. What the liberal must insist on, however, is that we should only reject his ideas if we have something better to put in their place: that is, it is not acceptable to reject something merely because it falls short of the ideal.

Social democracy, while allowing for a market sector of the economy,[46] puts great emphasis on the political. Now, of course, liberalism has a political sphere, too; but the liberal regards this with some suspicion, not only as a concentration of power, but because politics usually involves the imposing of the ideas and ideals of some people upon others who do not agree with them.

And while the liberal admits that in some cases this may be necessary, because of (a) the need for unanimity in our conventions, (b) the need for the imposition of our (tentative) knowledge where the ignoring of it might do harm, and (c) the need to protect some individual's freedom from others who do not recognize it, *any* coercive overriding of an individual's opinions is to him an evil, if sometimes a necessary one.

The social democrat, by contrast, is typically and most urgently concerned with the implementation of his policies. These need not be, and very often will not be, in his immediate self-interest, and will typically concern those situations which seem to him most urgently in need of alteration. Accordingly, they will reflect his value-judgements as to what society should be like. Now, because both the social democrat and the liberal are, presumably, democrats in their politics (not least for the reasons that Popper advances) they will go along, perhaps complainingly, with the decisions of the majority if it is opposed to them. But there is an important difference between their attitudes when in power. For the liberal will not be willing to impose his value-judgements (other than in the area of the political framework of the market order, which of course includes property rights, and the limited additional areas mentioned above), while the social democrat sees the *raison d'être* of politics as the achievement of his social goals. In the context of Popper's political philosophy, however, some qualifications must be made to this account. On the one side, the substantive agenda of public policy, on Popper's account, has a more consensual character to it than would be usual within social democracy: it would be constituted by a consensus directed at agreement as to the things most calling out for remedy. On the other, as we have stressed, his own argument would have us take very seriously the moral autonomy of each individual.

Another important theme is the issue of criticism and learning in the realm of politics. There is, I think, a problem here for the social democrat, just because his favoured institutional instruments – bureaucrats and politicians – do not make for effective monitoring. It is difficult for the bureaucrat to change his actions merely because there is less demand for his product, just because the kinds of monitoring that are operating within the system in which he is functioning do not naturally attune him to such things. And even if he wished to respond, it would be difficult for him to know how to respond, as he would be lacking the detailed information about preferences that is transmitted to the entrepreneur through the price system. Accordingly, other than in cases where we want matters pursued largely for their own sake (as, indeed, is arguable in the case of the legal framework of a society), a bureaucratic form of operation seems undesirable. Political control of the operation of a bureaucracy seems also an intrinsically weak form of control – as, indeed, does that exercisable by the electorate over the political realm itself. And, if one assumes the worst – an element of self-interest on the part of those participating in the institutions in question – then the operations of political and bureaucratic forms of organization appear to be less responsive to the public interest than do market forms of organization.[47]

There is also a serious problem about Popper's own argument concerning democracy. For, in *The Open Society*, it is accorded three broad functions. First, it has the role of enabling us to change our political regime by means of elections, rather than by violence. This seems to me of the greatest importance; but it is also important that we see how limited it is in its consequences. Some control will be exercised over politicians by such means, assuming that they wish to continue in office. But it is a very blunt weapon, considering the way in which we can exercise preferences only for bundles of political goods. Further, it is also ripe for manipulation – by politicians who find ways to bribe us with money taken from our own pockets, and by their advertising agents who, as in the United States, have found ways to present political issues on television through the use of images in ways which make rational discussion almost impossible. All this, to be sure, concerns matters which in principle are ripe for improvement by way of 'piecemeal social engineering'. The problem is that it is the politicians who would have to be responsible for agreeing to set up institutions which would then serve to constrain themselves.

Second, there is the theme of the critical scrutiny of the performance of government by its citizens. This is also a very worthwhile ideal. But it is one which, understandably enough, neither politicians nor civil servants welcome. It is also one which, in various ways, politicians within different Western democracies seem adept at evading, by one means or another. What seems to me particularly insidious here, however, is the way in which, with the expansion of the role of government, key decisions seem all too often to be made by negotiation between public servants and interest groups, or in so-called policy-making communities, in ways that are simply not open to the critical scrutiny of the general public (in whose name the resulting decisions are taken, and who also foot the bill).

In some regimes – such as the Presidential system of the United States – criticism, while it may be voiced, is frequently ineffectual, because of the weakness of the public forum in the United States, and because the various internal divisions within governmental responsibility make it difficult to hold anyone politically responsible for anything. While in some parliamentary systems, the combination of the party system, close interrelations between the press and government, together with restrictive libel laws, can also limit the effective power of criticism.

The most pressing problem about Popper's own ideas, however – as opposed to the practical difficulties of realizing them – is that he accords other functions to political democracy, without explaining which institutions could exercise them, and by what means. In particular, as I indicated in Chapter 2, Popper is concerned that there should be political control over the exercise of economic power. Much also, in his account, will depend on the proper exercise of what I there termed 'democratic vigilance'. I have no doubt that politicians and public officials do have considerable power over other aspects of society (although this has doubtless been significantly limited through the development of a so-called 'global market economy'). What is not so clear is how ordinary citizens could make sure that it is *their* concerns that are pursued by such means. At the same time, given the genuinely technical character of much of what government is now involved in, there are obvious problems about simple democratic accountability, and whether it could, in fact, be achieved.

All told, while Popper's ideas about democracy are attractive, and while he is raising important issues, I do not know what real-world institutions could even approximate to by playing the kind of role that he would be asking of them.

I do not wish to give the impression that the balance of this argument is one-sided. First, the aims and codes of conduct of those engaged in politics and in bureaucratic public service (if not necessarily the results of their actions!) may well be more inspired by altruism and a sense of duty towards the welfare of the public than is the case in a purely business operation, and one would also hope that there will be monitoring relationships oriented towards these ideals.

Second, because morality, for the social democrat, is not a private matter, the democratic institutions of a social democracy may perform a useful monitoring role, in the sense that they will constitute a forum within which virtually any feature of the society in question may be held up for critical scrutiny on moral grounds. They also allow for a measure of argument and critical discussion in this area. This seems to me to raise an issue of the greatest significance. For the institutional arrangements of classical liberalism might have the consequence that we treat all issues as if they were simply matters of taste, the content of which is protected from interpersonal scrutiny, and upon which people have the freedom to act, subject only to certain formal restrictions relating to the liberty of others. However, as I have suggested above, the content of people's preferences is something which may be in need of scrutiny, both in itself, in terms of its consequences, and also in terms of the processes through which it is formed and maintained. Further, if we wish to argue that individuals should be recognized as having rights, and in most cases freedom of action even on the basis of their bare preferences, we stand in need of a forum within which the case for this can be made, and mechanisms through which the results of such discussion can become part of people's day-to-day attitudes towards one another. Yet the thrust within classical liberalism towards privatization, while it is (at least in my view) of considerable positive significance in some areas, seems to me here highly problematic. For it risks not only closing off from scrutiny some things which may be in urgent need of it, but also of undermining the very basis that classical liberalism itself requires: that people come to recognize one another as having rights, and as being entitled to various freedoms, and so on. These issues, concerned with a public forum and legitimation and scrutiny within it, seem to me of key importance, and are a topic to which we will return.

There is also, of course, the whole issue that I raised at the end of the previous chapter: of our concerns for, and of our responsibility for, the overall character of the social order within which we are living. Before addressing this, however, we need to look at one further issue.

POPPER'S ANTI-ESSENTIALISM

An opposition to essentialism plays an important part in Popper's early work on the philosophy of social science.

The idea of essentialism is introduced early on in *The Poverty of Historicism*.[48] In that connection, Popper draws on an important theme in *The Logic of Scientific Discovery* which does not figure significantly in his later work.[49] This is his strategy of replacing metaphysical theories with methodological ones. In *The Poverty of Historicism*, Popper discusses the problem of universals, and proposes the term 'essentialism' as an alternative to 'realism' in that context. However, he turns almost at once from metaphysics to methodology. He is critical of the idea that the methods of the social sciences should be essentialistic in their character, identifying methodological essentialism with the following approaches: (a) the search for properties that lie behind the use of universal terms; (b) the asking – and answering – of 'what is?' questions, in respect to such terms; and (c) the concern to identify an unchanging essence, which persists through change.

Popper also argues that one reason why essentialist explanations had seemed attractive – but were in fact mistaken – related to the role played by models in explanation; something that, Popper suggests, had been misidentified as concrete things lying behind the appearances.[50]

In *The Open Society*, Popper has an extended discussion of essentialism, which centres on ideas in the theory of knowledge that he attributes to Aristotle: all knowledge must start from premises, which describe the essence of a thing by way of a definition. Such definitions are arrived at through a process of intellectual intuition, and are known with certainty.[51] By way of contrast with this, Popper gives an account of the methods of the natural sciences. In this (now familiar) account knowledge is hypothetical, and, he argues, we have replaced scientific certainty with scientific progress. Definitions, in Popper's account, are concerned not to disclose the character of essences, but are to be read the other way round: as giving short labels for some more complex phenomenon in which we are interested. He is also critical of the idea that intuition brings with it any kind of infallibility.[52]

Now it is interesting to contrast *The Poverty of Historicism* and *The Open Society* with Popper's later writings on the topic of essentialism in the philosophy of natural science. For in his paper on Berkeley as a precursor of Mach and Einstein[53] – Popper, after presenting Berkeley's critique of Newton and relating it also to the ideas of Mach and of Einstein, also goes on to advocate a 'third view', between positivism and essentialism.[54] This sees science as aiming for truth, and as attempting to explain the known by the unknown, and perhaps the unobservable.[55]

This is a theme upon which Popper subsequently elaborated in his discussions of essentialism in the context of the physical sciences; for example, his 'Three Views Concerning Human Knowledge',[56] and, most notably, in 'The Aim of Science'.[57] In his discussion there, he stresses the way in which, as distinct from the approach of instrumentalism, science may aspire to a knowledge of the structure of the world, and also to explanations which have the characteristic of 'depth'; an idea that he relates to the notions of simplicity, wealth of content, and also to a less easily describable notion of 'organicity', a notion that he elsewhere has described in terms of the importance of a 'simple, new and powerful unifying idea'.[58] In 'The Aim of Science', Popper also suggested that what might be called a 'fact-correcting' explanation might form something like a 'sufficient condition for depth'.[59] The correction of Galileo's and Kepler's laws by Newton's theory, which also explained them, provides a key example.

These ideas are interesting and suggestive; and they are of considerable importance as background to Popper's own suggestions about propensities.[60] However, there seems to me every reason to suppose that the same approach should hold good in the social sciences, too. Accordingly, I will suggest that Popper's ideas about anti-essentialism in *The Poverty of Historicism* and *The Open Society* (which, as should be clear from our discussion in Chapter 2, are found alongside ideas about the physical sciences which are closer to instrumentalism than to his later 'third view') stand in need of modification, in the light of the idea that, in the social sciences, too, we can properly aspire to knowledge of structure, and also 'depth'.

STRUCTURE AND DEPTH IN THE SOCIAL WORLD

If one were to seek to apply the realist approach of Popper's philosophy of natural science to the social sciences, two objections might be raised. First, it might be asked: what kinds of explanation could have such a character? Second, it might be objected that such an approach is incompatible with Popper's methodological individualism. I will address these points in turn.

The easiest way to explain what such an approach might amount to is by way of an example. Friedrich Hayek, in his Inaugural Address at the London School of Economics, offered some reflections on his discipline of a character that are suggestive both of such a parallel with realistic explanation in the natural sciences, and of some of the implications of such a realism for political philosophy. In that address, Hayek discussed the way in which the impetus to the development of economics had been 'a wish to reconstruct a world which gives rise to profound dissatisfaction'. However, he further argued that '[i]t was only when, because the economic system did not accomplish all we wanted, we prevented it from doing what it had been accomplishing . . . that we realized that there was anything to be understood.'[61] He then goes on to argue that the coordination of economic activity is accomplished by a complex mechanism, which turns out to involve, as an essential part, human behaviour which considered in itself is morally unlovely.

This account seems to me interesting for a variety of reasons. First, while it does not have quite the element of 'fact correction' which we met in the natural sciences, there is an important correction to Hayek's initial ideas involved. Not only does his account speak of the discovery of a structure behind the appearances as responsible for some familiar effect – a structure, what is more, that has some features that seem to have come as a surprise to Hayek. But the idea that such a structure exists has important implications, in its turn, for how he then views, morally, certain phenomena of the social world. Self-interested behaviour exhibited in commercial settings, while still unlovely, becomes something that we have to put up with because we want the consequences that it brings, rather than something the elimination of which has a place on our political agenda.

Now, of course, Hayek's account may well be incorrect. But that is not the point. For just as Popper has argued that we must distinguish between the truth and the realism of, say, Galileo's scientific theories, the same is true of Hayek's views, too. Even if Hayek's specific theories are incorrect, he has, I believe, given us good arguments to suggest that we can aspire to realistic knowledge in the social sciences. Further, we may be led, by the development of theories of such a character, to reappraise radically our views about what we think political action should be aiming at, in the light of revisions in our knowledge. In this connection, Popper's argument against Marx for the priority of politics over economics seems to me in one respect incorrect. Popper was surely right, against Marx, that politically generated improvements could be made – and have been made – within a 'capitalist' economy.[62] But there seems every reason to suppose that Marx was right that there may be structural relationships within economics and politics which may limit our ability to realize our ethical goals, politically.

To this it might be objected: but is Popper not an advocate of methodological individualism, and thus someone who rejects such ideas? In my view he is, but it is methodological individualism that stands in need of modification. For, as Robert Nozick has argued when discussing 'filter mechanisms',[63] there are good grounds for thinking that methodological individualism is defective. When we act, we act in social settings which are formed by the products of prior human action, and these may, at crucial points, act as filter mechanisms exercising a selective effect upon our conduct. For example, the wish that someone has to run a small business in a certain manner (say, by behaving paternalistically towards his employees) may be crucially affected by the current interest rate – or a change in the interest rate – which may itself be seen as an emergent product of the actions of many other individuals. This emergent product, however, has a 'thing-like' character, such that one may have to explain the success or otherwise of the person's plans in part in terms of his interactions with this phenomenon. And in some explanatory tasks we may need to refer to filter mechanisms and the conditions they impose rather than to the specific motives of individual agents.

Second, other social phenomena, while not having the dramatic character of Hayek's example, also seem to me to play a structural role in the social world. Consider the role played in the social world by the meaning of human behaviour. It might seem strange to raise this point against Popper, in light of his methodological individualism. However, there is a sense in which the meaningful actions of human beings form the stuff of the social world, in a way that has consequences of which, it seems to me, Popper does not take full note. As I have stressed earlier in this volume, each of us has our personal concerns, and ways of conducting ourselves, which have both meaning and moral significance to us. Now the kinds of issues with which Popper is concerned in his political writings for the most part arise from the unintended consequences of our actions, or are emergent products of the actions of many of us. In my view, Popper is right to emphasize that we have a proper concern – both practical and moral – with many of the macro-level characteristics of this material. But at the same time, I would wish to emphasize, against him, that the material out of which our existing institutions and practices are formed, and from which any new institutions and practices must be built, is not 'terra nullius':[64] rather, it is already full of our prior practices. Anything that follows must be a modification of these; and there are some things that, practically and morally, it may simply not be possible to achieve, given the position from where we start, even though, other things being equal, we might have found these things very attractive.[65]

All these points, I would suggest, indicate ways in which we might see the social world as having a structure, much as does the physical world. And explanatory theories which enable us to identify and understand such things would seem to me as interesting and illuminating theoretically as are comparable theories in the natural sciences. But this in turn suggests the possibility for a non-technological social science, just as there is a natural science. (Although clearly, the subject-matter of such a social science would be dependent upon our choices and prior activities in a way that the subject-matter of natural science is not.[66]) Such knowledge would be pertinent to our wish to make changes to our institutions, and to realize our various purposes in the world. But there seems no more reason why social science should be directed primarily towards these things, as a technology, than biological science should, say, be seen primarily as a theory of food production, or as a technology instrumental to the meeting of our other practical needs.[67]

Against all this, two lines of argument might be advanced, and it is important that I explain and meet them before I continue.

The first is an argument against realism. It can be put most simply in the following terms. Realism suggests that we may understand the world as it presents itself to us, in terms of structures which lie behind the appearances, yet which may serve to explain them. But, it might be argued,[68] while such structures may exist, will our conjectures about them not always be arbitrary, in the sense that it could have been the case that there were different conjectures as to their character, which would have been equally compatible with all the tests which we have performed, to date?[69]

While I would *like* to agree with those critics who suggest that such arguments are not to be taken too seriously,[70] I do not know of an acceptable way of handing them with respect to the natural sciences. In the social sciences, however, there is an approach which seems to me fruitful. It is suggested by the work of Gaventa, which he undertook in the course of his discussion of the work of Steven Lukes.[71] Lukes had argued that we could understand power, not only in terms of one person being able to impose his preferences upon others when they are in conflict, but also, for example, as a result of structural factors which play a role in the formation of people's preferences.[72] Gaventa offers what seems to me a most interesting line of argument, which is pertinent also to our problem. For he argued – by way of detailed historical discussion – that one might see power, as Lukes is concerned with it, as the product of the exercise of power in other, more obvious, senses. That is to say, the danger of epistemological arbitrariness is overcome, by telling a story of the genesis of the structure from other, less problematic, components.[73] Such an approach – which one might dub constructive realism – would seem to me available to us in the kinds of cases discussed by Hayek and by Nozick, so that on this score, the objection seems to be overcome.

The second objection was offered by Barry Hindess to rational choice theory,[74] and a related point has been made by James Beckford in the course of critical discussion of what might be termed a hermeneutical approach to sociology.[75] Hindess objected to the idea, beloved of rational choice theorists, that we have a bundle of preferences which we bring to decision-taking. May our preferences, rather, not be seen just as easily as the product of the choices that we are offered? Beckford argued, in the course of a discussion of the sociology of religious sects, that we may be mistaken to try to understand the actions of their members as if they were directly inspired by the, at times complex, theological beliefs of the sect. Rather, what they valued were, more typically, the social relationships and spiritual experiences which membership brought with it.

These objections seem to me highly suggestive. In the first case, it might be argued that economists[76] have been misled by their own theories, in the sense that they have treated what are, in fact, features of their own theoretical models as if they were features of

129

the individuals whose behaviour they wished to explain. (This is something which, if correct, would have interesting implications for the welfare consequences that are drawn from choices supposedly made on the basis of such preferences.) As far as Beckford's point is concerned, the error is an easy enough one for academics to make, in that it involves attributing to other agents a highly intellectualized way of looking at the world which may be much more common among academics than those whom they are studying.

I do not think, however, that these points are telling against the ideas which I wish to champion here. For my concern is, very much, to treat individuals as acting in ways that are shaped by their history and by the institutional settings within which they are acting. My claim is simply that, as we encounter them in these settings, they have various preferences and concerns, which may range both over particular actions that they may now be able to take, and over wider social outcomes, but that they are limited by virtue of their history and current institutional involvements as to what actions they can now coherently take. These preferences and concerns, however, while tied up with their history and the various institutions with which they are involved, are very much theirs, and they are not a *tabula rasa* upon which a social engineer can simply work, at his or her will. (This is not at odds with the arguments offered by Lukes and by Gaventa. Others may offer criticisms of our preferences and so on; ones which we may ourselves come to accept.[77] But the fact that we may have accepted such criticisms does not, in itself, necessarily even mean that we stop having them, or that we can act differently.[78])

It is also in this context that the ideas from Popper's 'Towards a Rational Theory of Tradition', which we discussed in Chapter 3, show their importance. For insofar as tradition matters, insofar as what people do is seen as, in part, a product of their history and of the history of the institutions in which they have participated, it will be clear that it is one thing to wish that we had institutions that performed a particular function, quite another for us to be able to create them. Here, I would like to return to the issue that I raised in the Introduction to this volume: that once one takes such a view of human conduct, the task of social engineering becomes both more difficult and more dangerous than it might seem from *The Open Society*. I have described it as 'more difficult' because one is dealing with people whose lives are full of meaning and concerns of their own, and who also enjoy autonomy in their moral judgements, rather than simply being 'stuff' upon which collective purposes can be imposed, at will. It is also more difficult because those people are socialized: they are, in significant ways, the products of their history, upbringing, expectations, intellectual involvements and entanglements with world 3, rather than virgin material onto which some purpose can be pressed. I have described it as 'more dangerous' because, clearly, to give someone power to alter such things is to give them a kind of power which can easily be misused, and which we would normally be extremely reluctant to accord to anybody, over another adult.

POLITICAL PHILOSOPHY REVISITED

But what has all this to do with political philosophy? It is because it is with an eye to these problems that the issue left open from the previous chapter – the problem of large-scale moral concerns, and of social engineering – must be addressed.

If one allows for the parallel that I have suggested between the 'modified essentialism' of Popper's approach to the natural sciences and our approach in the social sciences, some important consequences follow for Popper's political thought. In particular, some of the structural elements that I have highlighted should serve to qualify the 'social engineering' approach that he adopts towards politics.

First, insofar as there exist structural constraints upon our actions of the kind with which Hayek has been concerned, important problems face Popper's approach. It is, to be sure, open to Popper to interpret Hayek's work along the lines of his own ideas about 'social engineering'.[79] But to do so poses a problem for Popper's account of an 'open society'. For the kind of knowledge with which Hayek is concerned – and the sorts of constraints that his work suggests exist upon our actions – may not be at all easy for the population at large to grasp. There is an element in this of Plato's revenge. For while Popper can dethrone the would-be philosopher king, on the basis that his knowledge is fallible and stands in need of critical input from the population as a whole, the philosopher-king can respond that he may still have (fallible) knowledge which is vital to the well-being of a society, yet not something that it is easy to share with all citizens. It may involve the kind of issue that it is particularly difficult to address on the hustings of democratic politics. (Or even worse, through the largely hidden workings of pluralist politics, within which attempts may be made to obtain resolution for problems, without the over-all consequences of these measures ever becoming the business of anyone to bring into the light of day.[80]) Accordingly, Popper's politics is left with the problem: how do we make use of such (fallible) expert knowledge within a democratic society?

Second, there is an issue posed by the subjective meaning, to individuals, of those actions with the products of which the social engineer wishes to be concerned. Individuals can well say: the material upon which you wish to work is simply not up for grabs; it represents, rather, the products of various actions of ours, which we are taking for good reasons of our own. You – who wish to make various social changes – may have good reasons for wishing to be able to produce the kind of outcome that you desire. But what you do not have is the knowledge of our actions that you wish to alter. You thus have no way of judging whether what you are proposing we should do is possible for us to achieve, or morally appropriate for us to undertake. It makes not one whit of differ-ence, they might add, whether lots of people have voted that this action should be effected; for they have no knowledge of the relevant circumstances either. To put this another way, to treat us as objects of social engineering – democratic or otherwise – would seem to be failing, radically, to treat us as ends in ourselves. This would seem an odd view for someone to take who, like Popper, was in many respects profoundly influenced by the moral ideas of Immanuel Kant.

There are, in fact, two different elements to the problem that I have just raised, and to spell them out may, I hope, indicate that there is more to the issue than one of some people imposing their will upon others, in ignorance of what it is that they will be asking them to do. For essentially the same problem arises if a group of people are unanimous in their wish that some large-scale consequence be realized as a product of their actions. Unless the goal in question is one that can be the direct object of their actions, they may have no idea what they would have to do in order to bring it about. Further, if they could determine what they would have to do, they might be led to reconsider whether it was a goal that they in fact wished to achieve, once they under-stood what, at the level of particular actions, would be required in order to bring it about.[81] What is more, the point that we have discussed in connection with Popper's 'Towards a Rational Theory of Tradition' also holds good. The actions that people would need to take would have also to be actions that they could take, given who they are – i.e. in the light of their prior histories, habits, traditions and values, and the institutions that are available to them.

These two arguments are, in my judgement, powerful. But they cannot serve as a final resting-place. The former leaves us with the difficult problem of the political role that is to be played by expert knowledge. The second alerts us to the fact that the area within which the social engineer wishes to operate is not free of prior ethical concerns. It is perhaps suggestive of the classical liberal view that the proper concern of politics should be the determination of general rules, within which individuals are then free to pursue their particular moral concerns. However, such an interpretation of the argument of this volume would leave us with an important problem. For such individuals are blind to the large-scale and longer-term consequences of their actions, and to the consequences that will arise when they and others interact together. However, these issues may be of the greatest importance to them, and quite properly so. But by what means can they pursue them if – for reasons that I have indicated – a democratic version of 'piecemeal social engineering' seems morally problematic, when directed to such specific institutions and goals?

ABSTRACT INSTITUTIONS AND SOCIAL ENGINEERING IN AN OPEN SOCIETY

During the course of this volume, we have accumulated various problems which have not been resolved. Here is the place where this must be done. The problems which must be addressed here are as follows.

First, what, morally, do we owe one another – and, more specifically, how are specific claims about this to be assessed? Second, we have concerns about the overall character of the social order within which we live, and how this is to be maintained. In part, these may relate to issues of the first kind: if we have obligations towards others which are not, as it were, naturally disaggregated, we face the problem of how some collective responsibility is to be discharged. In part, they may relate more simply to characteristics of a society in which we would like to live which are, as it were, of the status of properties which emerge from the actions and interactions of various individuals.

Concerns of our second kind pose additional problems, too. First, as we have indicated earlier in this chapter, there seems every reason to believe that desirable social institutions may have features which are undesirable, but where it may be difficult for individual actors to understand the links between these things and the forms of social order that they find attractive. Second, as we have discussed in some detail in connection with Popper's work, once we take on board his ideas about tradition, the task of social engineering – of the development of social institutions aimed at producing some overall effect which we believe to be desirable – becomes problematic. For the task of social engineering becomes one which may involve the engineering of people's conduct, and almost of their souls.

I will proceed in the following way. First, I will go back to some themes in Popper's philosophy. Then I will raise some specific problems about social institutions, and suggest an approach to them which draws on these Popperian ideas. Finally, I will turn back to what remains of these questions, and will address them. The way in which I will do this will lead me to some departures from Popper's own political ideas. I will follow this somewhat crab-wise path for the following reason. Popper was himself familiar with the initial line of argument that I will be offering, and indeed, gave me some suggestions about it. While it certainly does not involve views which I can attribute to him, I have no reason to suppose that he would take particularly strong exception to it; at any rate, he professed to find the line of argument interesting, and if he had major reservations he did not – perhaps out of kindness, or so as not to discourage a young and not very confident student – voice them to me. I have every reason to suppose that he would have objected to my extensions of it, in the final part of this chapter, although I nonetheless believe them to be compelling.

Abstract institutions in an open society[82]

I will start by highlighting some themes from Popper's work.

First, according to Popper, philosophy is concerned with theories; especially with cosmological theories: theories about the universe, our place in it, and our knowledge of it. Philosophical theories also play a role as regulative ideas – as formulations of our aims or goals, and of their related methodological principles. The various activities of all of us are dominated by philosophical ideas, whether held consciously or as tacit presuppositions. This includes, especially, the pursuit of any theoretical discipline. Empirical and philosophical elements here form a complex whole.

Second, philosophy falls within Popper's fallibilism: the Socratic insight into our ignorance. But it may also share in that epistemological process of pluralistic, critical, non-justificatory improvement that Popper characterized by saying that we may pull ourselves up by our bootstraps.

Third, for Popper, the quest for secure foundations for our knowledge is mistaken. Popper also places us within Neurath's boat – or, rather, as he is a pluralist, within one of a whole fleet. But not only have we to improve our knowledge while embarked, we ought also to tackle the most pressing problems first. This admission of pluralism, however, and our own involvement in it, obviously poses a problem. Doesn't this necessarily lead to dogmatism, or else to relativism? And is it incompatible with objectivity? To this, Popper's answer is no. We share the human situation. This includes the problems of cosmology; our ignorance in the face of them; and the possibility of *creating* a realm of objectivity. For we may decide to set ourselves standards – standards which we may fail to meet – and we may try to bring such standards to bear on the problem of improving our knowledge. We may, further, expose our ideas to such criticism if they are challenged. We may hope to make progress by attempting to articulate systematic theories, and by confronting them progressively with all the relevant problems. And we may do so in a spirit of critical cooperation with those who may be working on other boats: on other ideas and on other programmes.

Fourth, those engaged in such activities act as intellectual trustees for other people, for all people are importantly influenced by philosophical theories. It is a sobering thought that other people may accept our ideas uncritically, for our ideas affect their day-to-day lives and well-being. This should give us pause, and bring home to us the ethical dimension to intellectual activity.

Liberalism offers an interesting approach to the problems of social and political philosophy. Popper has contributed to and thrown light upon liberalism, by relating it to his epistemological ideas. This has involved both particular suggestions and general analogies. It leads, obviously, to Popper's criticism of the view that we should be ruled by philosopher-kings: by the proud possessors of knowledge. It also provides a general (and Kantian) theme for his work: the rational unity of mankind. Freedom is related to reason by pointing to all individuals as possible sources of criticism; criticism which may help us discover where our theories are wrong. Such ideas are suggestive and also, I think, very appealing. It is therefore important to try to discover where problems may lie, and, especially, where these ideas themselves may have undesirable consequences.

Popper himself recognized that the blessings of the open society are mixed – recall his discussion of the 'strains of civilization'. But Popper argued that to try to return to a closed society is to court disaster, and that the path to the open society is a fit one for mankind to travel.

It is therefore of some importance that it has been suggested that the pursuit of the ideals of liberalism, of the Enlightenment, of 'rationalization' or of 'instrumental reason' leads to disaster; especially if such misgivings are more than the expression of concern for vested interests threatened by change, or of a romantic nostalgia. Unfortunately, those who have been most vociferous (e.g. the older Frankfurt School) have presented their ideas in a manner that makes them almost useless. Their way of writing makes it difficult to discover just what their criticisms are; their more interesting points seem to depend crucially on the acceptance of various highly tendentious economic, social and philosophical theories; and these writers also seem to make a point of not offering any positive suggestions.

Nonetheless, the idea that an open society may be inherently self-destructive is a challenging one; and I will explore here one aspect of this theme. I will suggest that there *is* a problem here that liberals should take seriously, as it can even be posed using ideas drawn from the liberal tradition itself. It also relates to problems concerning knowledge and society: to problems raised by Popper's deposing of the philosopher-king in his political philosophy.

Our problem – the self-destruction of an open society – might be introduced as follows. Popper's book contains a programme for the critical improvement – the rationalization – of a partly closed or partly organic society. All institutions (in the widest possible sense) are opened to critical appraisal by members of the society in question: as individuals, or collectively, through the ballot box.

This appraisal forms a sort of filter through which institutions, if brought forward for consideration, must pass if they are to survive. In addition, Popper accepts a (partly) free market, and emphasizes the importance of consumer choice.

The problem might initially be posed as follows. The possibility of creating a more open society depends on certain traditions and institutions being present (at least embryonically) in our partly closed society. But the means by which institutions are sustained in a partly closed society may not function in an open society. Beyond this, critical appraisal by members of an open society may actually destroy these institutions. An open society may thus initially prosper, but be living on capital inherited from its past. This, however, it will gradually use up – and in so doing, destroy itself. I will now suggest that there is something to this idea, by reference to the liberal tradition itself.

In his *Theory of Moral Sentiments* and his *Lectures on Jurisprudence*, Adam Smith discussed the way in which individuals are led to comply with the institutions of partly closed societies.[83] His theory emphasized the role of the approval or disapproval of the other members of the society around one – of social pressure. He discussed the way in which individuals are influenced by people in certain special positions – by what he called 'authority'. This included, in different situations, our reaction to such things as age and wisdom, bodily strength and wealth. All these influences formed a system of negative controls on an individual's behaviour (in part internalized) which served to keep it in line with the institutions of the society in question.

However, Smith also noticed that the economic liberalism which he favoured (and which, to a degree, Popper shares) affected these mechanisms. The mechanisms have, in fact, two components: psychological dispositions possessed by the individuals who are being influenced, and the situations in which they find themselves. Economic liberalism affects these situations. It brings with it increased independence for the individual, and the possibility of increased mobility. If a man becomes more economically independent from his family or from a particular employer, or a wife from her husband, the authority of these figures will be diminished. The sheer possibility of getting away from figures of authority or from social pressure also obviously diminishes their influence.

I have referred to all this for two reasons. First, because these developments would seem to increase the autonomy of the individual in a way very much in line with the ideals of the Enlightenment. I will quote a passage from Kant, which Popper himself has cited with approval:[84]

> Enlightenment is the emancipation of man from a state of self-imposed tutelage. This state is due to his incapacity to use his own intelligence without external guidance. Such a state of tutelage I call 'self-imposed' if it is due not to lack of intelligence but to lack of courage or determination to use his own intelligence without the help of a leader. . . . Dare to use your own intelligence! This is the battle-cry of the Enlightenment.

However, I wish also to mention Adam Smith's reaction to the developments I have described. In *The Wealth of Nations*, Smith contrasted the situation of a man living in a village where everyone knew him and he had 'a character to lose', and what happened if he moved to a big city. Here, freed from social pressure, Smith thought that he would fall into degeneracy and vice, and that there would be adverse social consequences, too. Smith was so concerned about these matters that he took up the mantle of the philosopher-king, and advocated various measures to constrain people, against their natural inclinations, for their own (and for their society's) good. These measures included compulsory education and even military training.

Is such a reaction understandable? I will suggest that it is, and that institutions vital for an open society are endangered; not just on the level of individual action, but also by collective action through the ballot box. I will refer to Mandeville, to Hume and also to Hayek, to whose discussion of the two other authors I am greatly indebted, and whose own work contains a fuller treatment of the problems which I will discuss here.[85]

My starting point is with Mandeville's idea that social institutions may function as systems, in which features which are valuable may be related to features which are considered undesirable. Such institutions may be complicated and, if the society is large, diffuse, so that members of the society may not perceive how they function. They may not appreciate the systematic connection between inconveniences they suffer and benefits they receive. They may act to remove the inconveniences, and in so doing, inadvertently get rid of the institutions. It is here that the ideas about social development discussed in connection with Smith and the theme of knowledge come together to pose a problem for the open society. Individuals, liberated from traditional authorities and leaders, may take actions – personally, or through the ballot box – which a philosopher-king could see are not to their advantage.

The problems are perhaps most acute where the institutions in question have what might be called an abstract character: where they consist, to an important extent, of the institutionalization of abstract rules. Consider, first, a system of social roles. Such a system ideally enables us to interact easily with people whom we know very little about, which is important in what Popper calls an 'abstract' society. It also provides a useful scaffolding for work on the construction of deeper relationships. However, we take these benefits for granted to such an extent that we may not even be consciously aware of them. But the *disadvantages* of the system are easy enough to perceive, just because the system itself consists of the imposition of certain stereotyped patterns of behaviour onto very different individuals in very different concrete situations. In an open society, the very battle cry of the Enlightenment – 'Dare to use your own intelligence' – may inspire people to dismantle such institutions when, if they could only see what they were doing, they might wish either to retain the institutions or, if it could effectively be done, to modify them.

The difficulties of a social role system most commonly lead to action on an individual rather than a legislative level.[86] Also, they might be thought not to be very serious. (Although, if one includes within them issues raised by feminists, this is far from the case.) The difficulties are perhaps more grave in a system of justice. Here, as Hume argued in the *Treatise*:[87]

> 'tis only the concurrence of mankind, in a general scheme or system . . . which is advantageous . . . [and while] the whole scheme . . . of law and justice is advantageous to . . . society [if we consider particular cases we may find that] Judges take from a poor man to give to a rich; they bestow on the dissolute the labour of the industrious; and put into the hands of the vicious the means of harming both themselves and others.

There are some special problems concerning relations between the legal system of a large open society and individuals in the concrete situations in which they encounter the system. The ideal of the rule of law – to say nothing of the effective conduct of a market economy – requires the articulation of law in such a way that one can tell how in principle it would apply to new cases. The individual encountering such a system will, therefore, find his case treated *qua* legal abstraction. He, however, will be immersed in its concrete details. He will, in a sense, know too much, and is also likely to expect a judgement that will accord with his intuitions concerning the case; something that the system can hardly provide. While he cannot individually do much, his resentment – and that of those who sympathize with him – may well find expression in direct action, or in the support of a political programme that promotes a particular interest (seen as an 'exception' or as a 'special case'), or which promises to rid us of all such difficulties – and thus, without intending to do so, of key features of an open society.

Finally, I will refer very briefly to one of Hayek's themes. The market, he suggests, is an immensely important institution for an open society. But it is in danger of being destroyed because it leads to consequences that people find unfair. Members of an open society can easily vote for measures to be taken to promote 'social justice', without realizing what their consequences will be for the functioning of the market as a system.

Let me try to sum all this up. I will do so in two parts. First, the more specific problem. An open society needs, for its effective functioning and possibly for its very existence, institutions like those to which I have referred. These would appear to exist in an embryonic form prior to the achievement of an open society, and the compliance of individuals with them there to be effected by means of mechanisms like those described by Smith. In an open society, these institutions themselves become extended in scope (so that role systems and the legal system both become more abstract: they are increasingly called on to govern our relations with people with whom we do not have personal relationships). At the same time, the maintenance of such institutions becomes more dependent on individual consent – and thus dependent on the perception, by individuals or groups, of the consequences of their actions. But it is just this that also becomes more difficult, because of the large-scale character of a modern open society, and the way in which, within it, the consequences of our particular actions may be exceedingly difficult to discern. As a result, the heritage from the past of a compliance with institutions may be eroded,[88] with bad consequences for useful institutions of a systematic character, and, thereby, for an open society itself. Such problems may be intensified by the very adoption, by members of an open society, of a 'critical approach'. Second, more generally, there is a problem of knowledge. The trouble here would seem to be that the unit of appraisal is wrong. Individuals are appraising bits of systems, rather than systems as a whole. And it is difficult for them to do otherwise in a large, open society.

How might these problems be met? I would like, initially, to explore a few possibilities which are already to be found within the liberal tradition. A satisfactory solution must, I think, recognize three points. First, that to solve the problem by getting people to comply (uncritically) with *all* established social institutions would, if it could be achieved, hardly be satisfactory. There are many institutions which we would surely wish to discard, or to change radically, if we knew all about them. Our problem also involves individual freedom, which we would not wish to sacrifice. Above all, we want there to be innovation, and the critical improvement of even our best institutions: this is one of an open society's key features. Second, any solution that is proposed must actually work *within* an open society. We want minimal coercion; but we must also be realistic about what people will do if they are not coerced. Finally, we should not lose sight of our ignorance, both as a limitation on what we can do and as a pointer to the fact that we should aim for solutions in which we can try out and learn from different ideas.

I will present my suggestion in three steps, the first two of which consist largely of comments which set the scene for the third.

The first concerns the individual. Part of our problem is, I think, posed by such slogans as 'Dare to use your own intelligence!' For they may be understood as suggestions to individuals that they are not free unless they reject anything the rationale of which cannot be made plain to them. The formulation of a more satisfactory and clear idea of the sort of freedom that a member of an open society can exercise should, I think, be high on our agenda. We need some way in which an individual's freedom can be related to knowledge of the consequences of his or her actions. And, it might be said, we need some effective institutional means of realizing the idea of individuals exercising their freedom by contributing critical arguments.

The mention of institutions brings me to my second comment. It concerns collective action. I would here like to refer to work of Hayek,[89] in which he formulates proposals about constitutional measures which might prevent us from legislating vital and systematic abstract institutions out of existence. (His proposals represent an interesting attempt to find a practical way round the problem raised by Popper in his discussion of the paradoxes of freedom.) One of Hayek's proposals involves the suggestion that we should have a new division of powers, between a body concerned with specific measures, and a second body concerned with the principles of law. This second body (which would also be democratically elected, albeit in a slightly odd way) would place restrictions upon the kinds of legislation that could be enacted by the former. However, even if such ideas would in principle help us, there is still a serious problem. How could such ideas work *in* an open society: how could they be brought into acceptance? If we cannot at present see why we should not pass legislation that destroys particular institutions, it is difficult to see why we would accept such new constitutional proposals. As they would obviously have the effect of preventing us from doing things which we at present wish to do, would they not be just as unacceptable as the features of our society that we currently wish to change?

One way out of this problem is a suggestion that was put to me by Popper,[90] in discussion – though he is obviously not responsible for what I do with it here. It is that such an institution could initially be set up unofficially, and could then try to pull itself up by its own bootstraps, over a period of time, by the effectiveness of its criticism. If, after a few years, it could say 'We told you so', it might start to be taken seriously, and eventually win for itself an established if not a constitutional position. This also illustrates a general point relevant to our larger problem: that claims to knowledge may be able to show their worth in an open society if they can operate freely in an appropriate institutional setting.

I now turn to my main suggestion. It starts from another theme in *The Open Society*. One *might* say that, for Popper, the only legitimate philosopher-king is *his* Socrates. Or, rather, that the only knowledge that can be *dogmatically* institutionalized is that of the philosopher who knows how little he knows. Is there a constitution which we could offer to Socrates which would also offer a solution to our problem?

Here, the epistemological analogue is, I think, of some help. For

Popper's epistemology includes his theory of metaphysical research programmes.[91] In this, we can follow up relatively coherent, systematic – one could even say, dogmatic – approaches to the solution of problems, within the discipline of a wider system of standards by means of which our performance may be appraised. Is there, perhaps, a political analogue? I think that there might be, and will now present one such idea. It is related to that offered in the final section of Robert Nozick's *Anarchy, State, and Utopia*, and also to a suggestion made by Karl Menger, in his *Morality, Decision, and Social Organization*.[92] We could suggest to Socrates that he operates a minimal state within the framework of which individuals could set up, on a voluntary basis, communities run on whatever systematic lines they preferred. Socrates' constitution would ensure the non-interference of one community with another,[93] and would also monitor the rules that communities set up concerning individuals' joining or leaving them (for there may obviously be *conditions*). He might operate such a constitution within an open society, as the coercion that it involved would be minimal, and would relate only to the protection of individuals and voluntary communities, and to our ignorance; also, its principles concerning individual action are relatively simple. Within Socrates' state, the individual would have the freedoms allowed by the community of which he is a member, and also the freedom to leave: to join (or to set up, using such resources as were available to him and to those who would join him) some community conducted in another way.

Such communities might be, variously, traditionalistic, restrictive or 'permissive' in their attitudes. They could also instantiate different theories about how, if at all, to revise their rules – answers to our earlier problem about institutionalizing argument. Socrates' constitution would enable people to make their own choices and – under the constraints imposed on them by the choices that others made – to pursue their favoured style of life.[94] It would also enable us to learn. Experiments would be possible, so that even Popper's Plato could set up his ideal state, though people could not be forced to join it, and would presumably stay in it only if Plato's claims held good. Above all, the systematic consequences of actions would be more easily relatable to the actions in question, and one might thus avoid the destruction of useful systematic and abstract institutions.

Institutional design, communities, socialization and exclusion

But how are we to handle the problem of institutional design, in the light of the problems that we have raised about it, both in our introduction, and in the discussion of Popper's ideas about tradition? In the space available to me here, I can offer only a brief and in some respects uncritical sketch. This is, I think, worth attempting nonetheless.

One move is clearly open to us, in the light of the previous section. That is to say, could people not choose to impose upon themselves specific codes of conduct – and shapings of their character – if this is understood as something that takes place within a voluntarily constituted community, their possibilities of exiting from which are guaranteed? The term 'voluntarily constituted community', however, might be misleading, in the sense that such institutions may range from something that is relatively closed in its character, to a neighbourhood which, while privately owned and imposing certain distinctive requirements upon those who enter it, is in all other respects open to free access by others. Such communities might, by such means, be able to create certain kinds of emergent order which those who live within them favour, as a result of imposing the particular commitments which its creation would involve upon their members and upon those who visit.

The use of the word 'community' here, however, may also be misleading. For as the production of such effects would be accomplished on the basis of (conjectural) knowledge aimed at producing specific effects, one might better see them in proprietorial rather than participatory terms. People would typically join them because they wished to enjoy certain results, rather than to participate in the production of something they know not what, the content of which would be open to the vagaries of democratic determination. Of course, there would be nothing to stop a group of democrats forming a community the heart of whose concerns was procedural. And, in the light of Popper's arguments about the importance of feedback mechanisms, and Hayek's ideas about the social division of knowledge, one could well imagine that any prudent community would allow for a degree of participation and feedback on the part of its members.

Such communities could impose rules upon the conduct of their citizens, which are local in their validity. They would be binding upon those who were members or visitors, and not something that could be trumped by considerations of those people's wider rights. If they wished to exercise these, it would, primarily, be by way of exiting from the community, and finding somewhere else to practise the specific forms of behaviour which they favoured. In view of the fact that the production of the emergent order in question would in large measure need to become a matter of tradition and second nature on the part of members, one could well expect that the community would impose certain restrictions upon activities which could be undertaken within the community, of a kind the rationale for which would not necessarily be transparent to its members, but which would relate to the character of the product in virtue of which people had joined the community. One could also well expect that, in some cases, there would be a fair degree of informal mutual monitoring of the behaviour of members; in particular of children and young people. All this would mean that, if people so wished, they could choose to live in areas which had a strongly 'neighbourhood' feel to them – but also that they would have to bear the restrictions which would be required to create this. Others, however, might wish to live in settings of a very different character, and which would place a premium upon the freedom of individual behaviour within a minimal framework of rules, within which there might be a high degree of diversity, but a sense of community of only a very 'thin' character.[95]

If one were looking for parallels in the world as it currently exists to the relatively closed neighbourhoods to which I have referred, one might think, for example, of the Hasidic communities in some parts of New York, and of predominantly gay neighbourhoods in parts of San Francisco, as well as the distinctive features of particular suburbs and city areas. (Such examples, however, are limited in the extent to which they realize the kinds of things that I am suggesting, in that, in the United States, they are typically not proprietorial communities, and they are subject both to the external rules of local authorities, and to constitutional requirements concerning non-discrimination, which may limit the extent to which people can impose specific requirements on those within a particular geographical area.) However, and this marks the difference, under the arrangements that I am suggesting these groups could form proprietorial communities which would, to a considerable extent, be able to make their own rules, upon compliance with which they could insist. They would be limited, in this respect, to what they owned, so that they would not be able to use the institutions of local government to force their preferences upon others. But one might expect that, in many cases, ownership might involve entire neighbourhoods, or even, indeed, what is currently a county or even a state.[96] It would not be open to other people to claim more general rights on the basis of which they could move in and behave differently, thus disrupting the production of the effects which these people wished to produce. For other people would simply not have the right to do this. People could be excluded from membership of – or even from entering – such communities, if it was judged that they would be disruptive. Or they might be allowed to enter only if they complied as a matter of artifice with the codes of behaviour which people within them might – by this point – be following as second nature, or, at the very least, if they were to undertake not to behave in ways that would be judged disruptive by the management or the members of the community.

Members of the groups in question might see themselves as, variously, pursuing a favoured lifestyle, or behaving in ways that they thought were proper, or which they considered to be enjoined upon them by their religious beliefs. From the perspective of *other* people, they would be engaged in certain kinds of experiments in living, from which others might learn. How? Largely, I think, because while most people would not wish to impose restrictions upon themselves which were particularly onerous, they might, nonetheless, be interested in the offerings of entrepreneurs who were on the lookout for ways in which they might learn from those things which had proved successful, in the lives of more restricted communities. Features which had proved successful in such communities might, thus, be re-packaged in proprietorial suburbs, or apartment buildings.

Such ideas are suggestive – at least to me! – and would merit exploration in more detail than would be possible here. But there are obvious problems about them which it might be useful to bring out into the open, and to discuss explicitly, although I can, likewise, only discuss a few of these here.

The first relates to exclusion. For it might be argued that this would be discriminatory. In one sense, it seems to me that it would, but properly so. For it is not clear how one can hope to produce specific kinds of order upon a voluntary basis, unless there is the possibility of discrimination: unless people are free to choose not to associate with those who do not behave decently, or do not keep their agreements to follow the rules to which they have agreed. Why should people believe that they have a right to force others to associate with them, against their wishes?

However, three arguments might be advanced, which pose problems for the ideas that I am here advocating. The first relates to ideas about the rights of citizens, and to the idea that they should not be excluded from 'public' space unless they have committed a criminal offence. I have earlier offered some criticism of the idea of citizenship as having any moral significance. Indeed, the ideas which I am discussing here are compatible with the abolition of national governments, and are thus something that might be administered by a global authority, impartial between every human being (although I do not think that this would be a good idea, because of the danger that such a single authority might become a tyranny). It is also the notion of public space that is involved in such an objection – and which, notably in the United States, has been extended from that which is government owned to other areas, such as privately owned shopping malls and airports – with which I wish to take issue. I see no reason why any physical location should be of such a public character – in the sense of being owned by government – at all. Similarly, I am here taking issue with the idea that people have a right to behave as they wish on other people's property, or that government should have the power to over-rule the regulations that a community wishes to have in force in respect of its own property, other than in respect of some very restricted issues, which I will discuss below. (These relate to the situation of children, to freedom of movement between locations – and to certain other cases in which materially coercive restrictions might be generated as a product of voluntary activity – and to a distinctive kind of openness to criticism.) Second, it might be argued that an effective discriminatory boycott could have devastating consequences upon those who suffer its consequences. Third, discrimination might be exercised on the basis of, say, such things as a person's race or beliefs – which might be seen as morally pernicious; a view with which I have full sympathy.

I think, however, that these matters can be handled fairly easily, within the kind of institutional framework which I am here suggesting. For people have the right to discriminate only within property which they actually own, while the property and other rights of people are elsewhere protected. Some community of the lithe and beautiful may well not let me in. But this does not prevent me from associating with *other* people. And what has seemed to me the key characteristic of the grimmest kinds of discrimination with which we are familiar – the physical oppression of people, or the use of the powers of the state to render them second-class citizens, or worse – would not be available, just on the grounds that communities would have power to make regulations which would hold good only within areas which they actually owned. Those of us who are excluded from the select areas in which the rich and famous may choose to live, may feel unhappy about it. But it is not clear that we will not be able to live quite comfortably with one another, and with people who view such kinds of exclusion as in bad taste, or who prefer to have a measure of variety in their surroundings. We could, there, own property, and choose – within certain *limits* – the kinds of rules under which we wished to live. We would also have the satisfaction of knowing that those who were exercising discrimination against us would have to pay for the privilege, in the sense that they would have to exercise it through actual ownership, not by means of governmental regulation such as zoning laws. (Externalities would be internalized, typically by way of proprietorial communities owning all those things which would affect them or by negotiating agreements – which would continue in the event of a sale, as restrictive covenants, and thus have an effect upon the capital value of the property – with their neighbours. Clearly, communities would also gain protection by virtue of the legal protection of all property rights against certain kinds of overspill effects.)

The limits to which I referred in the previous paragraph concern not oppression – for we would still have full liberal rights, albeit as reinterpreted in the light of the suggestions that I am offering here – but economies of scale. For if people wish to live in a way that is relatively unpopular, it may be very costly – to the point where, if they want to enjoy the ordinary amenities of life, what other choices are open to them might be rather more restrictive than this approach might at first have suggested. But, nonetheless, one might expect that there would be more choices open to people than there are currently, and also that people would have more options to exclude those who behave in an anti-social manner.

To this it might be responded: but what about those excluded people's civil rights? Here, there is a genuine difference between what I am proposing and what is more usual today. For people would not have civil rights, in the sense of the right of unconditional entry to other people's communities. Those who are disruptive would bear the costs of their anti-social behaviour, in the sense that they might end up excluded from places where they would like to be, and, say, be re-admitted only subject to some kind of good behaviour bond. This, however, leads to the question: where would they go, and what would life be like for them? And, further, may not people be left in a condition of privation, if others will not deal with them? There would seem to me every reason to expect that there will be places to which there will be relatively free access, and where entrepreneurs will specialize in offering minimal services to the relative outcasts – after all, this is something that some people do, in particular districts in large cities, all over the world. At the same time, even such association would not be unconditional, and those who do not respect other people or their rights may indeed find that they suffer the full costs of their behaviour. In addition, the arrangements suggested here would allow even the people at the bottom of the social heap – who do not usually enjoy such rights – to exclude from association with them those people who make their lives a misery. One might expect, however, that some people – whether out of compassion, or in the hope of making a profit, or both – might specialize in helping people back into more ordinary forms of social life; for example, by providing the social equivalent of a secured credit card for them.[97] For, after all, we would all wish that people be in communication with one another, and contribute to one another's well-being, through friendship and mutual exchange on the basis of the division of labour. At bottom, however, we are dealing with behaviour for which people would usually be incarcerated or otherwise restricted under the kinds of regime with which we are more familiar. I would certainly be open to argument that, at a certain point, this would be a better way of treating them, should anyone wish to advance it.

But what, it might be said, of some agreement, say, not to trade with members of some unpopular group; and what of those people who are discriminated against for no good reason, or offered association only on exploitative terms? In the first case, I think that we may usefully take up a suggestion which Hayek discussed, when he considered what might be called the coercive use of people's rights; for example, the person who takes advantage of their (temporary) monopoly in the possession of things that other people need to live, such as, say, in the event of the failure of other springs in a drought, someone's ownership of the only regular supply of water in a desert. In such cases, Hayek suggested that a rule of uniformity in their commercial dealings with others might be forced upon them; and this, while untidy and imperfect, would seem to me as good a way as any of handling such questions.[98]

This would mean that certain conditions would be imposed in respect of economic exchange, such that those with whom others may not wish to associate socially would not suffer from extortion, or be in danger of starving to death. Similarly, certain minimal rights to freedom of movement might be enforced, lest people find themselves trapped within a restricted geographical area. At the same time, such safeguards are genuinely minimal, and if people use violence or the threat of violence towards others; if they choose to break agreements into which they have entered such that others no longer trust them; or even if they insist on speaking only a language that almost no one else speaks, or deliberately get on the wrong side of other 'network externalities', then they will have to bear the consequences of these choices themselves.[99]

But what of discrimination towards some minority group, the characteristics of which it is either not open to them to change or not reasonable to expect that they should change? They might be offered association with others only on highly disadvantageous terms. If their numbers are small, the option of forming their own community may not be of much use to them, because economies of scale would operate against them.

This problem seems to me all too real. But I would like to relate it to another rather different problem. This concerns the situation of children who are brought up within specific communities. This will most obviously pose a problem in cases in which the group chooses to isolate itself from the wider life of society, and in which socialization into the behaviour needed to sustain the institutions in question starts to get close to indoctrination. It seems to me that we are, here, in need of institutions which call various communities to account – and in terms which relate to the legitimation of the wider setting within which people and communities are operating. If people are to be able to exercise choice, they stand in need of the cultural prerequisites to it. And, as we have seen Popper arguing, this also is something into which they have to be socialized. We are dealing here not with things that are natural rights in the sense of being things which people enjoy – and accord to others – merely by virtue of their shared humanity, but with specific and valuable cultural artefacts. There is a sense in which members of each particular community have also to be members of the wider community, and for its rules and procedures to have priority over their particular ones. This does not mean that they cannot exercise the restrictions and forms of discrimination, which I have discussed. But communities would not be able to do so in ways which limit the ability of their members – and of those who grow up within them – to make genuine choices, informed by standards wider than those of their particular community.

We are here encountering essentially the same issue as was discussed earlier in connection with Popper's preference for liberal imperialism. It is the idea that toleration, and the welcoming of diversity, is to be understood not as a natural product of diversity, or of particular diverse communities, but, rather, that it is to be understood as a cultural achievement; something that is a product of a wider culture within which diversity is then accorded protection, *under certain conditions.*

How this might be achieved raises issues which go beyond what can appropriately be addressed in the present context. But one possibility that might be involved, among others, is the institution of a form of accountability to which communities would be made subject; namely, rational accountability for the choices that they have made, and the rules that they are following, to other people. They would, as it were, have to set out their rationale for doing what they are doing, and be willing to defend it against criticism. It is in this setting that those practising unjustifiable discrimination might be distinguished from those following a particular rule because of its plausible relation to consequences which they value. In addition, it is in such a setting that groups can be confronted with problematic unintended consequences that flow from their choices and institutional practices. Further, young people who grow up within such communities would have to be prepared for exposure to this forum in some depth – such that those concerned with instructing them within relatively closed communities would have to make sure that the explanations they offered for their differences could stand up to such critical scrutiny; while they could not accomplish this simply by indoctrination. This would still mean that people could make restrictive choices; but they would have to be genuine choices, rather than ones which are forced upon them by their upbringing.

It might be argued that, in some respect, the arrangements that I am suggesting would be less tolerant than are our current arrangements, under which considerations of the freedom of religion and its extensions into the secular realm allow people to insulate certain of their beliefs from criticism. (While it could also be said that their *inability* to exclude other people, on the kind of basis that I *have* argued for, means that their beliefs and conduct have to face the rough and tumble of everyday life; and that, if their chosen way of life is exotic – such as is that of the Amish – they become, willy nilly, a kind of tourist attraction.) I am indeed arguing here for something distinctive. It involves, on the one hand, a right to exclude. But – for reasons for which I would argue on the basis of Popper's fallibilism – I would not allow people the 'right' to insulate themselves from criticism. This does not mean that others would have the right to thrust upon them things which they would find abhorrent, in the course of their day-to-day lives. Mill's and Popper's fallibilist arguments for toleration do not, as far as I can see, provide a good argument for the right to confront and upset others, in the ordinary course of the pursuit of their chosen activities. But they would seem to me to point for the need for some place in which hard argument and criticism are offered, and to which everyone would, at some point, be exposed, if they are to be able to exercise informed choice between alternatives. Further, as the basis upon which people are understood as having a claim to liberty rests upon their ability to exercise such informed choice, an uncritical espousal of particular substantive views cannot successfully be invoked against such ideas.

As will be seen from all this, the options that are open for particular communities are in *some* ways restricted. For there are limits to diversity, imposed by the requirements of rational discrimination. And this, in the light of Popper's ideas about the social and cultural formation of the self – and thus of the self that can exercise such discrimination – will mean that there will be requirements imposed upon all communities, institutions and choices. Diversity will be possible; but only in ways that are not incompatible with socialization into the liberal culture which underlies the entire arrangement. Defenders of various forms of traditionalism might say: but this allows us only a kind of ersatz practice of the form of life which we believe to be the right one. To this, my response is: yes. But the underlying rationale for the entire arrangement is a fallibilistic liberalism, and again, one cannot, against this, offer arguments based on the presumption that one's substantive views are correct. There is also a clear parallel here with the argument that we discussed in relation to Popper's own leanings towards liberal imperialism; namely, that toleration is a feature of such a regime, not something that can be relied upon to be an integral feature of all other particular views. Such a regime is, indeed, intolerant of, and restrictive towards, what may be features of people's specific choices. But it can do this because of its insistence on our fallibility.

It will, of course, be open to any individual or group to argue that features of the existing wider culture, or of the institutions which relate to it, unfairly stack the argument against them. A fallibilist culture must be open to such objections, and be willing to take them seriously. But, at the same time, such objections must themselves be open to critical scrutiny by others; and their acceptance must rest upon those arguments being found telling by them.

One other task which would have to be handled by the government of such a regime would be the determination of the character of externalities. That is to say, while individuals, groups and proprietorial communities would, to the greatest extent possible that is compatible with the overall character of the system, have the right to do what they wished on their own property, there is a problem concerning the overspill effects of their activities upon others. What such externalities may consist of, and whether they should be permitted, may clearly be a matter of dispute between different groups. For example, a puritanical group may be concerned about the effects, on their young people, of a more permissive neighbourhood near by. While one may discover problems – such as damage to the ozone layer and, more generally, limitations on the environment's ability to cope with pollution – solutions to which had not been bundled into existing conceptions of property rights. Such issues would seem to me to stand in need of decision by the wider governmental body, on the basis of expert, but open-ended, consensus. While the procedures involved might in part parallel the ways in which such issues are currently handled by law courts, the need for genuine public consensus would seem to me to point to the need for institutions of a rather different type. In particular, it would seem undesirable that issues should have to be decided only on the basis of specific cases; that argument can be advanced only by those who are party to a specific dispute or to whom the courts choose to accord recognition; and that judges are not accountable, in argument, to the rest of the community, in the sense that, as a matter of tradition, they do not respond to criticisms of their decisions or the grounds that they offered for them.

Essentially the same kind of openness would seem to me desirable in respect of public policy issues; that is to say, decisions which are to be imposed upon other people. Deliberations here would need to be shifted from private negotiations between interest groups and public servants, or policy-making communities, to the public forum. An argumentative basis for *all* governmental decisions would have to be a matter for public record. Lest this seem a simply crazy suggestion, I would remind the reader that most issues which are at present matters of public policy would no longer have this character if my suggestions here were to be accepted, in that they would, instead, become matters for private decision on the basis of the characteristics of different proprietorial communities, and would apply only to those living within them.

The wider liberal regime must thus be seen as the bearer of specific, if fallible, judgements as to how the world works. What, say, constitutes an externality or overspill effect will be determined on the basis of its distinctive forms of argument, and (fallible) judgements about this imposed on the different communities. If, to take up an issue raised by Bertrand Russell,[100] a religious group believe that they will suffer hellfire if they permit the practice of homosexuality not only within their own group, but by anyone else, they must be asked to make a telling case for this in a *public* forum. And if they cannot, they can only impose their rules upon themselves.

In a similar manner, we must take seriously the fact that we are dealing with people who, within specific groups, are socialized into specific forms of behaviour. However, the fallibility of the ideas which inform what to the outside observer look like various different experiments in living, also means that we can expect certain of them to fail. The wider liberal government will, to a degree, have the responsibility for handing failures. This may involve negotiating the revision of rules, if they fail to deliver the wished-for results, but the people involved want to try again. Or it may involve handing the re-integration of the products of the failures of such groups, into the wider community. Not least because of the costs that this will impose upon other people, it would seem reasonable either to demand that there be some kind of financial provision made for this contingency – possibly through the purchase of insurance, or through a lien on the group's property – or that the wider government can impose restrictions upon what kinds of behaviour members get up to, in the light of the current state of public knowledge as to its likely consequences. And this, clearly, would limit the activities in which such groups could engage. Once again, fallibilism does not mean relativism; and while anyone has the right to challenge accepted opinion, this does not mean simply saying that they do not like it. There is every reason for not invoking such controls other than in fairly extreme cases, just because the knowledge on the basis of which the government would be acting would, indeed, be fallible. But it would seem important that the government can do this, not least because of the inequity of a situation in which the adverse consequences of the behaviour of some group, against which everyone else had been cautioning them, have in the end to be paid for by those very people who had been issuing the warnings.

All this would amount to the creation of arrangements which would allow for the possibility of (limited) islands of voluntarily maintained restriction, within what is very much a wider liberal and fallibilist setting. The purposes for which such islands might be set up could range from the construction of specific, valued institutions, through a concern for some form of emergent social order, to the pursuit Popper's ideas about the creation of specific social institutions.

One interesting problem is that these liberal and fallibilist framework arrangements would themselves seem to have institutional and economic prerequisites. Some of what we have discussed here relates to ideas similar to Habermas's notion of a public sphere – although we have, perhaps, heightened the *problem* that we face by referring specifically to Burkean themes about the specific forms of socialization upon which the operation of its institutions may depend, and by our insistence on a relationship between individual freedom and classical liberal ideas about property rights.

If one thinks of societies such as the United States, Great Britain and Australia – to name places of which I have had personal experience – it would seem to me plausible to think of the operation of their public spheres as resting, in different ways, upon interactions between their political and legal institutions, the traditions of behaviour within specific areas of commerce and public service, and the operation of their media, both commercial and government funded.

Different arrangements clearly give rise to public spheres with different specific characteristics. All arrangements known to me fall short of anything that might instantiate adequately the ideas about public accountability, which I have discussed here. Further, I face a massive problem, in the sense that decisions affecting the existence and the character of a public forum are currently taken on a variety of political and commercial grounds which are blind to the kinds of consideration that I have raised here. All that it might be appropriate for me to say is that I am acutely aware of the fact that these issues raise difficult questions. These include the relationship between what one might hope to make plausible by means of philosophical argument, and what would be accepted as desirable by individual citizens. There is also the relation between all this, and the disaggregated actions that those very people may take in the different areas of their lives – not least, in their economic decisions – as well as how they would relate to the internal logic of larger-scale economic decision-taking, and its consequences. The reader will hardly be surprised that I do not venture any resolution of these issues here. All that I will say is that, in facing these problems, I believe that I am in good company in that, as I have suggested earlier in this volume, they seem to me to be problems that face Popper's ideas, too.

What, however, of the remaining problem which I promised to address – the problem of what we owe to one another. Here, I am in disagreement with Popper. I would fully agree that both the well-being of others (in the sense of their being freed from avoidable suffering) and also their enjoyment moral autonomy are highly desirable. At the same time, it is not clear to me that these are things which each of us has any general responsibility to bring about. This is because, on the one hand, I am simply unconvinced that we have moral *responsibilities*, over and above those that are recognized in the classical liberal tradition, for people with whom we do not have some kind of personal relationship, or a shared identity of a kind which we have *chosen* to sustain. The kinds of factor with which the negative utilitarian is concerned are typically bound up with people's choices, decisions and their involvement with particular institutions. If people make such choices, and join together with others in the pursuit of a particular goal, those who are part of this enterprise can clearly lay claim to their agreed share of its benefits, and to others that may be extended to them by other participants, if they should happen to fall on hard times. In my view, we should respect the freedom of the individual to choose to participate – or not to participate – in such arrangements. There would also seem to me good grounds for instituting general schemes for social insurance, to cover cases in which we may be unlucky, or in which the ideas upon which we have shaped our lives turn out to be incorrect. But it seems to me unfair to allow people the freedom to make such choices and then, if they choose not to take up the obligations and restrictions which they would involve, nonetheless to demand that those who have taken them up should also extend benefits to them. Clearly there is room for compassion. But this is not a matter of obligation; and those who would benefit from it would seem to me to have to take their chances among the petty concerns of other people's day-to-day moral lives which I discussed earlier.

There clearly is a need to address wider moral issues, relating to the overall character of the society in which we are living. But these, it seems to me, if they are to be handled in ways that are compatible with individual moral autonomy, are best handled by means of the kind of voluntary communities which I have discussed in this chapter.

What, the reader might wonder, is he or she supposed to make of all this? I will conclude this chapter with the following points.

First, I am not suggesting that the arrangements that I am discussing here are part and parcel of Popper's own approach; indeed, as I have explained, I am in some respects explicitly at odds with his views. Also, as I have had occasion to mention repeatedly, the ideas which I have set out here are merely a sketch. However, I would see them as addressing what seems to me a serious problem; something that is pressing not only in Popper's work, but in liberal democratic arrangements more generally. If the kinds of arrangement that I have suggested should prove acceptable or not, I would suggest that they are directed at genuine problems. And insofar as they differ so markedly from the arrangements towards which we are drifting today, this seems to me a measure of the way in which complex but interrelated problems of individual freedom, interpersonal accountability for our substantive views, social engineering and the maintenance of complex institutions have been lost sight of.

Second, it might be asked, am I *serious?* My answer is: yes. However, I currently take the view that the ideas that I have set out are to be seen, essentially, as a programme for further research. At the same time, I would strongly favour small-scale experiments in this direction, to see if there is, indeed, anything to these speculative ideas. To this end, I would favour the idea that – if appropriate financial guarantees can be given, and in return for laying themselves open to a measure of public scrutiny – private groups should be allowed to opt out of existing forms of local governmental organization, and be allowed to practise the kind of discrimination for which I have here argued. Indeed, the very fact that they would be experimental and that there would be many people around who would be dubious about the whole exercise would, in my view, make sure that they were submitted to public scrutiny and, in turn, make it that much more likely that the only forms of discrimination which they practised would be benign.

6

THE CONTEMPORARY RELEVANCE OF POPPER'S WORK

INTRODUCTION

One of the major themes of this book has been the development of an argument that Popper's ideas should be more closely related to classical liberalism than Popper's own writings would themselves suggest. In addition, I have been much concerned with raising some distinctive problems about social engineering, and suggesting what readers might have found slightly strange solutions to them. I (of course) fully stand by the ideas for which I have argued, and take the view that they are highly relevant to contemporary politics.

I would not, however, wish what readers might draw from this book to stand or fall with some of the more distinctive ideas that have preoccupied me, not only because of their obvious fallibility, but because there is clearly more to Popper's work than just these themes. In this final chapter, I will discuss why I consider Popper's ideas to be of wider contemporary relevance. In doing so, I will not recapitulate further on Popper's own views, or even on those aspects of his work which have been so ably stressed by such commentators as Bryan Magee and Roger James.[1] Rather, I will discuss a few themes which seem to me of interest, and which, for the most part, do not depend on the specific arguments about Popper's work that I have advanced in earlier chapters.

In doing this, I will touch briefly on a number of highly controversial issues of a kind which I cannot sensibly explore in a single chapter. What I will have to say here is, in consequence, both sketchy and highly programmatic. I think, however, that it is nonetheless worth breaking a lance for what seems to me a perspective which flows naturally from Popper's work, but which

159

is very much at odds with many ideas which are currently highly fashionable. What I am offering is thus an indication of an argument that I believe should be pursued in a way that is rather different from what is possible here. And indeed, I hope in a subsequent work to turn from what, in this book, has to a great extent rested upon a description of Popper's epistemological ideas to a more serious defence of them; both from their critics in the philosophy of science, and from points that are made in the work of recent post-modernist, post-structuralist and feminist writers. The following may at least serve to indicate the conclusions to which I currently suspect that such work may lead.

BETWEEN DOGMATISM AND RELATIVISM

Popper occupies a territory which most contemporaries seem not to realize exists. In a work such as Rorty's *Philosophy and the Mirror of Nature*,[2] one has a critique offered of traditional, foundationalist approaches in philosophy – with the assumption that, if this critique is accepted, the alternative is a kind of pragmatism. Much the same perspective seems to be found in the work of many post-modernists. What is striking about Popper is the way in which he offers a non-foundationalist, and non-justificationist, theory of knowledge, which nonetheless admits the possibility of progress. Popper argues that it is possible to impose upon ourselves restrictions such that our claims to knowledge are thereby rendered open to inter-subjective criticism. Fallibility and the possibility of the growth of our knowledge are not, as it were, facts of nature; they are artefacts – the construction of which requires that we behave in ways that may not come very easily to us. From such a perspective, not only our specific claims to knowledge but the procedures under which we are operating must be open to critical scrutiny. We also make progress only if we are lucky. At best, our views may withstand criticism. In the event of their not doing so, we may require of ourselves that our new conjectures 'save' the respects in which our previous theories have seemed to be successful so far, and also that they deal, constructively, with at least some of the criticism.

Popper's work seems puzzling to some people who favour views such as Rorty's, just because it contains some of the very arguments which have led them to embrace their own ideas – for example, a critique of foundationalism, and an advocacy of the idea that our descriptions even of the simplest matters of fact are theory-impregnated. Why, they might well ask, has Popper continued to uphold ideas about truth, self-emancipation through knowledge, and, more generally, the heritage of the Enlightenment, when his work also contains the very ideas which have enabled others to emancipate themselves from all that claptrap?

Popper, as I have indicated, has suggested that it is open to us to adopt various procedures, the results of which we can reasonably interpret as involving us in the discovery that our previous views were wrong, as a result of encounters with the criticism of others, and with a world which exists independently of ourselves (even though we have no unmediated experience of it). Why does he *wish* to take such a view? (Whether it will ultimately turn out to be *tenable* is, of course, another issue.) His concern, I believe, is ethical.

One of Popper's deepest-seated concerns was with the moral significance of suffering, and of the moral importance of relieving it and of responding to various forms of injustice and oppression. His complaint against the views of his recent critics, as it was against the positivists of his own day, would be that their views render this unreal. If one takes their views seriously, then there is no such thing as an encounter with the suffering and oppression of others. Rather, our concern must be understood as a response to our own feelings, and a view which we project on to the world; something that Popper felt was utterly unacceptable.[3]

To this, I believe that one can add an additional argument. It is that what might be termed the political benefits of a non-realist epistemology are illusory. One move, popular among contemporary post-modernists, is the exposure of various realist claims as conventional. Rather than, as they would see it, people being able to read truths off the world, armed with which they can then oppress others, post-modernists take a resolutely conventionalist view of human knowledge. There is no reality, no truth, that can inform people's views; there are simply varieties of discourses and perspectives. Not only are oppressors disclosed as simply imposing their ideas upon us; but it is open to us to choose those perspectives which we favour. We become liberated to see the world in terms of *our* political perspective.

This, however, seems to me a disaster. It is of course true that the proponents of some theories may have represented as truths things which, in fact, are conventional. It is also open to us to choose our way of looking at things, in those areas in which a conventionalist epistemology is appropriate. But such a choice, it seems to me, is politically pointless, once we see that *any* option is open to us. To draw encouragement or succour from seeing the world from our perspective in such circumstances is as futile as drawing encouragement at how rosy things look as a result of having put on rose-tinted spectacles.

Further, to treat our most important concerns, and our moral endeavours, as exemplifying merely one such perspective seems to me also to devalue them. It amounts to treating them as if they were simply matters of taste. It is difficult to see how we could accord to them the gravity with which we treat them, if we see them as having this degree of contingency. This, however, might seem to conjure up exactly what the post-modernist dislikes most: the picture of people who claim to know the truth about the world, and who then try to impose these views on to others. I wish to argue that, from Popper's perspective, the situation is in fact completely the other way round.

First, Popper's fallibilism has the consequence that one cannot presume that one has the truth. One is aiming at it, to be sure. But one has always to be on the look-out, to see what may be raised against the ideas that one favours, so that one might learn. As I have indicated, such a view provides an argument for toleration,[4] and indeed some suggestions as to why one should treat each person as something like an end in themselves. Popper's approach is also resolutely anti-authoritarian. No one is an authority in the sense of being above criticism, including the powerful. And the trappings of power, and the ways in which it is institutionalized, may be criticized, as removing people from such criticism. By way of contrast, a non-realist approach serves to insulate one's perspective from criticism: there is simply no basis on which such 'perspectives' can be criticized – or, to look at this from another perspective, in which criticism can be distinguished from oppression.[5] And this seems to me worrying, insofar as such perspectives are not only the basis on which people conduct themselves in self-regarding actions (if there are such) but upon which they also interact with others.

There is also a problem about conflict. Popper's approach involves us in the construction, together with other people, of a (tentative) basis upon which our various claims are to be validated. Our claims about the world, and for the correctness of our moral perspectives, are to be made in such a way that they are open to the critical scrutiny of everyone. And it is also open to anyone to challenge the procedures that we have, hitherto, used for the evaluation of such claims, and to suggest ways in which they might be improved. This offers us a way in which we may learn from others, and through which our faults may be corrected, and our prejudices overcome. It also offers a basis on which competing claims might be resolved: they have to be opened to critical scrutiny within such an inter-subjective forum.

One problem about post-modernism seems to me to be that it does not resolve our problems and disputes. Conflicts still exist. Indeed, as I have suggested above, the parties to them seem reassured in the (subjective) correctness of their views, and have to hand intellectual procedures which render them invulnerable to criticism. But what, then, is to happen in the event of there being conflicts? In part, they seem to me to be handled by way of people's writing of cheques upon the very liberal universalism which they have been repudiating – of suggesting, albeit implicitly, that in some sense everyone's rights (where rights are interpreted in a highly extensive fashion) should be respected by others. However, given their own views about the *status* of such appeals, it is not clear why others should take them seriously. And what of conflict? If this is to be resolved pragmatically, may this not include the oppression of the weak by the strong? An approach such as Popper's invites the strong to make their case on a field in which their claims may not hold up: for them to do so would require everyone to admit that they are reasonable. Without this, it is not clear why they should be interested in what others may think about what they are doing or why they should pay any attention to what others are claiming as their rights.

In *The Open Society*, Popper drew some encouragement from the fact that even those who were opposed to humanitarianism had, typically, come to couch their arguments in humanitarian terms.[6] From this point of view, there is room for further encouragement. Aside from the resurgence of nationalism – with its predictable consequence that people are willing to see and to treat others as not being on a par with themselves, morally – there has been an increased willingness for us not only to hold others accountable to liberal and humanitarian standards, but to take seriously criticisms of ourselves made by others, and even in cases in which we may have some misgivings about the basis upon which this is done.[7]

This is certainly not to say that, in our personal conduct, or at the levels of national or international politics, we always do very well; and there is a worrying complacency about the fate of those who are losing out as a result of economic globalization. But it does seem to me significant that there is a widespread view that it is appropriate that we and others should be called to account. Yet it is exactly this notion that there are interpersonally binding standards to which we should be held to account that is undercut by the arguments of post-modernism.

In concluding this section, I need to clarify what I am and what I am not arguing here. I am not arguing that Popper's approach is correct. There has been much argument about the cogency of his views, and I do not know how much will turn out to be tenable. I am arguing that Popper's approach opens up an interesting and attractive possibility – of a non-foundationalist, fallibilist approach, which would apply in all areas of our knowledge, factual, moral, political, aesthetic and even religious.[8] Such an approach seems to me attractive, both intellectually and morally, and well worth the investment of some intellectual effort,[9] to see if it can be made viable. At the same time, I am not denying that some of the *arguments* offered by post-modernists and post-structuralists are most interesting, and that they deserve to be taken *very* seriously. It is the idea that they are offering substantive positions that are either attractive or which make any real sense of the world in which we are living which seems to me highly resistible.

CRITICAL THEORY

Popper is well known for what might be described as his non-encounters with Critical Theory. Popper gave a presentation on 'The Logic of the Social Sciences' at a sociology conference in Germany, to which Adorno responded, in turn. Their papers became the subject of other papers by, among others, Habermas, to which Hans Albert responded. The results, together with other material, were reprinted in a volume entitled *The Positivist Dispute in German Sociology*.[10] To this, Popper appended another essay,[11] which he had written as a comment on the German version of the volume, and he has subsequently written a few other brief critical comments.[12] Popper clearly felt that his critics had not engaged with his original essay; he also made various morally charged criticisms of their obscurity, yet it is not clear that his readers will

164

have appreciated *why* he thought these points to be so significant. (The reason is, as we have seen, because of their relation to rationalism: in Popper's view, the rational unity of mankind and the possibility of learning from one another depend upon us going out of our way to make our work as accessible to others as we can. One might say that, from his perspective, what he was criticizing was *objectively* irrationalist in its tendencies.) At the same time, those who followed the discussion may well have thought that Popper had not really responded to his critics; and while Hans Albert did make some good points, his own interpretation of Popper's work seems to me somewhat positivistic in its tenor. As a result, it is no surprise that, in his recent *Juergen Habermas: Critic in the Public Sphere*, Holub comments that:[13] 'Although Habermas's comments were addressed mainly to Popper's arguments, he received no reply'; and Holub – and I imagine others – may well have concluded that no answer was given because Habermas's criticisms could not be answered. Because of Habermas's ever-growing significance, I will here suggest what such a response could have been.[14]

My discussion will be brief. It has three elements.

The first is that Habermas's initial response to Popper, which presented itself as a defence of Adorno's criticism of his work, does not, in fact, seem to owe *anything* to Adorno's perspective. Rather, his criticisms are drawn from the hermeneutical tradition, and from Peirce. Here, I think that Habermas does make some good points. But those points are made against the subjectivism and 'decisionism' which, as we have seen, represents but one strand in Popper's ethics. And, as I have suggested, Popper already had to hand, at the time at which he was writing *The Open Society*, arguments which would have enabled him to make essentially the same criticisms of these aspects of his own work, and offered, in their place, something that does not seem open to the same criticism.[15]

The result of all this, however, is striking. For when these themes from Popper's work, which we have discussed in Chapter 4, are given their full weight, it turns out that Popper and Habermas share a perspective drawn from the Kantian theme of objectivity as inter-subjectivity, which we met there. There is a sense in which much of Habermas's work can, in this light, be seen as close to Popper's 'critical rationalism' – and as resting on a fallibilist, inter-subjectivist epistemology of the kind that Popper set out. There is even a sense in which one can see the early Popper as sharing some of Habermas's political concerns, in that, if one recalls Popper's correspondence with Carnap, one may recall his expression of concern about the effect of business interests upon (consensus-directed) political deliberations. *If* one so wished, one might even describe this in terms of the colonization of the life world! It is also worth noting that Popper was willing to suggest that this might need to be controlled by means of the socialization of production.

I do not intend that these ideas about the convergence between Popper and Habermas should be taken *too* seriously. But I have been struck by the extent to which themes in Habermas's work can be made good sense of in terms of Popper's work, when the latter is interpreted with a stress upon the Kantian theme of inter-subjective consensus. It does, however, indicate the limits to the force of Habermas's criticism, given that the issues that he is raising could themselves be accommodated within Popper's own writings.

But what of Habermas's own wider concerns? Here, I will address two issues. The first concerns his well-known distinction between different cognitive interests. From Popper's perspective, two comments on this seem to me in order. The first is that, as Hans Albert indicated, Habermas's own reading of the 'cognitive interest' of science is unduly pragmatist in its character.[16] Popper has argued that it is open to us to take a realist approach to science, and from such a perspective one may take *natural* science as concerned with understanding. Indeed, one of the major themes in Popper's work is the way in which, once one takes such a view, many of the features which are argued to be distinctive of social science may be paralleled within the natural sciences. This does not mean that Popper's view of social science is positivistic: although there are some themes in his earlier writings which might seem to be interpretable in such a way,[17] the views with which he ended up lay stress on the role of rational action in the constitution of the material with which the social sciences deal, and, as we have seen, his epistemology lays stress upon inter-subjective consensus.

What seems to me more problematic is Habermas's view of emancipatory social science. It is modelled on that theme within psychoanalysis and Marxism in which an awareness of the character of the constraints upon us also serves to break their hold. Two points here are worth making. The first concerns the status of the theories in question, neither of which we have the *slightest* reason to believe to be correct, and which, as a result, seem a somewhat dubious basis for such a conception of knowledge.[18] Second, the idea that such emancipation is always desirable is also problematic, for reasons which relate to the discussion in the previous chapter of Popper's own invocation of the Kantian idea of emancipation through knowledge. To put the matter most simply – and thus in a manner which contrasts better with the ideas of Marcuse than Habermas – there would seem to be every reason to suppose that, in the large-scale societies of the kind within which I would imagine that most people wish to live, we must conduct ourselves on the basis of conventions and roles, the very best of which may not fit particular individuals too well. While I am all in favour of the idea that we should be able to revise them, it is not clear to me that *this* is best done by making us too directly aware of the conventional character of our social institutions. For while we may, in some respects, gain from becoming aware that they are conventional, and that their continuation depends upon our compliance, all this faces us with a massive problem. How are we to move to *better* shared conventions, which we can again take for granted? Our problem, as it were, is not to *shed* most of what has become 'second nature',[19] but to improve on it, and in such a way that we can swiftly come to take for granted this new, improved 'second nature', at every stage. It is by no means clear that the path to this is by way of our being made strongly aware of the conventional character of the restraints which we had been under, hitherto; not least, because this may lead to their simple rejection, or to individual experimentation of a kind that leads us away from any shared conventions. The problem, it seems to me, with an 'emancipatory' approach, is that it loses sight of the real problem – of improving our conventions, institutions and habits, which can hardly be made fully transparent to all of us – and of the difficulties that are involved in this, given that, in many cases, we can well expect that the best we can achieve will be highly imperfect.

It could, of course, be the case that we are adversely affected by things which have become second nature to us, such that their simple abandonment is to the good. But there seems to me no reason to suppose that this is actually true. The kind of belief in Freud that is involved is itself problematic (in the sense that it is not clear that understanding does, in fact, liberate[20]), while there is a danger that the idea will be interpreted in a way that Freud himself avoided: as suggesting that a society can function without, or with only minimal, repression,[21] something which would have to be shown rather than presupposed. Similarly, the idea that the laws of economics would no longer bind once they were seen as a human product is itself false. It may, doubtless, be useful to understand that economic constraints are the products of the actions of ourselves and other people, and thus that they can, in principle, be changed. But at the same time, we would be foolish if we were not to appreciate that what we experience as constraints are, typically, the products of institutions that seem to be needed, if we are to be able to coordinate our activities with those of other people with whom we do not have face-to-face relationships.[22] At the very least, this suggests that we need to understand that the discovery of the conventional character of conventions will not necessarily mean that we would be well advised to 'liberate' ourselves from them, and, further, that an awareness of them as conventional may, in some circumstances, make it difficult for us to conduct ourselves in ways that are in the interest of all of us, or to improve on the conventions from which we start. While self-emancipation has its attractions, it also has its problems, as I hope that the ideas that I developed in the previous chapter may have made clear.

All told, my conclusion – at the end of this extremely brief engagement with the work of someone who in my judgement is, despite everything that I have said, easily the most significant living social philosopher – is that Habermas's criticisms of Popper are limited in their force. His early arguments from totality seem to me poor, and his hermeneutical arguments, while interesting, can, I believe, be met from within Popper's own work. I would, indeed, see significant parallels between their views, and possibilities for their mutual cross-fertilization. However, for reasons that I have indicated elsewhere in this volume, I would urge that the social democratic tendencies with the work of each of them be corrected in the light of issues that emerge from the work of Hayek.

TOWARDS A NORMATIVE SOCIOLOGY OF KNOWLEDGE

Popper is well known as a critic of the sociology of knowledge, although the perspective from which he writes – that sociologists of knowledge are typically not sufficiently aware of the inter-subjective character of knowledge, and of objectivity as a social product – is highly distinctive. More generally, one might say that, from Popper's perspective, what is wrong with the sociology of knowledge is that its devotees seem unwilling to accept the idea that different social practices may give rise to different kinds of knowledge, and that we may wish to exercise choice with respect to our social practices, in the light of what products we value.

To take such a view involves, of course, that one does not accept an epistemological relativism. This, to be sure, is itself a view that has been embraced by some proponents of the sociology of knowledge – such as the 'Edinburgh School' – but not, I believe, consistently. (One problem is that they oscillate between presenting their own view as a form of 'science', the procedures of which somehow they do not seem to see as requiring legitimation, and presenting the objects of their study – which could, in fact, also include their own activities – as being social practices, the products of which, epistemologically, are all seen as being on a par.[23]) It also requires that we can attain at least a degree of autonomy and self-awareness: that we may reflect upon our practices, and make adaptations to them, in the light of what outcomes we desire.[24]

From such a perspective, one may see our habits, customs and institutions as functioning as methodological rules: as exercising constraints over us, which may lead to epistemological products, and patterns of legitimation, of distinctive kinds. But it is open to us to investigate these, and to make changes to them in a piecemeal manner (albeit one which is tempered by our theoretical knowledge of what the consequences of some of these changes may be). Or investigations will themselves be piecemeal: we are, again, very much in one of Neurath's boats, making changes to some parts of our knowledge, while standing on others. We may also only become aware of presuppositions, and the consequences of particular practices, in a piecemeal manner. From this perspective, the critical rationalist can welcome critical investigations of all kinds, from those of the micro-sociologist to the post-structuralist, but interpret them as part of a continuing process in which we may discover assumptions which we may wish to challenge and to modify, once we are aware of their character. Critical rationalism is not dismayed by the idea that there may be such assumptions, just because it does not believe that we have access to 'pure' sources of knowledge, or that we can be sure that our current ideas do not involve mistaken assumptions which stand in need of criticism. But it does require that specific claims about such presuppositions – and their problematic character – be explicated, and that it then be debated how we might do better.

Critical rationalism will also, thus, lead us to a critical sociology of knowledge; it will lead us to look at the patterns of organization, accountability, funding and authority in the production of knowledge, and to ask: are these leading to the kind of results that we want? It is at the moment strange that these matters do not receive much scrutiny from the perspective that I am here suggesting, even when there may be misgivings about how things are working.[25] While when there is discussion of the funding and organization of the production of knowledge, it seems all too often to be based upon a stupid pragmatism of a kind that has learned nothing from prior discussions of these issues.[26] At the same time, the making of changes and improvements is clearly problematic, for exactly the reasons that we have discussed in connection with the problems facing Popper's ideas about social engineering, and Habermas's views, above, and one would need to address the problems which I have there discussed for such approaches to have much hope of success.

The final issue that I would like to raise in this context, and which clearly bears the mark of cross-fertilization from Habermas, relates to the notion of a public sphere.[27] In Popper's writings, much is made of criticism. But one may ask: where is this criticism to take place, and on what basis? The main lines of Popper's work suggest the importance of a certain kind of critical accountability. But on the face of it this is not something to which we are usually subjected, other than by people who may well not ask us particularly searching questions. Further, wealth, power and authority often enable those for whom such scrutiny is most pressing to escape it. From Popper's perspective, the need for such scrutiny holds pride of place; yet we cannot assume that it will simply occur because he has argued for it, or even if lots of people think that it is desirable. The maintenance and indeed the construction of a public sphere is of vital importance. We need to bear it in mind when we look, critically, at our various institutions; not least because there is every reason to suppose that people will try to avoid such scrutiny, if they can. Further, many decisions which we may wish to take for other reasons will have implications for the maintenance of a public sphere. For example, the multiplication of television channels through satellite and cable broadcasting may have the effect that notions of a shared culture of critical account-ability are weakened. We also seem to me to face a particularly serious problem, in that the most effective institutionalizations of a public forum seem, for all their defects, those which operate at a national level and, in particular, those associated with parliamen-tary institutions and the ramifications that the existence of these has for the national media in the countries in question. But at the moment we are experiencing forms of economic change which limit the effectiveness – and thus the accountability – of national institutions, while decision-making is showing signs of migrating to international institutions which are hardly subject to pressure from public critical scrutiny at all. How such issues are to be handled presents a difficult problem. The issues that I have raised in the criticism of Popper, relating to tradition, custom and the disaggregated character of individual decision-taking, are also relevant here, in that while accountability is important, there is much in our lives which must be local or particular and may not be able to face the full force of such scrutiny.

My suspicion is that there is no *general* solution to be found to these problems of accountability, and that there is perhaps nothing for it among those who value these things than to practise a kind of democratic vigilance concerning the public spheres upon which we may make an impact. This would involve the scrutiny of institutional change from the perspective of openness to criticism, while at the same time being on the look-out for, and ready to spot, those institutions which seem to work particularly well, and to discuss how they may be adapted to changes which may be taking place, or which we may wish to make for other very good reasons.

More generally, and within this framework of public account-ability to criticism, my preference would be for private rather than public approaches to problem-solving. First, they would allow more readily for the kind of experimentation which I have discussed in the previous chapter; experimentation of a kind that seems to me too dangerous to leave in public hands, where it can be forced upon people. Second, insofar as critical scrutiny can make for the better operation of enterprises, one would think that there would also be pressures towards it in the private sphere. As Adam Smith noted long ago, good management may be encouraged through the competitive pressure of others. Third, the private sphere typically has less legitimacy than government, so that, it seems to me, provided that we have an effective public forum, private initiatives can be held up to criticism more effectively in terms of their long-term deleterious effects than can the operations of government itself.

POPPER'S CRITIQUE OF ROMANTICISM

The final issue that I would like to discuss here relates to Popper's critique of romanticism. This has two aspects to it, both of which are important.

The first concerns Popper's stress on the social and cultural constitution of the self. Insofar as Popper is correct about this, it would seem to me that we need both to examine critically the culture that is playing this role and to cherish those aspects of it which need protecting. In this connection, it is particularly important that we look at this culture not as being 'ours', but at us as being 'its'. I am acutely aware, as I write, of the way in which I personally have been shaped in the course of my education and my subsequent experiences; of the way in which I have come to question so much of what I once believed, and by the way in which I would both hope and expect that this process will continue until I die. Much of what I have learned – not least, through my encounter with Popper and with his work – has consisted of the discovery of new and vast areas of exciting ignorance, of countless new things to be learned about and to be explored. Much else has involved the discovery of problems: of ways in which I have discovered that ideas that I had hoped were in order are not, and of the problematic character of so much that had initially presented itself as solid and secure.

The possibilities for such discovery and enrichment are endless. Indeed, one of the sad things about growing older is the realization of just how much there will be no time to explore. But at the same time, we may well find that what we encounter seems to us defective; for example, established views in some area may involve things which we believe to be incorrect, or to rest on assumptions which seem to us uncompelling. This points to the need for criticism. Indeed, that by which we may be formed represents not something static, but something that is in flux, within which there are, at any one time, numerous and significant disagreements, and with which we can interact.

However, what we will be interacting with critically is, in my view, best seen as a complex but common culture. If one believes

172

that there is something wrong with how things operate, this requires investigation and then, to the best of one's ability, critical engagement. In the course of this, one *may* well discover that one was wrong, or perhaps that while the things which seemed to one significant but neglected are indeed so, but the reason that they are neglected is that they are not realizable at the same time as are other things of even greater importance. If, however, it should turn out that we were right, then what we have done is to highlight some problem about a shared culture; and we may even be able to suggest ways in which the problem may also be solved, and thus how things might be improved.

All this, while it might seem trite, is of some importance in itself, and is also pertinent to issues that have been raised by feminists, by gay activists, and by members of – or those with a concern for – minority groups who have a distinctive cultural perspective.[28] For there seems to me a danger that these groups, rather than stressing their criticisms of, and the need for an accommodation with, a wider culture, have instead moved in the direction of cultural expressionism. A wider culture has been rejected as if it was the expression of others, and stress has been placed, instead, on the significance by these groups of the creation of a culture of their own. However, insofar as this strategy is pursued, not only does it seem to me to risk the cultural impoverishment of those who pursue it – insofar as their resources may be limited – but there is the danger, also, that one may reach a point where what is said by these groups will be so distinctive that it begins to lose its critical impact upon the wider culture. For insofar as human rights are themselves a cultural artefact – both the product of a shared culture and something that is extended to those who share it – there is a risk that a strategy of self-imposed marginalization, rather than of engagement with the wider culture, may be seriously counter-productive. At the very least, it may result in the production of demands, specific to one's own culture, which those who do not share it simply do not recognize. Yet this is a disaster, just in the sense that what, typically, is needed is a re-negotiation of inherited conventions that are shared within a wider culture, the defective character of which is typically most apparent to these very people. If they are not willing to face the genuine hardships involved in making the appropriate criticisms, in ways that can be comprehended by others, there is a danger that they may be disregarded and the opportunity for improvement lost. At the same time, there is an obvious obligation on the part of everyone else to welcome such criticism and to do everything possible to make it easy for others to advance it.

The other issue relates to our fallibility. This we need to take seriously, not just in respect of our institutional arrangements, but in respect of ourselves. Whether we wish it, we all stand in need of criticism, in respect of virtually everything we do. We need to take this into account in respect of our institutional arrangements. And we should not presume that we are correct in respect of any assumption we make, or any course of action we propose to take. (Of course, in many circumstances the gains to possible criticism, and the lack of interest to anyone else of most of what we are doing, may mean that there is no point in actually exposing our activities to criticism; and I have also discussed institutions in terms of which those aspects of our cultures and identities that may not be suitable for such scrutiny might be protected.)

The key issue, however, is to distinguish a recognition of our fallibility from timidity, a lack of competence, or culpability. Rather, we all need to be open to the need to make changes in respect of our institutions, our personal style, and indeed our personalities themselves. We need, in effect, to become people with characters that fit an open society. We thus need to adjust to life in such a setting not only our self-understanding and self-presentation, but also our expectations of others. We need to value not those who pretend – to themselves and to others – that they make no mistakes, but instead those who are open to learning from other people, who are competent, care for others, run through the appropriate checks in advance of acting, but who can also *happily* admit that they were wrong. This requires change not just at the level of personal attitude but at that of institutions and of culture. Yet what is required seems to me to point in a direction very different from the concern not to be 'judgemental', which is so common today. Rather, we need to develop a culture within which we can all *encourage* judgement and criticism from others, and as much as we can obtain, but at the same time to become the kind of person and to inhabit the kind of culture in which such criticism can be distinguished from a personal assault, and in which the giving and receiving of such criticism is seen as something positive.

More, however, is needed than just this. For while we are members of an open society, we will also (whether or not my specific suggestions about this are found acceptable) be members of smaller communities, with their own particular and distinctive cultures and patterns of interaction. How different such memberships are related to one another, and to membership of an open society and its distinctive culture, presents many and interesting further problems, towards some of which I hope that I may have made a contribution in this volume.

If there is something to my argument here, it suggests that we face further, and important, problems of social engineering: the reshaping of ourselves, and of many facets of our traditions and culture in the light of fallibilism, of life in an open society, and also of the problems of sustaining our more particular involvements and associations. Such problems arise at every level, from the practical to the theoretical. And they, together with the more specific challenges that speak to us from Popper's work, moral, practical and intellectual, suggest to me, at least, that we are to be lucky to be living at a time when things are so interesting and there is so much that is so challenging to be done.

CONCLUSION

In this volume, I have discussed Popper's work in political philosophy and some issues concerning its interpretation. I have also raised some problems about it. At the end of the previous chapter, I offered some speculations about how these problems might be resolved. In this chapter, I have offered some very broad suggestions about differences between the views that seem to me suggested by Popper's work, and some ideas that are currently fashionable. I would not, however, wish this volume to conclude with that material just because, for good or ill, the ideas are my own rather than Popper's, and they are highly speculative. It would seem to me more to the point if I were to conclude by reaffirming some points about the importance of Popper's work.

Much of contemporary politics in democratic countries consists of attempts at what Popper would call piecemeal social engineering. Yet it is not informed by his awareness of our fallibilism (where fallibility is, emphatically, shared as much by those in political office as by public servants), and of the need for critical assessment as to whether, in fact, political initiatives have achieved what was wanted. More generally, we typically do not even take seriously the idea that our actions will have unintended consequences, and thus the need for critical feedback from all citizens.

During the course of this volume, I have offered some criticisms of Popper's ideas about our ability to form a consensus as to what are the most pressing cases for governmental activity – as to what, as it were, is most urgently in need of relief. However, in my view it would nevertheless be salutary if we were to look at government activities and expenditure from such a perspective, and to question very hard why funds were going elsewhere, when urgent suffering went unrelieved. (In making this point, I am not suggesting that there may not be a good case for expenditure on other matters; only that this would be a useful exercise for us to go through. Further, and this is an important consequence of the argument that I have offered in the present volume, just because something is even a terrible problem does not mean that we will be able to solve it. I suspect, for example, that some of the problems posed for Aboriginal peoples who have had Western society thrust, unwanted, upon them may be of this character.)

Popper's idea of openness to criticism also seems to me of the greatest practical importance. Our political institutions are often woefully under-equipped to perform such a function, while too much governmental activity – notably, interrelationships between government and interest groups, and the activities of policy-making communities – is not subject to genuinely public scrutiny at all. As I have argued earlier, the whole issue of the reconstruction of a public sphere, in the sense of a forum within which such activities are opened to scrutiny, seems to me particularly pressing.

These are among the practical issues that arise from Popper's work. But there are many important theoretical issues, too. I do not know whether, in the end, Popper's ideas in the theory of knowledge will be viable. But they certainly seem to me worthy of more intensive exploration than they are currently receiving, not least because they suggest a possibility that looks particularly attractive. For Popper, as I have suggested above, offers us a path between dogmatism and relativism, and a view which does not claim that there are foundations to knowledge, but which nonetheless offers us the possibility of progress. Popper's fallibilism also seems to me attractive. For as I have argued, his approach is radically anti-authoritarian. On his account, there are no authorities, in the sense of people whose claims to knowledge are beyond the need for critical scrutiny. And the claim that something is true, or that some standard or moral judgement is correct, opens up the person making it to just such scrutiny.

These ideas also suggest that we should scrutinize our existing institutional arrangements and practices, to see if they are compatible with such criticism and, more generally, to see if the incentive structures and patterns of accountability within them lead to the kinds of product that we actually want, including those in the field of knowledge. There is also the question of how our existing patterns of decision-making relate to the urgent task of the maintenance and reconstruction of a public sphere.

Popper's ideas, however, also seem to me to have important consequences for our 'selves'. The ideas which I have discussed in Chapter 5 have an important consequence in this field, which deserves to be drawn out explicitly. It is that, as selves, we are cultural amphibians. We have to live, in part, in the specific culture or cultures, with their local restrictions, which serve to give us our specific character and identity. While in part we live in the wider liberal culture of an open society. It is no mean task to construct a self – a cultural identity – which can handle these issues. But this is a task which we need to be able to accomplish, and in which it is important that we get as much assistance as possible from the culture into which we are socialized. There is, however, more to be achieved even than this. For at the heart of Popper's work there is his fallibilism, and his stress upon our need to learn from others. Yet, while this is so important, it is something that we typically find difficult. At every turn, we tend to pretend to have knowledge that we do not have, and we do not want the critical input from others that we so much need.

All this serves to highlight one of the most interesting tasks that flows from Popper's work: the idea that we may need to reconstruct our institutions, our culture, and indeed, our 'selves', so that we can thrive within an open society. We need both to live within an open society, and to develop a culture – and selves – which can relish the openness, fallibility and learning from others that this involves. At the same time, we need to partake, too, of the specific conventions and local practices which not only go to make up our more specific personalities, but which also give social interaction much of its interest.

These, to say the least, are interesting and challenging tasks, and ones to which, in our different ways, all of us may make our contribution. It is even possible that, in the terms of Popper's closing words from his autobiography, we might find that, in struggling with these ideas, we may find more happiness than we too could ever deserve.

NOTES

INTRODUCTION

1 It was also, clearly, Popper's view of Lakatos's interpretation of his own work. In writing this I have in mind not only Popper's response to Lakatos in 'The Library of Living Philosophers' (in P.A. Schilpp (ed.) *The Philosophy of Karl Popper*, La Salle: Open Court, 1974), but also an earlier version which I saw while working for Popper, in which he explicitly drew a parallel between what he was writing and Kant's response to Fichte.

2 Lest this seems all too confusing, my argument will be that: (i) Popper's early critique of 'essentialism' would seem in conflict with some aspects of the realism that he later espoused; (ii) that until after both Tarski and the ideas that he developed in his *Postscript* about the criticizability of metaphysics, while he was a realist, he was unhappy about espousing it in the public forum.

3 See *Objective Knowledge*, p. 40, with which one might usefully contrast his discussion of Whitehead in *The Open Society*.

4 See note 37 to Chapter 1, below.

5 Russell Jacoby, *The Last Intellectuals*, New York: Basic Books, 1987.

6 I have in mind here, especially, the consequences of the role of policy-making communities in the detailed development of public policy in areas such as health.

7 See *The Open Society*, note 21 to chapter 24. (*N.B.*: Unless otherwise indicated, all references to *The Open Society* are to the fifth revised edition of 1966.)

8 Popper's opening comment in the published version of 'Normal Science and its Dangers' (I. Lakatos and A. Musgrave (eds) *Criticism and the Growth of Knowledge*, Cambridge: Cambridge University Press, 1970, p. 51) was: 'Professor Kuhn's criticism of my views about science is the most interesting one I have so far come across.' Compare, on this, Ian Jarvie's 'Popper's Conception of the Social', *Revista Mexicana de Ciencias Políticas y Sociales*, 1995; it has also been discussed by Joseph Agassi in *The Philosopher's Apprentice*, Amsterdam: Rodolpi, 1993. My own suspicion is that Popper was no more than being (over-)polite to Kuhn and that Jarvie and Agassi are reading

too much into his comment. At the same time, it seems to me that Kuhn's work raises an issue of real significance for Popper's work, as I suggest in the text. On these issues, see also Jarvie's article referred to above; Bartley's *Unfathomed Knowledge*, La Salle: Open Court, 1990, and also my 'Epistemology Socialized', *et cetera*, Fall 1985.

9 See *The Myth of the Framework*, p. 107.
10 *Ibid.*
11 *Ibid.*, pp. 107–8.
12 Popper, however, also argued powerfully that even day-to-day science *could* have a non-routine character.
13 See his contribution to I. Lakatos and A. Musgrave (eds) *Criticism and the Growth of Knowledge*, Cambridge: Cambridge University Press, 1970, and his responses to Kuhn and to Wisdom in *The Philosophy of Karl Popper*.
14 Now in *The Myth of the Framework*.
15 See *The Open Society*, volume 2, p. 218.
16 'Towards a Rational Theory of Tradition', in *Conjectures and Refutations*, pp. 121–2.
17 *Ibid.*, p. 122.
18 See, for an example, D. Hobbs, *Doing the Business*, Oxford: Oxford University Press, 1986; and, for discussion, P. Edwards and J. Shearmur, 'Street Level Jurisprudence', delivered at American Political Science Association, Chicago, 1992.
19 See M. Lipsky, *Street-Level Bureaucracy*, New York: Russell Sage, 1980 and, for some useful discussion, C. Ham and M. Hill, *The Policy Process in the Modern Capitalist State*, Brighton: Wheatsheaf, 1984.
20 See *The Open Society*, chapter 3, p. 23.
21 In this respect, Geoff Stokes's emphasis in his 'Politics, Epistemology and Method', *Political Studies* 43, No. 1, March 1955, pp. 105–23, on the key role played by Popper's ideas about human nature seems to me open to objection.
22 If the more libertarian among my readers are concerned about the term 'engineering' here, and if what I say in my text does not reassure them, they might think about these matters in the following terms. Consider, say, Jane Jacobs's discussion of what makes for a good – as opposed to a bad – city locale, in *The Death and Life of Great American Cities*, New York: Vintage Books, 1961. It is, say, open to those people who would like to live in the kind of city setting that she describes as successful, to accept that its production might have to be understood as the result of a form of social engineering, in the sense that Popper describes. That is to say, it would typically involve a form of learning by trial and error, in which changes are made, by those to whom this task is entrusted, to the rules and regulations on the basis of which citizens conduct themselves, with the aim of reaching an outcome that those involved wished to achieve, but which they were not themselves able to bring about directly.
23 See, for example, Elihan Goldratt and Jeff Cox, *The Goal: A Process of Ongoing Improvement*, Croton-on-Hudson, NY: North River Press, 1987, and Robert J. Kriegel, *If It Ain't Broke – Break It*, New York:

Warner, 1991. My colleague David Adams has also drawn to my attention Charles Heckscher's 'Defining the Post-Bureaucratic Type', in Charles Heckscher and Anne Donnellon (eds) *The Post-Bureaucratic Organization*, Thousand Oaks, CA: Sage, 1994, pp. 14–61, which would seem in part to be dealing with similar approaches.

24 If this is not well known to any of my readers, may I recommend my 'Political Thought of F.A. von Hayek', University of London PhD dissertation, 1987? I am not claiming that Hayek's work is the origin of these developments; rather, that they are usefully to be understood in relation to points that he has made. See also, for a most suggestive discussion, Richard Cornuelle, 'The Power and Poverty of Libertarian Thought', *Critical Review* 6, No. 1, Winter 1992, pp. 1–10.

25 My understanding of these issues has benefited from discussion of the application of market-based management in a non-profit setting, at the Institute for Humane Studies, George Mason University, during 1991–2.

26 There is here, clearly, a whiff of Hegel's discussion of the relations between master and slave. At the same time, the positive effect might well depend on the institution's limit in its scope. For there are training programmes and other forms of 'total' institutional conduct – such as those which used to be used on Army recruits, and procedures in hospitals and retirement homes – in which the person's independent identity can be almost completely destroyed, rather than accorded an opportunity to develop, by regimes which are also oppressive in the old-fashioned sense.

27 See *The Open Society*, chapter 21, p. 193.

28 *Ibid.* See, in Popper's account of the problem to which I referred at the start of this paragraph, the interpolation 'especially of any direct intervention', which suggests that his preferred form of (institutional) action might be less problematic.

29 See *The Open Society*, chapter 17, p. 132.

30 See, on this, my 'Religious Sect as a Cognitive System', *Annual Review of the Social Sciences of Religion* 4, 1980, pp. 149–63.

31 And aside from medical science taking the problem of obesity seriously, and offering remedies, rather than unhelpful comments which seem to me the equivalent of suggesting that a goal that pertains to an emergent product which is the result of a complex of factors – as indicated in the text – can be pursued directly.

32 I am, in fact, unhappy about according *any* role to the state at all, and would prefer it if such tasks as I here mention could be undertaken by other bodies. I am also acutely aware of the fact that I have here offered (and will, in Chapter 5, expand upon) a wish-list as to functions which I suggest need to be performed, without providing an account, the production of which is incumbent upon anyone who makes any such suggestion, explaining *how* such functions are to be performed. All that I can plead here is that such a task could not be accomplished lightly, and that even a first attempt would not be appropriate in a volume that has, as its main concern, the discussion of the work of another figure.

1 THE DEVELOPMENT OF POPPER'S POLITICAL PHILOSOPHY

1 W. W. Bartley, 'Rehearsing a Revolution: Karl Popper: A Life; selection entitled Music and Politics', written for Mont Pelerin Society, 1989.

2 M. Hacohen, *The Making of the Open Society*, Columbia University PhD dissertation, 1994.

3 *Unended Quest*, p. 39.

4 Compare, for some discussion, my 'Political Thought of F.A. von Hayek' and my *Hayek and After* London and New York: Routledge, 1996.

5 See Popper, *op. cit.*, p. 32, and Bartley, *op. cit.*, p. 27.

6 Popper, *op. cit.*, p. 33, and Bartley, *op. cit.*, p. 32.

7 Bartley, *op. cit.*, p. 34.

8 See Bartley, *op. cit.*, pp. 47–9. Bartley argues that, rather than a demonstration, what took place was in fact part of an attempted coup.

9 See Bartley, *op. cit.*, p. 32, in which connection he refers to an early draft of Popper's autobiography.

10 See Popper to Hayek, 14 March 1944 (Popper Archive 305–13).

11 Compare *Unended Quest*, pp. 39ff., and also Bartley, *op. cit.*, p. 27.

12 Compare *Unended Quest* and also *The Self and Its Brain*. See, for discussion, W. Berkson and J. Wettersten, *Learning from Error*, La Salle, IL: Open Court, 1984; J. Wettersten, *The Roots of Critical Rationalism*, Amsterdam: Rodolpi, 1992; Hacohen, *op. cit.*, and also Bartley's 'The Theory of Language and Philosophy of Science as Instruments of Educational Reform: Wittgenstein and Popper as Austrian Schoolteachers', in R. Cohen and M. Wartofski (eds) *Methodological and Historical Essays in the Natural and Social Sciences*, Dordrecht: Reidel, 1974.

13 *Ratio* 4, 1962, pp. 2–10.

14 See *Unended Quest*, pp. 20–1; 74–5; 81–3.

15 See *Unended Quest* and *Conjectures and Refutations*, chapter 1; but compare Hacohen for a different interpretation.

16 See *Unended Quest*, pp. 89–90.

17 Compare Hacohen for some suggestions about the possible role of Neurath as a target for Popper's writings on historicism.

18 Compare Popper's introductory remarks to Ayer's public lecture, 'Man as a Subject for Science' (Popper Archive 101–13).

19 See his 'Response Upon Receiving the Award of the Fondation Tocqueville', 29/10/84 (Popper Archive 253–3, p. 1). He also makes other self-deprecating remarks about his knowledge of the literature in the field.

20 See Bartley's paper cited in note 12; but compare also Popper's letters to Gerschenkron of 24 August 1974 (Popper Archive 298–31) and to Hargrove of 28 February 1975 (Popper Archive 304–9), for some critical commentary.

21 See Popper to Hayek, 15 November 1943 (Popper Archive 305–13); also the book edition of *The Poverty of Historicism*, p. iv, and *Unended Quest*, section 24.

22 Popper Archive 300–14.
23 Compare Popper to Carnap, 25 April 1946 (Popper Archive 282–24), where Popper refers to having seen Hayek only four or five times.
24 See Hayek to Popper, 1 December 1980 (Popper Archive 305–17), which refers to and cites a passage from the 'Introduction' to F.A. Hayek (ed.) *Collectivist Economic Planning*, London: Routledge, 1935, p. 10.
25 F.A. Hayek, *The Road to Serfdom*, London: Routledge, 1944.
26 See A.J. Harrop to Popper, 2 January 1936 (Popper Archive 366–3).
27 See Colin Simkin, *Popper's Views on Natural and Social Science*, Leiden and New York: E.J. Brill, 1993.
28 See Bartley (note 1 above), p. 8.
29 Compare, on this, the letter from Hennie Popper to the Gombrichs of 29 July 1943 (Popper Archive 300–2). Popper also gives a breakdown of his budget, in his letter to Hellin of 29 June 1943, in order to stress the opportunity cost of (unanswered) cables to the USA.
30 Material relating to both activities is to be found in the Popper Archives.
31 *Unended Quest*, p. 113.
32 See, on all this, the historical note to *The Open Society; Unended Quest*, p. 117; Popper to Larsen, 23 August 1945 (Popper Archive 319–1); and Popper to Hayek, 15 November 1943 and 14 March 1944 (Popper Archive 305–13).
33 See Popper to Carnap, 31 March 1943 (Popper Archive 282–24).
34 Popper, it might be noted, took his interpretation of Plato seriously, and responded to his critics; cp., in this connection, his letter to Robinson of 14 November 1952 (Popper Archive 342–50), in which he also refers to a detailed critical response from Mabbot.
35 One striking example is to be found in Charles Taylor's 'The Poverty of the Poverty of Historicism', *Universities and Left Review*, Summer 1958, pp. 77–8. Taylor there claims: 'Popper is giving a statement of a widely held political view ... It is the view of liberal non-interventionism, the apology for an utterly negative view of freedom.' That this is incorrect will be clear enough from the present work; but it should have been glaringly obvious to any reader of *The Open Society*, a book which, Taylor says, 'should be read by all who are interested in political philosophy'. The context in which Taylor commends it makes it clear that he considers Popper's book to be an important example of a particular kind of ideological political theory. Taylor's article itself seems to me a striking example of how an intelligent man, who is clearly reading material carefully, can nonetheless *utterly* misunderstand its political character.
36 See also my 'Epistemological Limits of the State', *Political Studies*, 1990, and my 'The *Positivismusstreit* revisited', delivered at the Australasian Political Studies Association, Monash, 1993.
37 Compare *The Open Society*, chapter 25, and his 'Emancipation Through Knowledge'.
38 See, for example, Popper to Hellin, 29 June 1943 (Popper Archive

28–7) where, in the course of describing the book, Popper writes: 'the analysis is in nearly every case carried to a depths [*sic*] which need not shirk any comparison, although the terminology and the presentation is so simple and unimposing that superficial critics will surely complain about superficiality'. He continues, it might be noted, to disclaim any originality for the philosophical attitude expressed in the book.

39 Compare Popper to Hellin, 29 June 1943: 'I consider the destruction of the awe of the Great Names, the Great Intellectual Authorities, one of the necessary pre-requisites for a recuperation of mankind.'

40 The whole sad story can be traced through the Popper Archives. Compare, for example, the letter to Hellin, cited in note 38.

41 Compare Popper to Hayek, 1 June 1944 (Popper Archive 305–13); one finds the same themes by tracing Hayek's name in the index. (But, in pursuing such concerns, one must note the differences between the first and later editions of Popper's book, where the latter show evidence of revisions in the light of Popper's reading of Hayek's work.) It is also striking that, in this letter, Popper indicates that he will be toning down his 'unfair denunciation' of *laissez-faire* and its apologists, which he did in later editions.

42 See, on this, my 'Political Thought of F.A. von Hayek'. By what I have said in the text, I do not mean that Popper does not discuss the idea, and suggest that it is important. It is, rather, that he considers that it is an important piece of knowledge which social engineers need to possess about the limitations of their abilities. For Hayek, it was – at least in my view – the centre of his distinctive social philosophy.

43 Popper to Gombrich, 5 June 1944 (Popper Archive 300–3).

44 25 April 1946.

45 This would seem to be true enough if taken to refer to Hayek's social philosophy, although it is possibly a slight exaggeration if interpreted literally, in the light of the fact that Popper refers, in the original text of *The Open Society*, also to 'Scientism and the Study of Society', and 'The Counter-Revolution of Science'. (I am also not sure if Popper was, in making such statements, distinguishing between the text and the notes of the book.) In addition, in the first part of *The Poverty of Historicism*, Popper refers to Hayek's Inaugural Address at the LSE and there are also references to some of Hayek's other papers (e.g. his contributions to *Collectivist Economic Planning*, and his paper in *Ethics* of 1943), in the last two parts of *The Poverty*. These, however, were rewritten by Popper when he knew that the paper was to appear in Hayek's journal, so it is difficult to judge what role they might have had in the development of Popper's thought. In *The Open Society*, Popper also refers to Hayek in connection with the 'pure logic of choice'. He does not indicate a source for this, and it is possible that it might refer to Hayek's characterization of Mises's approach to economics, in these terms, in the context of Hayek's own critical discussion of Mises's work, in his 'Economics and Knowledge'.

46 25 April 1946.

47 Compare Popper to Gombrich, 8 August 1944 (Popper Archive 300–3).
48 See Popper to Hayek, 28 May 1944 (Popper Archive 305–13).
49 Compare Popper to Hayek, 28 May 1944 (Popper Archive 305–13).
50 Compare also my 'Popper, Hayek and Classical Liberalism', *The Freeman*, February 1989.
51 Compare his letter to Hayek on 6 May 1946, commenting on this as it arises in Hayek's 'Individualism: True and False' (1946) – subsequently included in F.A. Hayek, *Individualism and Economic Order*, London: Routledge, 1948 – although Hayek seems to have reassured him (see Popper to Hayek, 22 May 1946 (Hayek Archive 44–1)).
52 See Popper to Dahrendorf, 28 August 1977 (Popper Archive 287–5).
53 See Hayek to Popper, 28 December 1946 (Popper Archive, 305–13).
54 See Popper to Hayek, 11 January 1947; the idea that there should be such a *rapprochement* in fact goes back to Popper's letter to Hayek of 15 March 1944 (Popper Archive 305–13).
55 Carnap to Popper, 17 November 1946 (Popper Archive 282–24).
56 6 January 1946.
57 See 'Freedom: A Balance Sheet' (Popper Archive 49–22, pp. 10–11). (The date of the original lecture is not indicated; but his theme of the achievement of Western societies seems to me reminiscent of papers from the 1950s, such as 'A History of Our Time'.)
58 *Ibid.*, p. 11. Compare also, for similar sentiments, Popper's 'Preface to the [second] Italian Edition' of *The Poverty of Historicism* (Popper Archive 298–34).
59 See Popper to Berlin, 17 February 1959; Popper Archive 276–10.
60 Compare, for example, Chandran Kukathas, 'Defending Negative Liberty', *Policy* 10, No. 2, Winter 1994, pp. 22–6.
61 Popper Archive 305–15.
62 F.A. Hayek, *The Constitution of Liberty*, London: Routledge, 1960, p. 15.
63 Popper Archive 39–17. While it is undated, there seem reasons to suppose that it was written shortly after the publication of *The Open Society*, not only because of its content, but because Popper mentioned to Gombrich that it was a paper which he was planning to write, in a letter of 24 October 1944 (Popper Archive 300–3).
64 Popper to Hayek, 15 March 1944; compare also Popper to Hayek, 28 May 1944 (Popper Archive 305–13).
65 Although Hayek clearly felt that Popper had not given *The Sensory Order* (London: Routledge, 1952) the attention that it deserved. See Hayek to Weimer, 16 January 1983 (Hayek Archives 57–22), Hoover Institution. My own suspicion is that Popper felt that the criticisms he had offered in the letters he sent to Hayek on this topic were sufficient.
66 F.A. Hayek, *Law, Legislation and Liberty*, London: Routledge, 1973–9.
67 See Popper to Hayek, 28 May 1944 (Popper Archive 305–13). It is clear, however, that Hayek did not consistently espouse the view that Popper is here criticizing, and that in many places his views seem

identical to Popper's. See, on this, my 'Political Thought of F.A. von Hayek' and my *Hayek and After*.

68 See Popper to Hayek, 28 May 1944 (Popper Archive 305–13) and 6 May 1946 (Hayek Archive 44–1).

69 Compare Hayek to Weimer, 16 January 1983.

70 *Unended Quest*, p. 35.

71 Popper, 'Response upon Receiving the Award of the Fondation Tocqueville' (Popper Archive 253–3), pp. 8–9.

72 Popper Archive 322–16. The (handwritten) letter is undated, but a partially typed version also exists, dated 12 March 1974. (For 'Modern Masters' see Bryan Magee, *Popper*, London: Fontana, 1973.)

2 *THE OPEN SOCIETY* AND *THE POVERTY OF HISTORICISM*

1 Compare A. Koestler and others, *The God that Failed*, London: H. Hamilton, 1950, and L. Althusser, *The Future Lasts a Long Time and the Facts*, London: Vintage, 1993.

2 See Ryzand Kapuscinski's brief account in 'The Philosopher as Giant-Slayer', *New York Times Magazine*, 1 January 1995, pp. 24–5.

3 It was, clearly, Popper's concern for social relevance which was responsible for why he discussed what he did, in respect to Marx. I would be the last person to say that the early writings of Marx are uninteresting (although, at the same time, I would find it difficult to understand how someone could maintain the truth of the theoretical perspective from which they were written). But criticism of Popper's work for not discussing them, given the time and place at which he was writing, and that he was addressing views which were of then-contemporary political significance, seems to me misplaced.

4 For the relation of this to his understanding of historicism, see Popper's discussion of music in his *Unended Quest*.

5 Compare, in this context, the continuing work of Malachi Hacohen.

6 I have frequently been struck by parallels between his work and that of Robert Goodin.

7 On the methodology of social science and social theory, see *The Poverty of Historicism* and *The Open Society*; on the theory of explanation, see also his 'Prediction and Prophecy'; on moral futurism, see *The Open Society*, and for the parallel argument in aesthetics, his *Unended Quest*.

8 See, on this, *The Poverty of Historicism*, and 'Prediction and Prophecy' in *Conjectuires and Refutations*.

9 Compare Hayek's *The Road to Serfdom* and his *Scientism and the Study of Society*.

10 See *The Open Society*, volume 1, p. 161, and also *Conjectures and Refutations*, p. 359. The argument is close to one which Hayek develops in *The Road to Serfdom*.

11 See 'Prediction and Prophecy', in Popper's *Conjectures and Refutations*.

12 'Prediction and Prophecy', in *Conjectures and Refutations*, p. 343.

13 See, in this connection, Chapters 3 and 4.

14 See *The Open Society*, volume 1, p. 285, note 3. Compare also *The Poverty of Historicism*, p. 68: '. . . the difference between Utopian and piecemeal engineering turns out, in practice, to be a difference not so much in scale and scope as in caution and preparedness for unavoidable surprises.'

15 See my discussion in Chapter 1

16 *The Open Society*, chapter 3, p. 32.

17 *The Open Society*, volume 2, chapter 11, note 54.

18 *The Open Society*, chapter 25, note 7.

19 *Ibid.*

20 See Chapter 4.

21 See, notably, his 'Three Views Concerning Human Knowledge', and his *Postscript*.

22 Popper, *The Poverty of Historicism*, p. 56, quoting Hayek, in *Economica* 13, 1933, p. 122.

23 See *The Poverty of Historicism*, p. 35.

24 *The Poverty of Historicism*, p. 20.

25 *The Poverty of Historicism*, pp. 56–7; Popper presents a further defence of such a view in section 20.

26 See *The Open Society*, chapter 9, note 7(3), pp. 290–1. I might mention that Popper himself objected to Rush Rhees's interpretation of his views on social science as different in this respect from his views on natural science, in Rhees's 'Social Engineering'; cp. his *Without Answers*, London: Routledge, 1969. (See Popper's unpublished response, 'Social Institutions and Personal Responsibility'. Popper Archive 36–22, p. 15.) Popper argues, rather, that his concern was with the idea that the theoretical social sciences might benefit from paying attention to practical problems as, indeed, he had suggested that the natural sciences had done. All that I can say is that this is not the impression that was given to me by what Popper wrote, and that if Popper did intend this, his view of natural science at the time at which he wrote *The Open Society* would be more instrumentalistic than I had supposed. If that is the case, I would then offer the same criticism of the views that he held then about the natural sciences, as well as of the social sciences, in Chapter 5 below. It is just possible that Rhees was wishing to make critical points similar to those that I make in that chapter. But I must confess that I find Rhees's views in this piece so difficult to understand as expressing a single, coherent line of argument, that I cannot be sure whether this is the case.

27 See F.A. Hayek, 'The Trend of Economic Thinking', in *The Trend of Economic Thinking*. See also, for some discussion, my 'Political Thought of F.A. von Hayek' and *Hayek and After*.

28 There are, perhaps, some signs of Popper's openness to such argument; compare, say, 'A Pluralist Approach to the Philosophy of History' and 'Epistemology and Industrialization' in *The Myth of the Framework*.

29 *The Open Society*, volume 1, note 20 to chapter 6, pp. 256–7.

30 I have benefited here greatly from discussion at a workshop on Ethics and Economics held at the University of Sydney in December 1994.

31 This, in turn, relates to an issue that goes back, within 'Kantian' approaches to these issues, at least to Rousseau's *Social Contract*! For there he discusses our transition from a state-of-nature situation into a political community, without addressing what would seem to be the crucial question as to which political community people enter; crucial, because the character of the general will would seem to be different, depending on who comprises the community.

32 Compare, on this issue, Robert Goodin's *Protecting the Vulnerable*, Chicago: University of Chicago Press, 1985, and *Reasons for Welfare*, Princeton, NJ: Princeton University Press, 1988, but see also Robert Goodin, 'What is so special about our fellow countrymen?', *Ethics* 98, July 1988, pp. 663–86, and Henry Shue, 'Mediating Duties', *Ethics* 98, July 1988, pp. 687–704.

33 *The Open Society*, chapter 21.

34 *The Open Society*, chapter 9, note 4.

35 *The Open Society*, chapter 6, p. 109.

36 *The Open Society*, chapter 6, text to note 42.

37 *The Open Society*, chapter 17, p. 124.

38 *The Open Society*, chapter 7, p. 123.

39 *The Open Society*, chapter 7, note 4.

40 *The Open Society*, chapter 16, note 10.

41 *The Open Society*, chapter 20, note 26.

42 See, on this, *The Open Society*, chapter 17, p. 124; compare also pp. 117 and 122.

43 Popper interprets bad social conditions as being the result of exploitation. For an alternative argument, compare F.A. Hayek (ed.) *Capitalism and the Historians*, London: Routledge, 1954; and M. Hartwell and others, *The Long Debate on Poverty*, London: Institute of Economic Affairs, 1972.

44 *The Open Society*, chapter 17, p. 122.

45 *The Open Society*, chapter 17, pp. 124–5.

46 *The Open Society*, chapter 17, p. 125.

47 *The Open Society*, chapter 17, p. 126. Popper also seems to have in mind counter-cyclic policy, aimed at the relief of unemployment. In the *first* edition of *The Open Society*, he states (chapter 17, p. 122) that: 'The two most concrete and most urgent tasks of economic inter-ventionism or piecemeal engineering at present are protection against exploitation, and measures against unemployment, such as control of the trade cycle.' In later editions, the passage – and the reference to this topic – is dropped, but that Popper expected that such policy would be pursued would seem clear from his discussion in chapter 20, pp. 181–2 and in chapter 21.

48 *The Open Society*, chapter 17, pp. 126–7.

49 See *The Open Society*, chapter 16, note 10, and chapter 20, note 26.

50 *The Open Society*, chapter 7, p. 126.

51 *The Open Society*, chapter 17, section VII, is not to be found in the first

edition; in section VII, note 29, Popper refers to Hayek's discussion of the distinction, in *The Road to Serfdom*. The points that Popper takes up are central to Hayek's work, although Popper's treatment of them – e.g. in his discussion of piecemeal social engineering – is sometimes different from Hayek's.

52 *The Open Society*, chapter 17, pp. 132–3.

53 For our present purposes, what matters is that such rights were taken to be morally valid claims, the validity of which could be recognized by all reasonable people, rather than that from which such rights are supposed to be derived.

54 *The Open Society*, chapter 19, pp. 161–2.

55 In putting things in this way, I am not wishing to disregard wider issues about social consequences. Rather, I would take claims about these to require, for their assessment, disaggregation into what their admission would mean for those upon whose actions their accomplishment would be dependent.

56 I am not, here, suggesting that all social issues should be discussed in terms of rights – something which seems to me a widely shared intellectual error of our day – but, rather, that the kind of argument that is involved in such an approach is useful, in respect of the particular issue being discussed in the text.

57 I will not do it here, but it seems to me that if one were to list all the things that Popper commends to us, at various places, one might find that they add up to a list which has shades of Borges's story about the Chinese encyclopaedia.

58 See, on this, *The Open Society*, chapter 17, pp. 122–3 – something the avoidance of which, on the face of it, is the moral responsibility of their parents or guardians.

59 See *The Open Society*, chapter 12, page 94.

60 *The Open Society*, chapter 23, p. 222.

61 *The Open Society*, chapter 5, p. 67.

62 See *The Poverty of Historicism*, section 26, in which connection Popper also refers, on the final point, to the discussion in *The Logic of Scientific Discovery*.

63 *The Open Society*, chapter 5, p. 68.

64 I am uneasy about such terminology, because it is suggestive of an account of human behaviour in which there are 'norms' which are socially shared. I would certainly agree that there are shared social practices, and typical patterns of behaviour within which people partake in specific institutions. Further, while I would follow both Adam Smith and Popper in the view that the self is socially constituted, I am sceptical of any account which claims that *the same* understanding of such practices is shared by all participants in such things.

65 *The Open Society*, chapter 14, p. 93.

66 I have in mind the argument that 'Keynesian' ideas worked because – and for as long as – economic agents did not adjust their wage and other demands in the light of the anticipated consequences of increased, unfunded, government spending.

67 See Robert Nozick, *Anarchy, State and Utopia*, Oxford: Blackwell, 1974.

68 See, on this, both *The Poverty of Historicism* and *The Open Society*, and also his 'Models, Instruments and Truth' and 'A Pluralist Approach to the Philosophy of History' in *The Myth of the Framework*.

69 This seemed to me most noticeable in respect of his discussions about historical explanation, in which connection his argument in 'Models, Instruments and Truth' might seem, on the face of it, a significant (but not total) retreat from his earlier ideas on the role of universal laws in historical explanation.

70 *The Open Society*, chapter 10, p. 186. Popper also quotes similar sentiments from Burke, in a motto to volume 1 of *The Open Society*, which I quote, in turn, in Chapter 5, but for which he does not give a source.

71 *The Open Society*, chapter 17, p. 127.

72 *The Open Society*, chapter 18, note 4.

73 *The Open Society*, chapter 17, pp. 130–1.

74 *The Open Society*, chapter 21, p. 193.

75 *The Open Society*, chapter 21, pp. 193–4.

76 See, on this, *The Open Society* chapter 25, and also Popper's 'The Bucket and the Searchlight' in *Objective Knowledge*.

77 I will not discuss Popper's ideas about the 'empirical basis' of knowledge here, other than to say that he offers a complex story, in which we can learn by opening our ideas to inter-subjective scrutiny, making sure that they are testable in terms of claims about the behaviour of publicly accessible objects, and deliberately setting out to conduct our exchanges with people who share views different from our own, in the simplest and clearest possible terms. Testability, and more generally rationality, are, for Popper, *artefacts*. (His complaints about the obscurity of the language of some of those with whom he has disagreed are, it seems to me, to be understood in the context of this theory: his claim is, literally, that unless we conduct ourselves in ways that may not come naturally to us, the rational assessment of our views cannot be undertaken.) See, on all this, Popper's discussion of the 'empirical basis' in *The Logic of Scientific Discovery*, and *The Open Society*, chapter 23, and, for further discussion of some of these issues, Chapter 6 in this volume.

78 See *The Open Society*, chapter 25, p. 261.

79 Compare, however, our earlier discussion of the way in which Popper's views have shifted on this point.

80 See, on this, *The Open Society*, chapter 25, and also *The Poverty of Historicism*, section 30.

81 *The Open Society*, chapter 25, p. 266.

82 *The Open Society*, chapter 25, pp. 266–7. Popper surely exaggerates the extent to which such pre-selection from a point of view will mean that such evidence cannot be used to evaluate other theories; but his general point about the consequences of the limitations of evidence holds good here. (Indeed, compare also Chapter 5, for an argument that his own scientific realism faces a similar problem.)

83 *The Open Society*, p. 266.
84 Popper in *The Poverty of Historicism*, section 30, refers to Weber's views, but it seems to me that he did not see just how close they, in some ways, are. Compare, notably, Weber's *Roscher and Knies*, tr. G. Oakes, New York: Free Press, 1975, and B.T. Wilkins, *Has History any Meaning?*, Hassocks, Sussex: Harvester Press, 1978, which also raises many interesting points about Popper's views about history.
85 *The Open Society*, chapter 25, p. 270.
86 Compare Hegel's *Lectures on the Philosophy of History: Introduction*, tr. H.B. Nisbet, Cambridge: Cambridge University Press, 1975, first draft 'The Varieties of Historical Writing'.
87 In Weber, there is a radical difference between history and science, which pertains to ideas that he developed from Rickert, while Popper's views would seem to depend on what, contingently, he believes to be the case with regard to the human world (i.e. the only limited extent to which, he thinks, priority is to be given to economic issues), together with epistemologically generated doubts about our ability to settle issues of the general interpretation of history.
88 Compare, on this, *The Open Society*, chapter 23.
89 *The Open Society*, chapter 25, p. 267.
90 Compare, on this, my 'Popper, Lakatos and Theoretical Progress in Economics', in M. Blaug and N. de Marchi (eds) *Appraising Modern Economics. Studies in the Methodology of Scientific Research Programmes*, Aldershot: Edward Elgar, 1991.

3 AFTER *THE OPEN SOCIETY*

1 Geoff Stokes, 'Politics, Epistemology and Method: Karl Popper's Conception of Human Nature', *Political Studies* 43, No. 1, March 1995, pp. 105–23; see also my reply, 'Epistemology and Human Nature in Popper's Political Theory', pp. 124–30.
2 The key problem, with which I do not wish to burden the present text, is that any such task would involve an attempt at the reconstruction of his views from several series of lectures which Popper delivered in the United States, and from which only notes seem to have survived. (And another series of lectures of which there is a recording, albeit one that was made on now-superseded recording equipment, which would require decoding and transcription.) In addition, material relevant to Popper's views on politics is also to be found in the transcriptions of his lectures and seminar proceedings from his time at the LSE. All this material would require integration with his various papers – published and unpublished – over the relevant period. This is a task pieces of which I hope to undertake, gradually; but it is not something that it would make any sense to try to anticipate here.
3 Compare the quotation from his *Unended Quest*, in chapter 1, text to note 67.
4 There is no reason to suppose that an author will be an expert on his own development, and there is every reason to suppose that an

account given by him of that development may be given a teleology leading up to his present views, which may do violence to actual historical developments. This was certainly the case with respect to Popper, when, for example, the editor of his *Die beiden Grundprobleme*, Troels Eggers Hansen, faced the difficulty that Popper, when annotating that work for publication, over forty years after it was written, could not get himself back into the thread of his older argument, and wished to write notes from his then current perspective. More generally, it is surely difficult to think oneself back to a situation in which one was grappling unsuccessfully with problems that one later thought that one had been successfully solved.

5 First delivered as a lecture, in German, on 13 June 1959, and published (in English) in *Ordo* 30, 1979, in an issue that was a *Festschrift* for F.A. Hayek. It is included in Popper's *The Myth of the Framework*.

6 *Ibid.*

7 Compare, in this context, his 'The Status of Science' and his 'Note on the Cold War' (Popper Archives, 6–6).

8 See, in this context, Popper's *The Myth of the Framework*, and also his 'Toleration and Intellectual Responsibility', in S. Mendus and D. Edwards (eds) *On Toleration*, Oxford: Clarendon Press, 1987, pp. 17–34.

9 See 'Towards a Rational Theory of Tradition', in *Conjectures and Refutations*, p. 121.

10 See, on this, Popper's explicit discussion of the fact that he is doing this in his 'A Pluralist Approach to the Philosophy of History', where he looks again at historicism to see if there is, in some sense, something in it; his comments in 'On the Sources of Knowledge and of Ignorance', in *Conjectures and Refutations*, p. 6, and also his similar approach to the problem of invariance, in his (still unpublished) 'Rationality and the Search for Invariants' (Popper Archive, Folder 80).

11 It would seem to me that this paper is a key text for Stokes's approach to Popper – in that many of the key themes that he takes up may be found particularly starkly in this essay. If I am right that it is usefully seen as a (partial) corrective of his earlier views, this would indicate that it is not a good point from which to commence an interpretation of Popper.

12 E.g. on the occasion of his delivering 'Prediction and Prophecy in the Social Sciences' at the Tenth International Congress of Philosophy in 1948.

13 See, on this, 'On the Sources of Knowledge and of Ignorance', in *Conjectures and Refutations*, p. 6.

14 'Towards a Rational Theory of Tradition', in *Conjectures and Refutations*, p. 120.

15 'Towards a Rational Theory of Tradition', in *Conjectures and Refutations*, p. 121.

16 'Towards a Rational Theory of Tradition', in *Conjectures and Refutations*, p. 120.

17 'Towards a Rational Theory of Tradition', in *Conjectures and Refutations*, p. 122.

18 See, on this, notably 'The Bucket and the Searchlight', in *Objective Knowledge*, and 'Science: Conjectures and Refutations', in *Conjectures and Refutations*.

19 This view may usefully be contrasted with Collingwood's views about absolute presuppositions, in his *Essay on Metaphysics*, Oxford: Clarendon Press, 1948.

20 'Towards a Rational Theory of Tradition', in *Conjectures and Refutations*, p. 132.

21 See, on this, also *The Open Society*; 'Back to the Presocratics', in *Conjectures and Refutations*; and 'The Myth of the Framework', in *The Myth of the Framework*.

22 'Towards a Rational Theory of Tradition', in *Conjectures and Refutations*, p. 130. See Stokes, *op cit.*, for some interesting suggestions about links between this material and Popper's ideas about our expectations concerning causality.

23 'Towards a Rational Theory of Tradition', in *Conjectures and Refutations*, p. 130.

24 'Towards a Rational Theory of Tradition', in *Conjectures and Refutations*, pp. 130–1.

25 'Towards a Rational Theory of Tradition', in *Conjectures and Refutations*, pp. 132.

26 'Towards a Rational Theory of Tradition', in *Conjectures and Refutations*, p. 131.

27 'Towards a Rational Theory of Tradition', in *Conjectures and Refutations*, p. 132.

28 Stokes, *op. cit.*

29 See 'Science: Conjectures and Refutations', in *Conjectures and Refutations*, and *Unended Quest*.

30 Compare on all this, my 'Popper, Lakatos and Theoretical Progress in Economics', in M. Blaug and N. de Marchi (eds) *Appraising Modern Economics. Studies in the Methodology of Scientific Research Programmes*, Aldershot: Edward Elgar, 1991. Also, while Popper is a critic of Mannheim's sociology of knowledge, it is worth noting that on more than one occasion in the course of *The Open Society* (for example, chapter 15, p. 107), he indicates that an economic or a sociological approach to the understanding of scientific or cultural phenomena may be fruitful. Indeed, he even suggests, in chapter 22, pp. 210–11, that his own treatment of Plato might be seen in this light.

31 See my 'Epistemology Socialized?', *et cetera*, Fall 1985, and also the Introduction to this volume.

32 Compare Popper's discussion of the 'principle of transference' in *Objective Knowledge*.

33 I have in mind the phenomenon of 'political correctness', which I would see as in part a response to the problem discussed in the text.

34 'Towards a Rational Theory of Tradition', in *Conjectures and Refutations*, p. 133.

35 *Ibid.*

36 *Ibid.*

37 While, as I have suggested in the text, these ideas seem to me to have some interesting implications for Popper's work, the overall quality of his argument here seems to me not up to the standard of *The Open Society*.

38 'Towards a Rational Theory of Tradition', in *Conjectures and Refutations*, p. 134.

39 Compare *The Open Society*, chapter 14, p. 94.

40 If a reader should find this statement surprising, I would suggest that they consider, first, pp. 289–95 of his *Objective Knowledge*, in which his general strategy concerning reduction is set out, and then section II of his reply to Watkins in Schilpp's *The Philosophy of Karl Popper*, and also Popper's *The Self and Its Brain*, section 26.

41 *The Open Society*, chapter 5, p. 65.

42 See, for example, *Objective Knowledge*, pp. 235–8.

43 See, on this issue generally, Popper's discussion of 'basic statements' in *The Logic of Scientific Discovery*, and also *The Open Society*, chapter 23. Some aspects of this issue are considered in more detail in the next chapter.

44 See, on this *Objective Knowledge*, pp. 180 and 254, in which Popper also refers to the work of Sir Ernst Gombrich.

45 See, on this, W.W. Bartley's extensive discussion, in his *Unfathomed Knowledge, Unmeasured Wealth*: La Salle, IL: Open Court, 1990.

46 *Objective Knowledge*, p. 180.

47 See *Unended Quest*, note 302.

48 *Unended Quest*, p. 196.

49 See *The Self and Its Brain*, section 31, p. 111, note 5.

50 *The Self and Its Brain*, p. 111.

51 See the reference to Smith's *Theory of Moral Sentiments* in *The Self and Its Brain*, p. 111, which Popper inserted at my suggestion, and also Andrew Lock, *The Guided Reinvention of Language*, London: Academic Press, 1980.

52 *The Self and Its Brain*, p. 144.

53 *The Self and Its Brain*, pp. 108 and 144.

54 *The Self and Its Brain*, p. 109.

55 *The Self and Its Brain*, pp. 144–5.

56 *The Self and Its Brain*, p. 145.

57 See, on this, *Objective Knowledge*, chapter 2. It relates, more generally, to the non-justificatory character of Popper's theory of knowledge.

58 Compare *The Self and Its Brain*, p. 22.

59 If such an account were correct, it would not show that we did not have the experiences in question; only that the relationship would have been one in which, in Austin's expression from pre-feminist days, the physical would have worn the trousers.

60 'Indeterminism in Quantum Physics and in Classical Physics', *British Journal for the Philosophy of Science* 1, pp. 117–33 and 173–95. See also *Conjectures and Refutations*, pp. 293–303; *Objective Knowledge*, chapter 6; *Unended Quest*; Popper's response to Watkins in Schilpp's *The*

Philosophy of Karl Popper; The Self and Its Brain; and The Open Universe, which contains material from the *Postscript,* together with some other relevant papers by Popper.

61 See the references in note 60

62 See Schilpp's *The Philosophy of Karl Popper,* volume 2, p. 1057.

63 *Unended Quest,* pp. 46–7. See also his contributions to H. Krebs and J. Shelley (eds) *The Creative Process in Science and in Medicine,* Amsterdam: Excerpta Medica, 1975.

64 *Objective Knowledge,* p. 260.

65 *Unended Quest,* p. 47.

66 *Ibid.*

67 *Unended Quest,* p. 58.

68 *Ibid.*

69 *Unended Quest,* p. 62.

70 *The Myth of the Framework,* p. 36.

71 See, on all this, *The Open Society,* chapter 23. This, it should be added, is the context in which his appeals for simplicity, against the use of pretentious language, etc. are to be understood: his thesis is that the possibility of learning from others depends upon us eschewing such behaviour.

72 See 'Toleration and Intellectual Responsibility', in Mendus and Edwards, *op. cit.,* pp. 17–34.

73 *The Open Society,* chapter 25, p. 278.

74 See the text, between notes 57 and 58.

75 *Unended Quest,* p. 196. Cp., also, 'Replies to my Critics', in *The Philosophy of Karl Popper,* and the conclusion to 'How I See Philosophy', in *In Search of a Better World.*

76 *The Open Society,* chapter 10, pp. 174–5.

77 *The Open Society,* chapter 10, p. 176.

78 *The Open Society,* chapter 10, pp. 176–7.

79 *The Open Society,* chapter 14, p. 98.

80 See, on this, his untitled, unpublished lecture on *The Open Society* (Popper Archive 27–7, p.3).

81 In fact, there is a clear, if critical, preference in his work for multi-national empires.

82 The positive interrelation between commerce, culture-clash, and the development of an open society is a significant theme in Popper's work.

83 Popper was also a consistent and hard-hitting critic of Zionism.

84 For example, as to which of the many different – and typically conflicting – bases is to be chosen as the definition of a nation; and, further, once one of these is chosen, how firm lines are to be made of things which are intrinsically fluid (such as, for example, between language and dialect).

85 It is, however, striking, in this context, that as Anna Bramwell notes, 'many National Socialist leaders . . . came from outside Germany'. See her *Blood and Soil,* Bourne End: Kensal Press, 1985, p. 13.

86 *The Open Society,* chapter 10, p. 181.

87 *Ibid.*

88 *The Open Society*, chapter 12, note 53.
89 See M. Hacohen, *The Making of the Open Society*, Columbia University PhD dissertation, 1994.
90 *The Open Society*, chapter 9, note 7. Popper also argues that one should be realistic as to what one could expect from such a body, and that it might hope to reduce, but hardly to abolish, international crime.
91 *Ibid.*
92 Interview with Shari Steiner (Popper Archive 202–15 p. 6). (It is striking that, earlier in the same interview, the interviewer clearly finds it strange that Popper is critical of the idea of national self-determination.)

4 VALUES AND REASON

* This chapter draws in part on my 'Epistemological Limits of the State'. In that connection, I thanked Michael Lessnoff, Larry Briskman, David Gordon and Emilio Pacheco for their comments on earlier versions of the paper, and also the anonymous referees of *Political Studies*. I would like to repeat my thanks to them here.
1   *Unended Quest*, p. 115.
2   *The Open Society*, chapter 5, p. 61
3   *The Open Society*, chapter 24, p. 232.
4   *The Open Society*, chapter 24, p. 233.
5   *Ibid.*
6   *The Open Society*, chapter 5, note 18.
7   *Ibid.*
8   In further discussion of the latter, Popper endorses Moore's criticism of naturalism, but then states, in a way that relates the discussion to his critique of essentialism, that: 'an analysis of good . . . can in no way contribute to an ethical theory which bears upon the only relevant basis of all ethics, the immediate problem that must be solved here and now'. See *The Open Society*, chapter 11, note 49.
9   *The Open Society*, chapter 5.
10 *The Open Society*, chapter 5, p. 64. I write 'stress' as the passage quoted is in italics in the original.
11 *Ibid.*
12 *The Open Society*, chapter 5, p. 61.
13 *The Open Society*, chapter 5, note 18.
14 *The Open Society*, chapter 5, p. 65.
15 *The Open Society*, chapter 5, p. 67.
16 *The Open Society*, chapter 5, note 5 (2).
17 *Ibid.*
18 I have in mind notably David McNaughton's *Moral Vision*, Oxford: Blackwell, 1988, which in its broad outline, if not in the full details of the position or argument, is the best account that I know of the kind of view to which, I would suggest, Popper's argument should lead us.

19 *The Open Society*, volume 2, p. 385.
20 *Ibid.*
21 *The Open Society*, volume 2, p. 386.
22 *The Open Society*, volume 2, p. 391.
23 *Ibid.*
24 Compare Popper's contributions to *The Self and Its Brain*, end of section 1.
25 *The Open Society*, chapter 24, p. 225.
26 *The Open Society*, chapter 24, p. 238. (Note the contrast between this, and Popper's earlier criticism of Kantian appeals to reason in connection with ethics.)
27 'A Non-Psychological Justification of the Categorical Imperative'. It is located in the Popper Archive at 366–14, in a folder marked 'Canterbury University College Lectures "Ethics" General', which also contains a memo dated 3 March 1940. I am somewhat circumspect about the use of this piece, and would not myself wish positively to attribute it to Popper. The front page attributes it to 'Professor POPPER', a title which Popper did not hold at the time. The typescript appears to be a transcript by some other party, which at some points clearly garbles the argument, and which has then been corrected in manuscript. The content of the lecture has many parallels with arguments in *The Open Society*; but at the same time, some of the terminology in which the argument is developed does not seem characteristic of Popper.
28 *Op. cit.*, p. 4.
29 *Op. cit.*, p. 5.
30 *Ibid.*
31 In particular, what we are offered is meta-ethical argument which parallels a particular interpretation of the categorical imperative. However, an acceptance of this meta-ethical objectivism would seem to me compatible with non-universalism at the level of particular ethical judgements, as I argue later in the text.
32 Notably, Hans Otto Apel. It is worth noting, however, that the kind of reservation indicated at the end of Popper's Appendix to *The Open Society* is also to be found in this paper, in that it suggests that 'if a man refuses to approach ethics reasonably, then he could not be persuaded of the validity of moral principles even if they were demonstrable in the way that geometrical theorems are demonstrable' (p. 4).
33 See *The Self and Its Brain*, sections 18 and 30 (of Popper's contributions).
34 Compare also Popper's note to section 8 of *The Logic of Scientific Discovery*, added to the work in translation. Commenting on a passage in which he relates objectivity to inter-subjective testing, he writes: 'I have since generalized this formulation; for inter-subjective testing is merely a very important aspect of the general idea of inter-subjective criticism'. In this connection, it is worth noting that Popper changed his terminology, when discussing ethics, from referring to 'decisions' to referring to 'proposals', in the light of the fact

that the latter were more clearly discussible. See *The Open Society*, chapter 5, note 5.

35 I. Kant, *Critique of Pure Reason*, Transcendental doctrine of method, chapter 2, section 3. Compare *Logic of Scientific Discovery*, sections 8 and 30, and Popper's references there to Kant's ideas about objectivity. The theme of 'communication' in this passage might also be usefully compared with *The Open Society*, chapter 23, p. 239.

36 The approach itself is worth comparing with similar ideas that Hannah Arendt draws from the third critique. Compare her *Lectures on Kant's Political Philosophy*, Chicago: University of Chicago Press, 1982.

37 Smith's own theory is, clearly, developed with a starting point in ideas about sympathy as a kind of emotional resonance. But as his argument develops, this is (thankfully) left behind, and his work contains various examples of judgements which could not possibly have such shared experience as their basis. I am here suggesting that if one takes a lead from such cases, the whole work can be reinterpreted as offering a model for a non-naturalistic ethical realism. (See, for a more detailed exploration of this argument, my 'From Brother Sense to Brother Man', delivered at the meeting of the AAPSS at the American Philosophical Association, New York, 1987.) I might also mention that the seriousness with which we would take the judgements of other people would depend on our willingness to take these judgements as attempts to capture what is *right*. However, just how far one might wish to push these parallels with scientific knowledge, and how we are to understand ethical realism, I am happy here to leave open. See, however, my 'Natural Law Without Metaphysics?: The Case of John Finnis', *Cleveland University Law Review* 38, Nos 1 and 2, 1990, for some further discussion.

38 Compare, on this, *Moral Vision*, and also J. Dancy, 'Ethical Particularism and Morally Relevant Properties', *Mind*, 92 1983, pp. 530–47.

39 For examples of this, see Adam Smith, *Lectures on Jurisprudence*, ed. R. Meek *et al.*, Oxford: Clarendon Press, 1978.

40 *The Open Society*, chapter 6, note 20.

41 *The Open Society*, chapter 5, note 13.

42 *The Open Society*, chapter 8, notes 48 and 50.

43 *The Open Society*, chapter 24, p. 245.

44 *The Open Society*, chapter 24, p. 240.

45 *The Open Society*, chapter 24, p. 234.

46 *The Open Society*, chapter 6, p. 89.

47 *The Open Society*, chapter 6, p. 94; see also pp. 109–10.

48 I have discussed this in my 'From Divine Corporation to a System of Justice', in P. Groenewegen (ed.) *Economics and Ethics*, forthcoming. See also my 'Scope and Status of Prudential Liberalism', *The Review of Politics* 54, No. 2, 1992, and also, for invaluable historical discussion, Knud Haakonssen, *Natural Law and Moral Philosophy: From Grotius to the Scottish Enlightenment*, Cambridge: Cambridge University Press, 1995, and Rebecca Lynn Reynolds, *Samuel Cocceji and the*

Tradition of Natural Jurisprudence, M.Litt. thesis, Cambridge University, 1993.

49 Compare my 'From Dialogue Rights to Property Rights', *Critical Review* 4, numbers 1–2, pp. 106–32.

50 Compare Frank Michelman, 'From Dialogue Rights to Property Rights: Reply to Shearmur', *Critical Review* 4, Nos 1–2, pp. 133–43. I have explored the extent to which the argument might be extended in response, in some detail in my *Hayek and After*. Michelman's counter-argument has, in my view, some interesting parallels to Cocceji's response to Grotius's argument from sociability to universality. See the reference to Rebecca Reynolds, in note 48, above.

51 Cp. my 'From Intersubjectivity Through Epistemology to Property: A reply to Michelman', *Critical Review* 4, Nos 1–2, pp. 144–54.

52 Of course, within a particular territory, one would expect the authorities to operate on the basis of the rule of law, and the police services to protect everybody in the same way; but this would apply to citizens and to non-citizens alike.

53 That is, that we may in fact be in a situation in which we believe that a duty is owed to everyone, but only be in a position to discharge it within the country in which we are living.

54 On which, compare *The Open Society*, chapter 5, note 6; chapter 9, note 2; chapter 11, note 62.

55 *The Open Society*, chapter 8, p. 138. Cp. also pp. 107–8.

56 One might here usefully compare the puritan classic, Joseph Alleine's *Alarm to the Unconverted*, London: Banner of Truth Trust, 1964, which, in a similar manner, exhibits the disruptive effect of deep religious concerns for others' spiritual well-being, upon ordinary moral life.

57 I have developed this argument at greater length in my *Hayek and After*.

58 See the text to note 23, above.

59 *The Open Society*, first edition, chapter 24, pp. 217–18. Popper's argument would seem to me to read better if the final word in the quoted paragraph were 'non-rational'. It should be noted that, on this issue, significant changes were made in later editions of *The Open Society*.

60 *The Open Society*, first edition, chapter 24, p. 218.

61 *The Open Society*, first edition, chapter 24, p. 219.

62 See Chapter 1, text to note 9.

63 *The Open Society*, chapter 24, note 6.

64 *The Myth of the Framework*, p. xiii.

65 Or, at least, that was the impression that I gained in conversations with Popper on this topic, when I worked for him, in the course of which he referred to problems similar to that discussed in *The Myth of the Framework*.

66 See *The Retreat to Commitment*, London: Chatto & Windus, 1964; La Salle, IL: Open Court, 1984 and also his 'Rationality versus the Theory of Rationality', in M. Bunge (ed.) *The Critical Approach*, New York: Free Press, 1964. Compare also the discussion of these issues

in W. W. Bartley and G. Radnitzky (eds) *Evolutionary Epistemology* . . ., La Salle, IL: Open Court, 1987, chapters 9 and 15; and David Miller's *Critical Rationalism*, La Salle, IL: Open Court, 1994, chapter 4.

67 Unless, that is, we are offered some more general *moral* theory as to why the preferences of each person are to be respected, which would itself have to be held open to criticism.

68 See *The Open Society*, chapter 5, note 6 and chapter 7, note 4 – where the reference to pistols and to related issues is reminiscent of Popper's later story of his encounter with the Nazi.

69 Although, of course, we may choose to hold our 'tastes' in such a manner; alternatively, they may receive protection, as matters of free choice, by virtue of their link with a view – which we hold open to criticism – of their significance for the autonomy of the person.

5 POPPER, LIBERALISM AND MODIFIED ESSENTIALISM

1 Compare H. Reiss (ed.) *Kant's Political Writings*, Cambridge: Cambridge University Press, 1970, p. 14; and R. Bubner, *Modern German Philosophy*, Cambridge: Cambridge University Press, 1981, p. 108.

2 Popper himself has however written that: 'I wrote about Hegel in a manner which assumed that few would take him seriously.' See *The Open Society*, volume 2, Addendum 1 (1961), section 17.

3 *Unended Quest*, p. 115.

4 *Conjectures and Refutations*, 'Introduction', section iv, p. 6.

5 Bryan Magee, *Popper*, London: Fontana, 1973, p. 84.

6 *The Open Society*, volume 2, p. 198.

7 *Unended Quest*, p. 36.

8 *The Open Society*, volume 2, p. 134.

9 *The Open Society*, volume 2, chapter 24, note 2.

10 *The Open Society*, volume 1, chapter 6, note 4.

11 *The Open Society*, volume 1, p. 102.

12 *The Open Society*, volume 1, chapter 5, note 18, part 1.

13 *The Open Society*, volume 2, p. 238.

14 *Ibid.*.

15 *Ibid.*

16 *The Open Society*, volume 2, pp. 238–9.

17 *The Open Society*, volume 1, p. iv.

18 *The Open Society*, volume 2, chapter 16, note 10; p. 179; and chapter 20, note 26.

19 Compare also, *The Open Society*, volume 2, pp. 124–5, and volume 1, note 3: 'Marx's prophecy of the victory of the proletariat is his reply to one of the most sinister periods of oppression and exploitation in modern history'. In *The Open Society*, volume 2, chapter 17, note 21 Popper discusses – but does not accept – a possible rejoinder: that these problems would be overcome if we assume perfect competition.

20 *The Open Society*, volume 2, p. 125.

21 *The Open Society*, volume 2, pp. 130–2.
22 F.A. Hayek, *The Constitution of Liberty*, London: Routledge & Kegan Paul, 1959.
23 *The Open Society*, volume 2, p. 125.
24 *The Open Society*, volume 2, chapter 20, note 26; see also volume 1, chapter 10, note 67.
25 *The Open Society*, volume 2, chapter 20, note 26.
26 *The Open Society*, volume 1, chapter 9 note 2.
27 *The Open Society*, volume 1, p. 131.
28 *The Open Society*, volume 2, p. 237.
29 *The Open Society*, volume 1, chapter 7.
30 *The Open Society*, volume 1, p. 4.
31 *The Open Society*, volume 2, p. 151.
32 *The Open Society*, volume 1, p. 125.
33 *Ibid.*
34 See the first part of my 'Epistemology Socialized?', *et cetera*, Fall 1985.
35 *The Open Society*, volume 2, chapter 20.
36 At least to me: see my 'Religious Sect as a Cognitive System', *Annual Review of the Social Sciences of Religion* 4 (1980), pp. 149–63, and my 'Epistemology Socialized?'.
37 What follows here in my text is merely a sketch; any serious study would have to call, *inter alia*, on the literature of the theory of public choice. Another treatment, in some ways complementary to the present discussion, is my 'Popper, le libéralisme et la démocratie sociale' in R. Bouveresse (ed.) *Karl Popper et la science d'aujourd'hui*, Paris: editions Aubier, 1989.
38 Compare Adam Smith, *Lectures on Justice*, ed. Cannan, Oxford: Clarendon Press, 1896, pp. 256–7; and *The Wealth of Nations*, Glasgow Edition, Oxford: Clarendon Press, 1976 and G.W.F. Hegel, *Philosophy of Right* (tr. T. M. Knox), Oxford: Clarendon Press, 1942, paragraph 239, p. 148.
39 Hegel, *Philosophy of Right*, paragraphs 241–2, pp. 148–9.
40 *Philosophy of Right*, paragraph 245, p. 150. The paternalistic elements in the writings of Adam Smith and other classical liberals should, I think, have given them more cause for concern than they actually showed. See, on this, my *Adam Smith's Second Thoughts*, London: Adam Smith Club, 1985, and 'From Divine Corporation to a System of Justice', in P. Groenewegen (ed.) *Economics and Ethics*, London and New York: Routledge 1996. As I have indicated earlier in this volume, I would be delighted if such functions could be discharged without there being a state at all.
41 Compare Adam Smith, *Lectures on Justice, op. cit.* pp. 253–4, and J. Shearmur and D. Klein, 'Good Conduct in the Great Society', in D. Klein (ed.) *Reputation: Studies in the Voluntary Enforcement of Good Behaviour*, Ann Arbor: University of Michigan Press.
42 Compare N. Rosenberg, 'Institutional Aspects of The Wealth of Nations', in *Journal of Political Economy* LXVIII (1960).
43 See, on this theme, Adam Smith's remarks in *Lectures on Jurisprudence, op. cit.*, pp. 253–9.

44 Compare F.A. Hayek, 'Economics and Knowledge', in his *Individualism and Economic Order*, London: Routledge, 1944.

45 Compare F.A. Hayek, 'Competition as a Discovery Procedure', in his *New Studies*, London: Routledge & Kegan Paul, 1978.

46 It is difficult to see how any form of large-scale social organization that did not possess a market economy could be considered to be compatible with Popper's ideas.

47 Compare, here, the growing literature on the theory of public choice and, for a defence of the use of self-interest models in the critical comparison of different institutional arrangements, G. Brennan and J. Buchanan, 'The Normative Purpose of Economic "Science"', in J. Buchanan, *Economics: Between Science and Moral Philosophy*, ed. R. Tollison and V. Vanberg, College Station: Texas A&M University Press, 1987, pp. 51–65.

48 Troels Eggers Hansen has drawn to my attention that essentialism is, in fact, criticized in *Die beiden Grundprobleme*, pp. 177 and 248.

49 One reason why it became less prominent was, presumably, because Popper later came to the view that metaphysical theories could be rationally assessed in their own right. Compare his *Objective Knowledge*, page 40, note 9.

50 See *The Poverty of Historicism*, pp. 135ff.

51 See *The Open Society*, volume 2, chapter 11, pp. 9–21.

52 *The Open Society*, volume 2, pp. 15–16.

53 The paper, subsequently reprinted in his *Conjectures and Refutations*, dates from 1953. It is striking that, when discussing the idea of essentialism there, Popper refers back to *The Poverty of Historicism* and *The Open Society*. (See note 5 on page 169 of *Conjectures*.) This would seem to bear out the view that this is the first published occurrence of the idea, outside of Popper's discussions in the social sciences; but see also note 48, above.

54 *Conjectures and Refutations*, p. 173.

55 *Conjectures and Refutations*, p. 174.

56 Also now in *Conjectures and Refutations*.

57 This paper, drawn from Popper's *Postscript*, was first published in *Ratio*, and then, subsequently, in his *Objective Knowledge*. It is now also available in his *Postscript*, volume 1, to which I will refer in the present chapter.

58 See 'The Aim of Science', chapter 15 of *Realism and the Aim of Science*; the other quotation is from 'Truth, Rationality and the Growth of Knowledge', chapter 10 of *Conjectures and Refutations*, p. 241.

59 *Postscript*, volume 1, p. 139.

60 See Popper's *Postscript*, volume 3.

61 See 'The Trend of Economic Thinking', in F.A. Hayek, *The Trend of Economic Thinking: Essays on Political Economists and Economic History*, ed. W. W. Bartley III and Stephen Kresge, Chicago: University of Chicago Press, 1991, p. 19. See also, for discussion, my *Hayek and After*.

62 See *The Open Society*, volume 2, pp. 119–20. Of course, one might defend Popper by saying that, on the 'Hayekian' account that I have

given, the structures in question themselves depend on human decisions of various kinds. But it is exactly on this point that it seems to me that Popper's account is open to criticism, in that – understandably enough, because he was discussing Marx – it conflated structural questions of the kind that I have here raised with issues of historical inevitability.

63 See his *Anarchy, State, and Utopia*, chapter 1.

64 This is an allusion to the British government's declaration of Australia as such, thus disregarding the fact that it was already full of aboriginal land rights (of a kind).

65 Compare, for further discussion, Paul Edwards and Jeremy Shearmur, 'Street-Level Jurisprudence', paper delivered at the American Political Science Association, Chicago, 1992.

66 There is, possibly, a parallel here with views that see the natural sciences as having as their subject-matter the products of God's prior activities.

67 In this respect, Juergen Habermas's characterization of science as instrumental seems to me mistaken. The development of scientific knowledge can, surely, just as easily be understood as a search for meaning, which has changed its idea of the kind of meaning that might be found in nature, as its search has progressed: compare my discussion in Chapter 6. Such a realist approach to science is not without its problems. But, in my view, it should not be dismissed out of hand.

68 See, for a fuller account, my 'Realism Under Attack?', *Philosophy of the Social Sciences*, June 1986, in which I should have referred also to S.F. Barker, *Induction and Hypothesis*, Ithaca and London: Cornell University Press, 1957, which was a starting point for discussion with a colleague which led to the paper, but of which I lost sight as the paper developed.

69 Most obviously, 'Goodmanesque' ones, if these are interpreted as describing actual characteristics of the world.

70 See David Miller, *Critical Rationalism*, and W.W. Bartley III, 'Ein Loesung des Goodmans-Paradoxons', in G. Radnitzky and G. Andersson (eds) *Voraussetzungen and Grenzen der Wissenschaft*, Tuebingen: Mohr, 1981. (Bartley was kind enough to send me an English-language version of his paper.)

71 See S. Lukes, *Power: A Radical View*, London: Macmillan, 1974, and J. Gaventa, *Power and Powerlessness*, Oxford: Clarendon Press, 1980.

72 Lukes's approach was notoriously ambiguous, in that he presented his own (realist) view as superior to other approaches, yet at the same time seemed to suggest that the adoption of one rather than the other such view could be understood as a product of a value-based choice. He also seemed to me needlessly to insist on the idea that power should be understood in terms of the exercise of personal responsibility.

73 It might be argued that under-determination problems also occur in respect of meaning (in which connection, one might point to the parallel between our 'Goodmanesque' problem, and Wittgenstein's

problems about rule-following). However, while, clearly, a rule – and hence meaning – is under-determined by evidence, *which* rule is chosen can be seen as a product of *our* interaction with evidence, where the outcome may be understood as determined by our physiology and socialization. This clearly does not affect the Goodmanesque problem – for there is no reason to believe that there is a correspondence between our predispositions and the character of things in themselves – but it does seem to me that, here, Hobbes's and Vico's ideas about the human sciences being different and epistemologically less problematic are perhaps correct.

74 See Barry Hindess, *Choice, Rationality, and Social Theory*, London and Boston: Unwin Hyman, 1988.

75 See James Beckford, *Cult Controversies*, London: Tavistock, 1985.

76 It is worth noting that those 'Austrian' economists who followed von Mises have consistently rejected this approach.

77 That we could – at least in principle – do so would seem to me an essential requirement. The 'in principle' here is to be understood in terms close to those involved in cases in which, for example, we might suffer from some form of mental derangement, and those who over-rule our judgements in this state would say that we would, in principle, have agreed. If I were to offer a theoretical account of this, I would do so in terms of ideas drawn from Adam Smith's ideas about an 'impartial spectator'.

78 This seems to me one of the many respects in which Habermas's model of 'emancipatory' social science is defective: see also my discussion in Chapter 6.

79 Compare note 40 to Chapter 1, above.

80 Compare, for some discussion, my 'Hayek and the Wisdom of the Age', in N. Barry *et al.*, *Hayek's 'Serfdom' Revisited*, London: Institute of Economic Affairs, 1984.

81 Compare, for more extended discussion, Edwards and Shearmur, 'Street-Level Jurisprudence'.

82 This section is based upon my 'Abstract Institutions in an *The Open Society*', in H. Berghel *et al.* (eds) *Wittgenstein, The Vienna Circle and Critical Rationalism*, Vienna: Hoelder, Pichler, Tempsky, 1979, pp. 236–41, which in turn was based on an invited paper on Popper's social philosophy, delivered at a meeting of the Austrian Wittgenstein Society in 1978. The first five paragraphs, which were written in 1978 but which have not been previously published and which offer an overview of Popper's approach, include the fairly extensive suggestions which Popper made when I asked him to look over this section of my manuscript.

83 For more extensive discussion of the interpretation of Smith which underlies these brief remarks, see my *Adam Smith's Second Thoughts*; and my, 'Adam Smith and the Cultural Contradictions of Capitalism' in N. Elliot (ed.) *Adam Smith's Legacy*, London: Adam Smith Institute, 1990, and also my paper with Dan Klein, 'Good Conduct in the Great Society'.

84 I. Kant, 'What is Enlightenment'. The passage that I have cited is

translated by Popper in his 'Emancipation through Knowledge', now in *In Search of a Better World.*

85 See also, on this, my 'Political Philosophy of F.A. von Hayek'.

86 I have left the text at this point as it was initially published. I would now, though, be inclined to stress the significance of an intermediate level: action through the courts, especially where they have a constitutional role, or are involved in the interpretation of international treaties with quasi-constitutional consequences (e.g. which pertain to human rights). The growing role of such bodies within contemporary politics seems to me one of the most sinister of contemporary political developments, especially insofar as it is often the vehicle through which people pursue something that on the face of it is highly desirable: greater moral accountability of governments, and of others holding power. I will not, here, launch into a diatribe on this topic, except to say that what is wrong with it is that such bodies are, effectively, exempted from having to answer criticism offered by the people upon whom their often arbitrary judgements are imposed.

87 Book III, Part III, Section 1.

88 There is a danger that I am here painting too sanguine an account of social order in the past – not least in the light of, say, the role of the mob in early nineteenth-century London. Compare, for a striking account, Paul Johnson, *The Birth of the Modern*, New York: HarperCollins, 1991.

89 See, on this, his *Law, Legislation and Liberty*, London: Routledge & Kegan Paul, 1973, etc.

90 This relates to the period during which I was working as his assistant. The paper containing this material was itself also written during this period (see note 82, above).

91 Compare, on this, Popper's discussion of the criticizability of metaphysics in his *Conjectures and Refutations*, the discussion of metaphysical research programmes in *Unended Quest*, and his *Postscript*.

92 See Karl Menger, *Morality, Decision and Social Organization: Toward a Logic of Ethics*, Dordrecht and Boston: Reidel, 1974; I would like to thank Popper for drawing my attention to this work, in the present context.

93 Such a constitution could not be neutral, in that what counted as interference would have to be decided by the framework government, and in ways that might well be in conflict with the ideals that particular communities might wish to espouse. Similarly, the overall grounding of the constitution in fallibilism and learning, would mean that communities would be constrained to educate their young people in ways which 'Socrates' judged would give them the opportunity of coping with diversity, and making judgements between competing alternatives, when they reached maturity.

94 For, clearly, the cost of pursuing some option which others do not favour, and of which they might actively disapprove, might be high.

95 I have been struck, in this context, by the way in which, in suburban areas near San Francisco in which I have lived, people are routinely polite and friendly towards those whom they meet, including

strangers. At the same time, such behaviour does not carry with it any deep concern.

96 If the reader should feel that I am dealing, here, merely with phantasies, I might mention Disney World. While in one sense this, too, is a phantasy, in another it is as real and as hard-headed an example as one might wish for. Compare, for an interesting discussion, Fred Foldvary, *Public Goods and Private Communities*, Aldershot, Hants: Edward Elgar, 1994.

97 This institution, common in the United States, allows people with a poor or no credit rating to hold a credit card, backed by money equivalent to the credit extended to them, which is held in a deposit account of the issuing bank. By this means, the people in question can re-establish their credit rating, by careful use of their credit card, and will in time have credit extended to them on an ordinary basis.

98 See F.A. Hayek, *Law, Legislation and Liberty*, volume 3, London: Routledge & Kegan Paul, 1979, pp. 81–8.

99 In the event of exclusion because of the claim that some specific action has been performed, one is dealing with something that might be contested in courts. In the event of discrimination against members of certain kinds of groups which people may plausibly argue (even on a statistical basis) would put valued features of their community at risk, entry might be secured by the posting of a good behaviour bond or a requirement that the people in question comply with certain conditions. In the event of the connection that is claimed being specious, and shown to be such via the kinds of accountability that I discuss, below, the community in question would be shown in a bad light, and one could well imagine that other people would be reluctant to associate with it, if it maintained the practices in question.

100 See the discussion in F.A. Hayek, *The Constitution of Liberty*, p. 451, note 18.

6 THE CONTEMPORARY RELEVANCE OF POPPER'S WORK

1 Compare Bryan Magee, *Popper*, London: Fontana, 1973 and R. James, *Return to Reason: Popper's thought in public life*, Somerset: Open Books, 1980.

2 Richard Rorty, *Philosophy and the Mirror of Nature*, Princeton: Princeton University Press, 1980.

3 Compare, on this, Popper's discussion, in *Unended Quest*, of the impression made upon him by suffering, as a young child, and his surprise at the continuing influence of non-realist epistemologies after the Second World War. See also the first five sections of chapter 2 of his *Objective Knowledge*.

4 See, on this, Popper's 'Toleration and Intellectual Responsibility', in S. Mendus and D. Edwards (eds) *On Toleration*, and also Mendus's introduction, which discusses this feature of Popper's fallibilism.

5   A point which is argued very effectively by Thomas McCarthy in 'The Critique of Impure Reason: Foucault and the Frankfurt School', *Political Theory* 18, 1990, pp. 437–69. (Indeed, it is striking that many of the points that have been made by critics of Foucault who have been influenced by Habermas are also points that follow from Popper's work.)

6   *The Open Society*, chapter 6, note 54.

7   I have in mind especially what seem to me some rather silly views to which international bodies have committed themselves, starting with the particular interpretation of human rights agreed to by the United Nations.

8   It is striking, in this context, just how few people with an active interest in Popper's work there are who currently hold teaching positions in philosophy or political theory in universities.

9   I say 'even religious' in the light of Bill Bartley's *Retreat to Commitment*.

10   T. Adorno *et al.*, *The Positivist Dispute in German Sociology*, London: Heinemann Educational, 1976.

11   On which see Popper's 'Reason or Revolution?' (1970), subsequently incorporated into the English edition of the *Positivismusstreit* volume.

12   See, notably, various pieces in Popper's *In Search of a Better World.*

13   Robert C. Holub, *Juergen Habermas: Critic in the Public Sphere*, London and New York: Routledge, 1991, p. 38.

14   My argument here draws on my 'The *Positivismusstreit* Revisited', delivered at the Australasian Political Studies Association, Canberra, 1993, and also on my 'Habermas: A Critical Approach', *Critical Review*, Winter 1988, which should be consulted for fuller details, although my concluding comments there about Habermas's politics stand in need of correction in the light of Stephen K. White, *The Recent Work of Jurgen Habermas*, New York: Cambridge University Press, 1988.

15   I argue this in some detail in 'The *Positivismusstreit* Revisited'.

16   See Hans Albert, 'The Myth of Total Reason', in *The Positivist Dispute in German Sociology*.

17   I have in mind especially his emphasis upon universal laws in the social sciences, in some of his earlier writings – on which compare both my comments on tradition, in Chapter 3, and also Popper's discussion of the rationality principle in his 'Models, Instruments and Truth', in *The Myth of the Framework.*

18   It is worth noting, in this context, Gellner's broad acknowledgement to Popper in the Acknowledgements to *The Psychoanalytic Movement*, London: Fontana, 1985, 1993, which indeed seems to me to offer the extended 'Popperian' critique of psychoanalysis that Popper himself did not produce.

19   On which compare Marcuse's *Eros and Civilization*, London: Routledge & Kegan Paul, 1956, and Russell Jacoby, *Social Amnesia*, Boston: Beacon Press, 1975, on the latter of which see also my review in *Philosophy of the Social Sciences*, March 1983, pp. 87–90.

20   That is, to what extent psychoanalysis actually *cures* anybody.

21   I am here alluding to Marcuse and Jacoby.

22 See, on this, F.A. Hayek, *Individualism and Economic Order*, London: Routledge, 1944.

23 I have discussed this in 'One Cheer for the Edinburgh School?', delivered at a plenary session of the British Society for the Philosophy of Science, Edinburgh, 1986.

24 Compare the final section of the previous chapter.

25 Compare D. Colander and A. Klamer, 'The Making of an Economist', *Journal of Economic Perspectives*, 1, no. 2, 1987, pp. 95–111.

26 I have in mind the reorganization and multiplication of British universities, and comparable activities conducted under the banner of 'economic rationalism' in Australia. The suggestion about 'learning nothing' relates to the debate on these issues in the 1940s and 1950s. This effort was odd in that it was not clear what was supposed to be *wrong* with the earlier arrangements, and thus what problem was supposedly being solved. Insofar as change is attempted, there would seem to me every reason to try to learn from success, and to see which practices are responsible for that, and the degree to which they can be adapted elsewhere, rather than proceeding as if people can produce whatever they are asked to (assuming, for the sake of argument, that what they are asked to do makes any sense), from scratch.

27 Compare J. Habermas, *The Structural Transformation of the Public Sphere*, Cambridge, MA: MIT Press, 1991, and C. Calhoun (ed.), *Habermas and the Public Sphere*, Cambridge, MA: MIT Press, 1992.

28 It is important in this context that we recognize that culture is an institution rather than something that is instantiated in the same way in each person, and also that it is silly to assume that there is a particular viewpoint or perspective upon the world which anyone should be expected to hold because of their particular social or cultural background.

NAME INDEX

209

SUBJECT INDEX

213